CHIPPEWA
CHILD LIFE and
Its Cultural Background

CHIPPEWA
CHILD LIFE and
Its Cultural Background

SISTER M. INEZ HILGER

With a New Introduction by
Jean M. O'Brien

Minnesota Historical Society Press · St. Paul

Borealis Books are high-quality paperback reprints
of books chosen by the Minnesota Historical Society
Press for their importance as enduring historical
sources and their value as enjoyable accounts of life
in the Upper Midwest.

⊗The paper used in this publication meets the mini-
mum requirements for the American National Standard for Information Sciences – Permanence for
Printed Library Materials, ANSI Z39.48-1984.

Minnesota Historical Society Press, St. Paul 55101

First published in 1951 by the Smithsonian Institution Bureau of American Ethnology as Bulletin 146

New material © 1992 by the Minnesota Historical
Society

International Standard Book Number 0-87351-271-5

Manufactured in the United States of America

10 9 8 7 6 5 4 3 2 1

Library of Congress Cataloging-in-Publication Data

Hilger, M. Inez (Mary Inez), 1891-
      Chippewa child life and its cultural background /
Sister M. Inez Hilger; with a new introduction by Jean
M. O'Brien.
          p.   cm.   – (Borealis books)
      Originally published: Washington, D.C. : U.S.
G.P.O., 1951.
      Includes bibliographical references and index.
      ISBN 0-87351-271-5
      1. Ojibwa Indians – Children. 2. Ojibwa Indians –
Social life and customs. 3. Ojibwa Indians – Psychol-
ogy.   I. Title.
E99.C6H46   1992
977'.004973 – dc20   91-44657

CONTENTS

ILLUSTRATIONS

PLATES
(All plates facing page 188)

14. Making birchbark canoe, Mille Lacs Reservation, 1940 (continued). 1, Placing birchbark. 2, Shaping canoe by means of poles and framework for bow or stern. 3, Placing bark into position by means of second set of poles.
15. Making birchbark canoe, Mille Lacs Reservation, 1940 (continued). 1, Framework for either bow or stern. 2, Binding edges with split roots of spruce.
16. Making birchbark canoe, Mille Lacs Reservation, 1940 (continued). 1, Canoe ready for gunwales, ribs, flooring, and binding of edges. 2, Filling cracks in bark with pitch. 3, Placing ribs and flooring.
17. Making birchbark canoe, Mille Lacs Reservation, 1940 (continued). 1, Canoe ready for use. 2, Transporting canoe. 3, Canoe on exhibition at Mille Lacs Indian Trading Post, Onamia, Minn.
18. Man's snowshoes collected on Lac Courte Orielle Reservation, 1935.
19. Josephine Gurneau making cord of basswood fiber, Red Lake Reservation, 1933. 1, Rolling strands of basswood fiber. 2, Softening strands by moistening.
20. Fishing. 1, Fish nets being hung to dry, Red Lake Reservation, 1933. 2, Shuttle and sample of fish net made on Red Lake Reservation, 1933.
21. Fishing. 1, A haul of fish, Red Lake Reservation, 1932. 2, Fish nets drying, L'Anse Reservation, 1935.
22. Emma Martin tanning deer hide, Lac Courte Orielle Reservation, 1935. 1, Wringing hide after soaking. 2, Last wringing of hide. 3, Second scraping of hide. 4, Stretching hide.
23. Emma Martin tanning deer hide, Lac Courte Orielle Reservation, 1935 (continued). 1, Hide stretched for final scraping. 2, Final scraping of hide. 3, Smoking hide.
24. Birchbark receptacles. 1, Anna Knott making wild-rice winnowing trays and teaching daughter to make them, Vermilion Lake Reservation, 1939. 2, Nonleakable birchbark receptacles, Red Lake Reservation, August 1933. 3, *a*, Work basket; *b*, makok'; *c*, winnowing basket.
25. Mary Gurneau making nonleakable birchbark receptacle, Red Lake Reservation, August 1932. 1, Holding bark over fire. 2, Fastening folded end. 3, Folding opposite end. 4, Completed receptacle.
26. Wigwams. 1, Mishiman and wife and their wigwam covered with birchbark and bulrush mats, Lac Courte Orielle Reservation, 1935. 2, Wigwam entirely covered with bark, Red Lake Reservation, 1932.
27. Wigwams. 1, White Earth Reservation, 1938. 2, Lac du Flambeau Reservation, 1935. 3, Lac du Flambeau Reservation, 1922.
28. Wigwams, Mille Lacs Reservation, 1940. 1, Coverings of cattail mats, tar paper, and flattened cardboard boxes. 2, Wigwam frame. 3, Coverings of cattail mats and birchbark. 4, Coverings of elm bark and birchbark.
29. Tipi. Women packing wood, Red Lake Reservation. 1, Tipi covered with birchbark − entrance view, Mille Lacs Reservation, 1940. 2, Same as 1; rear view. 3, Nancy Cain, 1939. 4, Mrs. Peter Everywind, 1932.
30. Fireplaces. Collecting herbs. 1, Mabel Daisy, Red Lake Reservation, 1932. 2, Red Lake Reservation, 1933. 3, Gathering medicinal herbs, roots, and bark, Lac Courte Orielle Reservation, 1935.

31. Fireplaces. 1 and 2, Lac du Flambeau Reservation, 1935 and 1934. 3, Mille Lacs Reservation, 1940.

FIGURES

INTRODUCTION TO THE REPRINT EDITION

Sister Mary Inez Hilger's study *Chippewa Child Life and Its Cultural Background* is a rich and detailed portrait of the Chippewa or Ojibway people in the 1930s. First published in 1951 by the Bureau of American Ethnology at the Smithsonian Institution, this monograph was constructed from Hilger's fieldwork on nine Chippewa reservations in Minnesota, Wisconsin, and Michigan. Her account, which focuses upon child rearing practices as central in illuminating "traditional" culture, remains valuable today; the present-day Chippewa who grew up on reservations have recognized it "as a valid interpretation of their own childhood experiences," according to one scholar.[1]

The title of Hilger's publication is actually quite misleading. Although child rearing practices are in the foreground, this study is in fact much more. Hilger views the Chippewa of the 1930s through the lens of child life, providing a remarkably full account of the culture of these northern peoples.

Born in 1891, Hilger was raised in rural Stearns County, Minnesota.[2] Her father immigrated from the Rhineland region in Germany, arriving in the United States at the age of twenty. Her mother was born in Minnesota. The Hilger family ran a general store, a grain elevator, and a lumberyard in Roscoe, Minnesota, forty miles southwest of St. Cloud.[3]

Hilger came to both anthropology and the Chippewa relatively late in life. In 1908 she had entered the convent of the Sisters of the Order of Saint Benedict in St. Joseph, Minnesota. After teaching for several years, she attended the University of Minnesota, receiving a bachelor of arts degree in American history and literature in 1923. Two years later she was awarded a master of arts degree in sociology and social work from Catholic University in Washington, D.C. Hilger then joined the faculty of the College of Saint Benedict, where she remained throughout her career.

The next years were busy ones, as she undertook responsibilities as dean of the College of Saint Benedict (1925–28) and head of the department of sociology (1925–32) in addition to her teaching assignments. Hilger drew upon the encouragement and professional direction of Father John M. Cooper, a professor in the anthropology department of Catholic University. Cooper and Hilger corresponded regularly as he pushed her to complete a doctorate in anthropology under his guidance and to conduct fieldwork among American Indians.[4]

Although it might seem natural for Hilger to have focused on the Chippewa for her dissertation, given the proximity of the reservations to her home town, the connection was actually much more accidental. Reflecting upon her career in 1958, she recalled being sent to the Indian mission at Red Lake Reservation in 1932 for a vacation. While there she became interested in investigating the history and culture of the residents.[5] Nevertheless she continued to consider other possible sites for her work. Ultimately Hilger wrote to Cooper: "I have almost decided not to ask to go among the Blackfoot [sic] but to do work at White Earth. One of our old Sisters,—a Chippewa,—is quite willing to be my interpreter. She herself will tell me all that she can remember. She lived with her tribe until she was thirteen years of age."[6] One year later, Hilger was given permission to continue her work at White Earth and Red Lake reservations for the coming summer. By then, her plan to finish her graduate work was crystallizing. "Some day I may be permitted to complete my residence work for a Ph.D. degree and in the meantime I should like to do the research work for the dissertation," she wrote to Cooper.[7]

In planning her fieldwork for the summer of 1933, Hilger considered concentrating upon a number of aspects of native culture. Because she had been advised to identify an area that had not been focused upon previously, she isolated "child life, music, and art" as not having "been covered to any great extent." Hilger wrote to Cooper, "Now I know I could not do justice to either art or music. But I do think, Doctor, that I could do a creditable piece of work on child life." She suggested that she use Cooper's own research on childhood education as a guideline for her investigation.[8] Cooper approved wholeheartedly of Hilger's plan and offered his guidance. Citing the recent work of Margaret Mead and Bronislaw Malinowski, he encouraged her to follow the functional approach that was then becoming important in anthropology.[9]

Hilger pursued her doctorate through the mid-1930s, encountering some disappointments along the way. In the fall of 1934, she concluded that meeting the residence requirements of Catholic University would be impossible.[10] In 1936, however, with the assistance of Cooper, she was awarded a scholarship to Catholic University, enabling her to finish her degree.[11]

Interestingly enough, the dissertation Hilger completed in 1938 had very little to do with Chippewa child life. Entitled "A Social Study of One Hundred Fifty Chippewa Indian Families of the White Earth Reservation of Minnesota," it is instead an analysis of housing and living conditions.[12] Her dissertation was in some ways both a significant and a puzzling departure, given Hilger's several seasons of fieldwork and increasingly well-developed focus on child rearing and culture. The explanation lies in the fact that the fieldwork for this study was done as commissioned research under the auspices of the Bureau of Indian Affairs, which was interested in obtaining surveys of each of the seven Chippewa reservations in Minnesota. She was allowed to use the material she gathered for her degree as well.[13]

In 1938 she applied for and received a grant from the Social Science Research Council to complete her study of Chippewa child life.[14] Two years later she wrote to the Bureau of American Ethnology, offering her finished monograph for publication.[15] Although the manuscript was accepted, Hilger was informed in 1942 that the Bureau was forced to suspend its publication activities because of the war effort.[16] Publication of the volume as *Chippewa Child Life and Its Cultural Background* finally went forward in 1951.

In the long run, Hilger's interest in child rearing and culture was more central to her life-long research work than were her ties to the Chippewa. Her experiences on the reservation, however, were formative and continued to have an impact on her anthropological approach. Several short seasons of fieldwork on Chippewa reservations followed, but her intensive commitment to the Chippewa was confined to the years between 1932 and 1940.

The fieldwork that formed the basis for *Chippewa Child Life* was conducted among a number of essentially separate groups residing on five reservations in Minnesota, three in Wisconsin, and one in Michigan. It is crucial to bear in mind the climate of the 1930s for the Chippewa, the larger historical context of the cultures with which Hilger worked, and the fact that, while there were certain common elements in the histories of these peoples, their experiences were nonetheless distinctive as well. The large and diverse peoples who came to be called the Chippewa have had a complex history of contact with Euro-Americans. They have been affected by vast migrations, changes in material culture, intermarriage with fur traders, and alterations in the social, political, and economic dimensions of their lives.[17]

The immediate backdrop of this study was the developments of the late nineteenth and early twentieth centuries. Although assimilation of Native Americans had always been the ostensible objective of policy makers for Indian tribes, between the 1880s and 1934 they intensified their efforts. Dissatisfied with the pace of assimilation, policy makers mounted an aggressive campaign to eliminate tribal cultures by implementing a program designed to break up reservation land bases, to root out tribal structures and leadership, and to immerse Indians in the Christian and capitalistic mainstream of American society. The centerpiece of the new policy, the General Allotment Law (or Dawes Act) of 1887, mandated that reservations be broken up into individual land holdings for tribal members. The government would hold land in trust until such time as Indians had become well versed in the market economy and could be expected to function easily within this system. The Nelson Act of 1889 extended the provisions of this policy to Minnesota.

The results of the policy were disastrous for Indians. Allotment, sale of "surplus" land, the subsequent relaxation of trusteeship, and an enormous amount of fraud resulted in the loss of approximately 65 percent of Indian-owned land in the United States between 1887 and 1934.[18] The impact on most reservations in Minnesota was even more catastrophic. By 1983 land loss for the Minnesota Chippewa ranged from 96 percent at Leech Lake Reservation to 21 percent at Grand Portage.[19] The process of land loss and fraud were legendary at White Earth, where swindlers devised countless schemes to extract allotments and reservation resources from Indians.[20] By 1934 only one in twelve of the Chippewa on White Earth Reservation retained his or her original allotment.[21]

Part and parcel of the allotment policy was an intensification of efforts to eradicate native cultures through immersion of children in Euro-American schools (especially boarding schools both on and off reservations), vigorous repression of traditional religious practices, and the replacement of traditional nature-based political and legal systems with Euro-American models. The implementers of this policy assumed that through these means, ties to "traditional" cultures and values could be severed, thus facilitating a transformation of Native Americans that would result in their absorption within white society at large. Such assumptions proved to be naïve.

Under Commissioner of Indian Affairs John Collier, the government finally recognized the tragic results of allotment and assimilation. Collier implemented policies in the 1930s that ended allotment, endorsed cultural pluralism as a positive good, and sought to provide institutional supports for the retention of traditional cultures. The 1930s signaled the ending of concerted assimilation programs that had been forced upon Indians since the inception of the United States. In some senses, this decade was thus transitional for the Chippewa and others, as Indians adjusted to the shift in policy from assimilation to the endorsement of cultural pluralism. Tribal governments were given renewed recognition by the United States under the controversial Indian Reorganization Act of 1934.

Indians were also affected by the economic depression that gripped the nation in the 1930s. Like people elsewhere, many Chippewa relied upon New Deal programs in order to survive. At White Earth and other reservations, positions with the Works Progress Administration, National Youth Administration, and Civilian Conservation Corps – Indian Division provided options after wage labor (particularly in the lumber industry) dried up.[22]

One consequence of decades of assimilation policy was the fragmenta-

tion of Indian societies. Confronted with the dilemma of cultural retention or cultural adaptation, the Chippewa and others made painful individual choices. They responded to the expanding United States presence in their lives in different ways. The result was the formation of
complex configurations that did not fall neatly into the dichotomy "traditional" or "progressive." As historian Melissa Meyer argued with regard
to the outcomes of the era,

> Social heterogeneity never broke down into neatly polarized con-
> tingents. The divisions separating the two ethnic groups at
> White Earth were not hard-and-fast, and individuals frequently
> crossed boundaries to create unique adaptations. An individual
> might simultaneously exhibit both "traditional" and "progres-
> sive" traits, especially if these terms are defined in rigid, categor-
> ical ways that fail to allow for change over time.[23]

Diversity characterized the responses of the Chippewa, both within
reservation communities and among reservations.

These monumental changes formed the backdrop of Chippewa experiences when Hilger began her fieldwork.[24] Because she witnessed a
culmination of decades of change — and a watershed as well — her portrait is valuable from this perspective alone. Although consciously focus-
ing upon "traditional" culture, especially through selecting for interviews
older Chippewas and those raised in "traditional" ways, Hilger nonetheless provided a snapshot of a society in transition. And while she placed
a priority on recording what she regarded as some kind of pure, but fad-
ing, culture, evidence of transition abounds in this monograph. Such
statements as "Today hardly anyone listens to parents," uttered by an informant commenting upon the "traditional" value of respect for one's
elders, reflect the change.[25]

Hilger's sensitivity to the differences present in the reservation communities and the carefully noted variations in practices detailed in her
monograph illustrate her powers of observation. At the same time, however, her language presumes the existence of a pure and static culture
represented variously by her choice of terms and phrases such as "traditional," "in the Early days," or the "primitive days." The timeless quality
conveyed in this kind of presentation is typical of the anthropology of her
era. The reader must be alert to the implicit value judgments in this sort
of portrayal. *Chippewa Child Life* captures these several Chippewa
groups at a particular point in time, and the historical context of each
community is central to understanding the dimensions of each culture.

Other issues regarding Hilger's assumptions and perspective are per-
tinent as well. In reading this work one wonders, for example, about the
impact her religious commitment may have had on her work. Did she
have an implicit or explicit agenda in conducting her fieldwork? Did her

vocation as a nun influence the responses she obtained from her informants? Did her own beliefs affect the interpretations she made of cultural practices? Certainly the Indians realized who she was. While on the reservations, Hilger stayed at missions, and she always wore her habit while conducting her fieldwork. If Hilger wondered how these issues might relate to the responses she got, she dismissed her concerns quite easily. She simply saw little conflict: "Sisters seldom disturb the basic economic and political culture pattern – at least the sisters that are most appreciated by the Indians are the ones that have not done so," she asserted.[26] "Religion" is conspicuously absent as a category from this statement.

In view of the fact that Hilger obtained and included information on Chippewa religion, it is tempting to conclude that she retained a healthy hold upon social scientific objectivity and also managed to gain at least a modicum of trust from a number of informants who had plenty of reason to suspect her motives and conceal all they knew. Yet her account needs to be read with caution. Her description of the Midewiwin and other traditional religious practices must be regarded as a minimal expression of the practices of her day, particularly given Hilger's position and the aggressive efforts by the United States government to eradicate traditional religions. Along these lines one should view Hilger's statement that "Belief in a Supreme Being was firmly rooted in the Chippewa culture" with suspicion.[27]

Hilger explored the problem of religious perspectives in an essay published in 1945.[28] This piece suggests that in many ways her concerns with regard to reservation Indians were more heavily influenced by her social science training than by missionary instincts. Acknowledging that reservation Indians faced many social problems (but were not *more* "socially disorganized" than other peoples), Hilger outlined a series of concerns for Catholic sociologists who were interested in helping Indians alleviate reservation problems. Reflecting her conviction that "American Indians should be assimilated into the general population as rapidly as possible," her prescriptions were geared toward fact finding and problem solving and fostering cooperation between interested professionals and individuals, including missionaries and Indian Service employees. The principal aims of the Catholic sociologist, she argued, should be to learn about traditional cultures in order "to make use of traits in each pattern that can be adapted to present-day life and education." Hilger apparently saw no potential conflict of interest in the myriad individuals who intervened in the lives of Indians for various reasons and with differing motives. Instead she stressed the good will and mutuality of interests that she assumed would prevail. At heart an applied anthropologist, she certainly believed in intervening and altering traditional cultures, but the sole recommendation she made involving religion was that interested children ought to be encouraged to attend Catholic colleges and universities. There does not seem to have been any blatant religious intervention motivating her work.

In the end, *Chippewa Child Life* is remarkably devoid of value judgments, particularly in view of Hilger's religious commitment. Yet appreciation for native cultures did not necessarily come easily to her. Reflecting upon her impressions of her summer on Red Lake Reservation in 1932, Hilger recalled, "It was there that I began to think of the Indian as something more than a savage without a country. As I lived with them I began to understand them. They were proud of their past and as filled with pride for their simple huts as we are for our spacious homes."[29] While expressing such sentiments was not unusual for the time, overcoming these kinds of expectations and value judgments was hardly typical. Not surprisingly, Hilger fell short of being entirely successful, despite her best efforts.

Such criticisms aside, Hilger displayed a remarkable sensitivity to cultural differences and a fundamental respect for other cultures that made her a penetrating observer. She realized the need for understanding and appreciating Indian cultures in their own right and knew that Indians had their own interpretations of the world and how it worked as well as their own sensible interpretations of white men. Clearly grasping the structural difficulties of reservation life in the early twentieth century, she confronted white stereotypes of Indians and offered explanations. For example, when Hilger addressed the often-voiced complaint that Indians were lazy, she pointed out that there were few economic opportunities on reservations and that training provided to Indians was often inappropriate. Answering the criticism that Indians did not act in economically rational ways in providing for the future, Hilger cited the traditional value placed upon sharing and the native assumption that storing foodstuffs was hoarding and antisocial.[30]

Like others of her day, Hilger regarded Native American culture as passing inevitably (and not entirely regrettably) into the past.

> The third generation on the White Earth Reservation stands on the threshold of American civilization from which there is no escape, no turning back. Tribal life has all but lost its hold under economic pressure and the forces of a new social order.[31]

Fieldwork and the production of ethnographic studies constituted "salvage" work and provided a service for future generations who would never have the opportunity to observe native cultures. Hilger used this idea to motivate one informant, suggesting that he was providing a "legacy to generations of his descendants . . . the day would come when there would be no member of his tribe left who would remember even one of their customs."[32] A strain of paternalism runs through her writings as well. Concluding that while many White Earth Indians were poverty stricken (although contented), most were motivated to change their orientations: "Their experience has been limited and they need to have patient, sympathetic, and helpful teachers."[33]

Despite her conviction that an understanding of child rearing practices and the socialization process was central to understanding a culture, Hilger did not use psychoanalytical or personality theories in her work. Inspired by her friend Margaret Mead, with whom she became acquainted while at Catholic University, Hilger drew upon ideas about the centrality of child rearing in understanding cultural systems. She offered no new theoretical perspectives. Her principal "contribution lay in the application of carefully controlled and precise techniques for the field," wrote anthropologist Robert F. Spencer.[34] Nevertheless Hilger was aware of the ways in which anthropology was changing and even investigated the use of Rorschach testing prior to embarking upon her fieldwork among the Araucanian. Her response to this investigation is revealing:

> One thing . . . has been bothering me ever since I have come home and thought it all over: Just what is the psychological approach in anthropology? Does DuBois *The People of Alors* contain a sample of it? – Truly I could not do that kind of thing to my informants. – I have been so frank with them that I would rightly be considered a two-faced person by them if I gave them Rorshachs [sic] and "fortune-tolded" their characters and personalities.[35]

Hilger left anthropological theorizing on personality to other scholars of the Chippewa, such as A. Irving Hallowell.[36]

Although Hilger acknowledged her discomfort with theory, she apparently harbored no doubts about the ability of ethnologists to uncover the essence of tribal cultures through observation and the strategic selection of informants. Nor did she seem to trouble much over the extent to which this sort of strategic selection might bias her results. Thus it made sense for her when conducting research for her dissertation to disregard Chippewa families who were "so situated economically and socially that they were distinguishable from whites only with some difficulty."[37] In her eyes and given her assumptions, such families were no longer Indian. Contemporary concerns about, for example, how the selection of topics and informants determine the results a researcher obtained did not occur to Hilger, nor in some senses could she be expected to consider such potential biases. She was convinced that extreme caution in the selection of informants, painstaking checking of information gleaned against information already available, and her own good judgment were sufficient to yield sound material that captured the substance of the tribal culture under investigation.

So confident was she in the essential soundness of her methods that she produced a *Field Guide to the Ethnological Study of Child Life* in 1960. Having conducted fieldwork among one South American and seventeen North American tribes, she had developed an approach to ethnography that was elaborate, systematic, and painstaking. A recognized expert in the field of child rearing, Hilger wrote that

> the impetus to my ethnological studies of the child came from the knowledge that there was no study of child life of any tribe or any so-called primitive people extant at the time, except Margaret Mead's *Coming of Age in Samoa* and her *Growing up in New Guinea,* and neither of these was like the study I was undertaking.[38]

Hilger acknowledged the influence of Mead as well as anthropologists Wilson D. Wallis, Truman Michelson, Regina Flannery Herzfeld, and Father John M. Cooper in producing her guide.[39]

Although Hilger's approach was certainly systematic and careful, creating a model for other ethnologists interested in child rearing practices and a lens for revealing the central assumptions, beliefs, and practices of a culture, her long-term contributions to anthropological theory are less apparent. She sought to let the information she gathered speak for itself, often providing rather lengthy passages in the words of the informants themselves, suggesting that "an interested psychologist . . . will be able to deduce certain psychological information from our studies."[40] A. L. Kroeber assessed Hilger's approach, as represented in a 1954 festschrift for University of Minnesota anthropologist Wilson Wallis:

> Sister Inez Hilger's field method is essentially field technique. . . . It is all sound; and it carries a strong personal appeal to me because I did ethnography with one of her tribes fifty-three and fifty-four years ago. The fundamental approach is still comfortingly the same; and so is the equipment: pencil and a stoutish notebook. Even the results attainable are astonishingly corroborative.[41]

In many ways, Hilger's emphasis upon accuracy, verification, and critical evaluation of the explanations provided by her informants constitute the greatest strength of her contributions. Because she was so concerned with these issues, the reader is able to evaluate critically the information provided. Her concern with indicating variation in beliefs and practices from different reservations, and even different areas of the same reservation (or among different age groups or classes of people), allows the reader to develop a comparative perspective.

Hilger set forward her own assessment of her ethnographic field method in 1954:

> A field assistant and I set out to record the ethnography of primitive Indian child life as reflected in the milieu of the tribal culture. Our method was that of personal observations and personal interviews with Indian informants in their native habitat. The method . . . grew out of what we set out to do. To a large extent it developed out of our field experience.[42]

Sound and empirical, "the work of Sister Inez represented a classic and substantive ethnography," commented Robert Spencer.[43]

Hilger's work with the Chippewa resulted in a number of publications in addition to *Chippewa Child Life*. These included studies of burial and mourning practices, of hunting and fishing customs, and of several crafts and were published in the journals *Primitive Man, American Anthropologist*, and *Indians at Work*.[44] Other publications by Hilger include book-length monographs about child rearing practices of the Arapaho of the Plains and the Araucanian of Chile and article-length studies of culture and child rearing among the Cheyenne, Arikara, and Menominee.

Although Hilger remained at the College of Saint Benedict throughout her career, she also traveled widely and was active in and recognized within the field of anthropology. She held a number of visiting professorships both in the United States and abroad, including the University of Tokyo, the University of Jerusalem, and the University of Heidelberg. She received research grants from the Social Science Research Council, American Council for Learned Societies, American Philosophical Society, Wenner-Gren Foundation, and National Geographic Society among others. Her study of Araucanian child life won an award for outstanding research from the American Catholic Sociological Society. She was honored by the Smithsonian Institution in 1955 when they recognized her career-long association with the Bureau of American Ethnology and scholarly contributions by designating her an Honorary Research Associate. Hilger retired in 1975 and died two years later.[45]

Hilger's meticulous approach to ethnography ensures that *Chippewa Child Life* will remain valuable. Her inclusion of lengthy passages in the words of the informants themselves and her care in indicating context and variation allow the reader to interpret anew many of her insights; they also provide a sense of the momentous changes experienced by the Chippewa in the early twentieth century.

Jean M. O'Brien

NOTES

1. Helen Hornbeck Tanner, *The Ojibwas: A Critical Bibliography* (Bloomington: Indiana University Press, 1976), 15. At the present time several tribal names are in use, including, but not limited to, Chippewa, Ojibwa, Ojibway, Ojibwe, and Anishinabe. Chippewa has been used in this introduction, as Hilger preferred.

2. The papers of Sister M. Inez Hilger are in two locations. Most of her research materials are on deposit at the Smithsonian Institution. An additional body of material containing correspondence, biographical material, lecture notes, and her writings are housed in the archives at the Convent of the Sisters of Saint Benedict, St. Joseph, Minnesota. I am grateful to Sister Ruth Boedigheimer for her assistance in finding material used in writing this introduction.

3. Sister M. Inez Hilger to Donald Giese, September 12, 1958, Box 6, Folder 86, Papers of Sister M. Inez Hilger, Archives of the Convent of Saint Benedict, St. Joseph, Minnesota.

4. John M. Cooper to Hilger, July 29, 1929, Box 5, Folder 67, Hilger Papers. In this letter, Cooper described his own interest in "child caring" and furnished a questionnaire for Hilger, who was about to make a trip to White Earth Reservation.

5. Donald Giese, typescript story of Hilger's life, 1958, Box 6, Folder 86, Hilger Papers.

6. Hilger to Cooper, May 26, 1932, Box 5, Folder 67, Hilger Papers.

7. Hilger to Cooper, April 13, 1933, Box 5, Folder 67, Hilger Papers.

8. Hilger to Cooper, April 13, 1933, Box 5, Folder 67, Hilger Papers. This statement is remarkable, given the fact that one of the recognized experts on Indian music, Frances Densmore, had published two volumes on Chippewa music. Frances Densmore, *Chippewa Music*, Bureau of American Ethnology Bulletins no. 45 and 53 (Washington, D.C.: Government Printing Office, 1910 and 1913). She had recently published an ethnography that depicted Chippewa culture more broadly; Densmore, *Chippewa Customs*, Bureau of American Ethnology Bulletin no. 86 (Washington, D.C.: Government Printing Office, 1929; St. Paul: Minnesota Historical Society Press, Borealis Books, 1979).

9. Cooper to Hilger, May 27, 1933, Box 5, Folder 67, Hilger Papers.

10. Hilger to Cooper, October 14, 1934, Box 5, Folder 67, Hilger Papers.

11. Hilger to Cooper, June 18, 1936, Box 5, Folder 67, Hilger Papers. Hilger was the first woman to matriculate at Catholic University with full privileges.

12. Hilger, *A Social Study of One Hundred Fifty Chippewa Indian Families of the White Earth Reservation of Minnesota* (Washington, D.C.: Catholic University of America Press, 1939).

13. F. Stuart Chapin to Hilger, October 21, 1937, December 27, 1937, Dr. Louis Balsom to Hilger, no date – all Box 5, Folder 73, Hilger Papers.

14. Frances Carol Locher, ed., *Contemporary Authors* (Detroit: Gale Research Co., 1978), 73–76:293.

15. Hilger to Matthew Stirling, April 5, 1940, Box 8, Folder 138, Hilger Papers.

16. Stirling to Hilger, December 16, 1942, Box 8, Folder 138, Hilger Papers. Her study, *Arapaho Child Life*, was accepted in 1944 but also became a victim of wartime cutbacks; Hilger to Stirling, September 5, 1944, Box 8, Folder 138, Hilger Papers.

17. There is a large historiography that treats the Chippewa southeast and southwest of Lake Superior. See especially William W. Warren, *History of the Ojibway Nation* (St. Paul: Minnesota Historical Society, 1887; St. Paul: Minnesota Historical Society Press, Borealis Books, 1984), and Ignatia Broker, *Night Flying Woman: An Ojibway Narrative*

(St. Paul: Minnesota Historical Society Press, 1983), for recorded oral histories as well as Harold Hickerson, *The Chippewa and Their Neighbors: A Study in Ethnohistory* (New York: Holt, Rinehart and Winston, 1970).

18. Francis Paul Prucha, *The Great Father: The United States Government and the American Indians*, abridged ed. (Lincoln: University of Nebraska Press, 1986), 305.

19. Elizabeth Ebbott, *Indians in Minnesota*, 4th ed. (Minneapolis: University of Minnesota Press, 1985), 25. Mille Lacs and Red Lake were virtually unallotted; Red Lake was specifically excluded from the provisions of the act.

20. This process is ably documented in Melissa L. Meyer, "Tradition and the Market: The Social Relations of the White Earth Anishinaabeg, 1889–1920" (Ph.D. diss., University of Minnesota, 1985).

21. 1935 Report of the Commissioner of Indian Affairs to the Secretary of Interior, from Hilger, *Social Study*, 10.

22. Hilger, *Social Study*, 27–29.

23. Melissa L. Meyer, "Signatures and Thumbprints: Ethnicity among the White Earth Anishinaabeg, 1889–1920," *Social Science History* 14 (Fall 1990): 334.

24. Although Hilger was well versed in the history of the Chippewa in Minnesota and sensitive to conditions in the 1930s that affected Indians there profoundly, her section providing historical background surprisingly omits any discussion of the 1930s. As a decade that saw many crucial changes, the omission is significant.

25. Hilger, *Chippewa Child Life*, 60.

26. Hilger, *Social Study*, viii; Hilger to Giese, September 17, 1958, Box 6, Folder 86, Hilger Papers.

27. Hilger, *Chippewa Child Life*, 60.

28. Hilger, "The Catholic Sociologist and the American Indian," *American Catholic Sociological Review* 6 (December 1945): 246–49 (quotations on p. 246, 249).

29. Giese, typescript story of Hilger's life, 1958, Box 6, Folder 86, Hilger Papers.

30. Hilger, "Catholic Sociologist," 248.

31. Hilger, *Social Study*, 127.

32. Hilger, *Field Guide to the Ethnological Study of Child Life*, Behavior Science Field Guides (New Haven: Human Relations Area Files Press, 1960), 1:ix.

33. Hilger, *Social Study*, 199.

34. Robert F. Spencer, "Obituary of Sister M. Inez Hilger," *American Anthropologist* 80 (1978): 650.

35. Hilger to Cooper, May 24, 1945, Box 5, Folder 67, Hilger Papers.

36. Hallowell's studies of the Ojibway, which focus mainly on the northern groups in Canada, remain classic. See especially his collection of essays *Culture and Experience* (Philadelphia: University of Pennsylvania Press, 1955).

37. Hilger, *Social Study*, vi.

38. Hilger, *Field Guide*, i.

39. Hilger, *Field Guide*, i. Hilger does not seem to have maintained much contact with other scholars of the Chippewa, although she acknowledged the assistance of Hallowell for reading her manuscript in the preface to *Chippewa Child Life*. Her preliminary remarks also stress the "considerable difference" between her findings and those of scholar Ruth Landes in her monograph *The Ojibway Woman*, Columbia University Contributions to Anthropology no. 31 (New York: Columbia University Press, 1938).

40. Hilger, "An Ethnographic Field Method," in *Method and Perspective in Anthropology: Papers in Honor of Wilson D. Wallis*, ed. Robert F. Spencer (Minneapolis: University of Minnesota Press, 1954), 25.

41. A. L. Kroeber, "Critical Summary and Commentary," in *Method and Perspective*, ed. Spencer, 288.

42. Hilger, "Ethnographic Field Method," 25.

43. Spencer, "Obituary," 650.

44. See, for example, "Chippewa Burial and Mourning Customs," *American Anthropologist* 46 (October–December 1944): 564–68, "Indian Women Making Birch-bark Receptacles," *Indians at Work* 3, no. 3 (1935): 19–21, and "Chippewa Prenatal Food and Conduct Taboos," *Primitive Man* 9 (1936): 46–48.

45. Leonard Carmichael to Hilger, April 12, 1955, Box 8, Folder 139, Hilger Papers; Spencer, "Obituary," 650–53; Locher, ed., *Contemporary Authors,* 73–76:293.

PREFACE

The purpose of this study is to record the customs and beliefs of the primitive Chippewa Indians of the United States as evidenced in the development and training of the child. Childhood among the primitive Chippewa began with birth and ended with puberty. It was divided into two periods. The period from birth to the event of walking was called dăkābī'nââswăn; the period from the event of walking to puberty, ábānōd'jī. From the event of walking to puberty, a boy was called kwīwī'sēns; a girl, ekwē'sēns. A child's age was not counted by years. Before it reached the dawn of reason, it might be described as having been "just old enough to remember," or "before it had any sense." Children between the age of reason and puberty were designated as having been "so high"—a gesture of the hand indicating the height.

From puberty to the birth of his first grandchild a man was called kwīwīsēns'sōk; a woman, ekwē'wōk. From the birth of his first grandchild to the birth of his first great-grandchild a man was called nimicō'mis; a woman, nōkōmis.

No monograph dealing with Chippewa child life is now available. Frances Densmore's (1929) Chippewa Customs, for which information was collected on the White Earth, Red Lake, Cass Lake, Leech Lake, and Mille Lacs Reservations in Minnesota, the Lac Courte Orielle Reservation in Wisconsin, and the Manitou Rapids Reserve in Ontario, Canada, contains some excellent material on child training and development. So does Diamond Jenness' (1935) study of the Ojibwa of Parry Island found in The Ojibwa Indians of Parry Island, Their Social and Religious Life. The findings of the present study are largely in agreement with those of Densmore and of Jenness regarding child life. The writer has noted considerable difference, however, between her findings and those of Ruth Landes (1938 b), whose research was done among the Ojibwa of western Ontario and is recorded in The Ojibway Woman. All other sources that have come to the writer's notice (listed in the bibliography) contain only scattered and scanty information on the child.

The first eight sections of this work are concerned largely with phases in the development and the treatment of the child; the last nine sections, with the milieu in which the child was reared. Since rather complete information on the cultural background of the child is already available in the literature (see bibliography), it was covered in the research of this study only to the extent of ascertaining its relationship to child life. Incidentally, at times, informants volunteered detailed information on such traits; sometimes, occasions or seasons permitted personal observation of them. Such information, being new, is included in the monograph.

The material for the study was gathered by the writer on the Red Lake Reservation in Minnesota in the summers of 1932, 1933, 1939; on the Lac Courte Orielle, the Lac du Flambeau, and the La Pointe Reservations in Wisconsin and the L'Anse Reservation in Michigan in the summer of 1935; on the White Earth Reservation in Minnesota in 1938; on the Vermilion Lake and the Nett Lake Reservations in Minnesota in the summer of 1939; and on the Mille Lacs Reservation in Minnesota in 1940.

Ninety-six Chippewa men and women on the nine Chippewa reservations named above contributed information included in this work. A list of their names is found on page   xxxi. Since many were willing to give information only on condition that neither they nor those of whom they were speaking would be identifiable in the published account, names are omitted in the text.

Great care was exercised in selecting informants. Commercial informants were avoided, as well as those who were suspected, even only slightly, of consciously giving misinformation. Of the first generation only those were included whose memory and mental alertness gave no signs of senility. Informants of the second and the third generations were chosen either because they had been reared by grandparents and therefore knew the old customs or because they were living in groups that adhered to primitive ways and participated in primitive activities.

Two or three interpreters were employed on each reservation. These were selected with the assistance of missionaries, of Indians and whites in the local service of the United States Bureau of Indian Affairs, and of educated resident Indians on the reservation. Interpreters were given an opportunity to select from the list of informants those for whom they wished to interpret. Their choice was usually a relative or a friend. Confidence was thus established from the outset and information was often given spontaneously owing to pleasant rapport. This method also eliminated loss of time and the withholding of information, which might have occurred had either an interpreter or an informant, or both, harbored feelings of antagonism or distrust toward the other. This method, furthermore, facilitated the checking of information on any one reservation, for interpreters relayed information, in most instances, as new information. Details, too, were recounted rather than the answer given, "This old lady said the same as did the one we saw yesterday." All information was checked. The final checking was done on the Mille Lacs Reservation in 1940 after the notes of previous field work had been compiled into manuscript. In order not to eliminate personal touches, direct quotations are freely used throughout the work.

It was exceedingly difficult to obtain detailed or complete information regarding items whose origin lay either in dreams or in quests for personal power, or that were associated with or obtainable only through membership in the Mīdē'wiwin, the native religion. In many cases it was impossible to obtain such knowledge; not even names were obtainable. Powers are lessened, or disrespect is shown to the spirits who granted them, if they are revealed. Medicinal or magic use of herbs, roots, and barks frequently fell into this class. For assistance in procuring some native names, the writer is under special obligation to John Kingfisher, of Lac Courte Orielle Reservation, and to Frances Sayers, of Red Lake Reservation, both natives who have acted as official interpreters for Federal, State, and local governments; and to Benno Watrin, Benedictine priest at Ponsford on the White Earth Reservation, who is known in the Chippewa country as the white man most conversant with the Chippewa language. In all instances where plants are not identified, it was impossible to do so. Urging the obtaining of names in these cases would have savored of a most discourteous act. In some cases, too, the price for the purchase of secret knowledge was high. (Selling it cheaply indicates that the owner of it does not prize it highly nor appreciate its spiritual powers.) One old man advised the interpreter to try the following way: "Make the approach by offering a half pound of tobacco; this will get the talking started. Then ask for the information and offer one or two quilts or blankets or some article of clothing of equal value, and see what will happen. I doubt that even then you will get it."

Pictures shown in plates 13 to 17 are from photographs taken by the Mille Lacs Indian Trading Post; all others, by the author.

The late Father Felix Nelles, Benedictine priest, of St. John's Abbey, Collegeville, Minn., 30 years a missionary among the Chippewa on the Red Lake, Leech Lake, and White Earth Reservations, assisted the writer with the correct pronunciation of all Chippewa words found in the study. Father Felix spoke and wrote Chippewa fluently. The transcription of Chippewa words is based on the Phonetic Transcription of Indian Languages (1916).

Father Felix Nelles also read the section dealing with the training in religion and supernatural powers and the section which describes the belief in life after death, and he gave valuable suggestions. The writer is sincerely grateful for his kind assistance.

The writer also wishes to express her indebtedness to the late Dr. John M. Cooper, head of the Department of Anthropology, Catholic

University of America; to Dr. Wilson D. Wallis, head of the Department of Anthropology, University of Minnesota; and to the late Dr. Truman Michelson, of the Bureau of American Ethnology, Smithsonian Institution, for their continued interest and many helpful suggestions; to Dr. Matthew W. Stirling, chief of the Bureau of American Ethnology, and Dr. A. Irving Hallowell, of Northwestern University, for reading the entire manuscript, and to Dr. W. N. Fenton, also of the Bureau of American Ethnology, for reading it in part, and to all three for valuable advice.

She acknowledges her obligation to both Chippewa informants and interpreters without whose fine cooperation and intelligent assistance this work could not have been produced. It is hoped that their descendants will be appreciative of the information this work contains; it was to be left to them as a legacy. Informants particularly were grateful for the opportunity of recording customs and traditions that had been so intricate a part of their lives, in order that their great-grandchildren's children might learn to know them.

The writer is appreciative of the courtesies shown her by the personnel of the United States Bureau of Indian Affairs on the Chippewa reservations. She is also deeply grateful to the Catholic Sisters on these reservations and to Mrs. Emily Weinzierl near Nett Lake and Vermilion Lake Reservations for their hospitality during the summers of ethnological research; to Sister Marie Hilger, Sister Immacula Roeder, and Sister Deodata Kaliher for assistance in field notes; and to Sister Corda Burfield and, most especially, to Mrs. Peter Lelonek for typing the manuscript.

The writer is obliged to her family for financial assistance in field work in 1932 and 1933; to Mr. Roy P. Wilcox, of Eau Claire, Wis., for field work in 1935 and 1938; and to the Social Science Research Council for grants-in-aid for the final work in 1939 and 1940.

St. Benedict's Convent,   SISTER M. INEZ HILGER,
      St. Joseph, Minnesota.   *Benedictine Sister.*

INFORMANTS AND INTERPRETERS

Red Lake Reservation of Minnesota:

Ella Bad Boy
Tom Barrett
Amos Big Bird
Cecilia Blackjack
Solomon Blue
Jane Bonga
Mary L. Brun
Nancy Cain
Mary Crawley
Mabel Daisy
Mrs. Peter Everywind
Mrs. Glasby
Josephine Gurneau

Mary Gurneau
Angeline Highlanding
Mary Iyubidud
Kah gay se goke
Eva Mountain
Naytahwahcinegoke
Frances Sayers
James Sayers
George Stateler
Mary Sumner
John Baptiste Thunder
Charley Johnson

White Earth Reservation of Minnesota:

Big Bear
Carrie St. Claire
Andrew Vanoss
Mr. and Mrs. Wilson

Gabriel Siace
Gimiwananakwod (Rain Cloud)
Sadie Rabbit
Mrs. Vivian Jones

Nett Lake Reservation of Minnesota:

Sophie Goggleye
Grandma Peterson

Sarah Wein

Vermilion Lake Reservation of Minnesota:

Jennie Boshey
Anna Chosa
James Gowboy
Anna Knott

Mary O'Leary
Mrs. Howard Pete
Mrs. Joe Pete

Mille Lacs Reservation of Minnesota:

Mrs. John Noonday
Mildred Hill
Emishewag

Benay
Susan Anderson

Lac Courte Orielle Reservation of Wisconsin:

Peter Cloud
Louis Corbine and wife
William De Brot
George Fleming and wife
Ellen Gockey
Alice Hall
Susie Homesky
Mary Isham
Mary Krokodak
Henry La Rush
Sister Syrilla La Rush
Emma Demare Martin

Peter Martin
Mishiman and wife
Nellie Olson
Mitchell Quagon
Mary Robinson
Frank Setter
Mrs. John Shogey
Mrs. Otis Taylor
Frank Thayer
Angeline Wolf
John Kingfisher

La Pointe Reservation of Wisconsin:

Mrs. George Arbucle	Mrs. Joseph La Pointe
Martha Cedarroot	Frank Scott
Margaret Greeley	Mary Twobirds

Lac du Flambeau Reservation of Wisconsin:

Grandma Ardeshaw	Mrs. St. Germaine
Margaret Christianson	Mr. and Mrs. Pat Williams
Ben Gauthier and wife	

L'Anse Reservation of Michigan:

Dan Curtis	Mrs. Peter Sharlifoe
Louis Gauthier	Lucy Shosa
Ana Johston	John Thayer
Charles Pappin and wife	Mrs. Ed Vashow

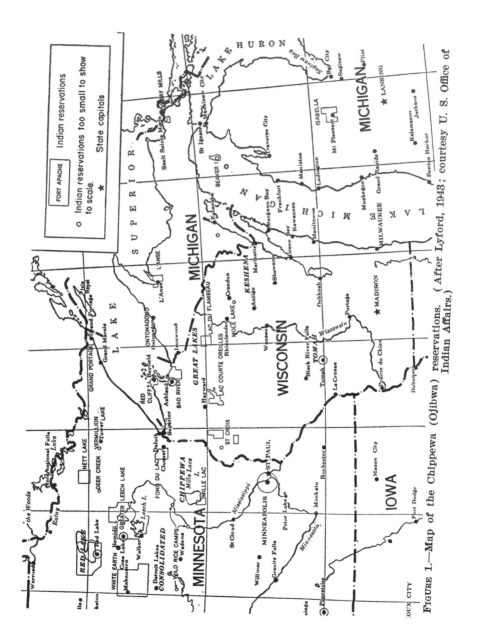

FIGURE 1.—Map of the Chippewa (Ojibwa) reservations. (After Lyford, 1943; courtesy U. S. Office of Indian Affairs.)

CHIPPEWA CHILD LIFE AND ITS CULTURAL BACKGROUND

By Sister M. Inez Hilger

INTRODUCTION: THE CHIPPEWA INDIANS

Copway, a native Chippewa, wrote in 1851 regarding the origin of the name of his people: "I have heard a tradition related to the effect that a general council was once held at some point above the Falls of St. Anthony, and that when the Ojibways came to this general council they wore a peculiar shoe or moccasin, which was gathered on the top from the tip of the toe, and at the ancle [sic]. No other Indians wore this style of footgear, and it was on account of this peculiarity that they were called *Ojibway*, the signification of which, is *gathering*" (Copway, 1851, p. 30). The word "Chippewa," which is now generally applied to this tribe in the United States, is the popular adaptation of "Ojibway."

Culturally, the Chippewa Indians belong to the woodland area of North America; linguistically, they belong to the large Algonquian family. The tribes of the Algonquian family, according to Michelson's linguistic classification, fall into four major divisions: Blackfoot, Cheyenne, Arapaho, and Eastern-Central, the last having two subtypes—the Eastern and the Central. The Eastern includes the Micmac, as one group, and the Abnaki, which comprise all the remaining extant dialects, as a second group. The Central subtype, the one including the Chippewa, is subdivided into the following groupings: The Cree-Montagnais; the Menomonie; the Sauk, Shawnee, Fox, and Kickapoo; the Ojibwa, Potawatomi, Ottawa, Algonkin, and Peoria; the Natick; and the Delaware (Michelson, 1906–07, pp. 223–290).

The first recorded word regarding the Chippewa is found in the Jesuit Relations of 1640 where they are mentioned under the name of Baouichtigouin. In 1641 Fathers Isaac Jogues and Charles Raymbault found them at war. In 1667 Father Allouez wrote of them as living on "the sault by which Lake Tracy empties into the Lake of the Hurons" (Kellogg, 1917, p. 135). In 1670–99 Perrot found them living south of Lake Superior (Hodge, 1907, pt. 1, p. 278). Mention of the Chippewa is found in most of the journals and narratives of the

1

early missionaries, travelers, and fur traders.   The tribe is recorded in historic literature under more than 70 different names, among them Achipoes, Chepeways, Odjibwag, Uchipgouin, Dewakanha, Dshipewe-haga, Ninniwas, Saulteur, and Saulteaux.

Contemporary Chippewa, basing their information on traditions recorded in the ceremonials of the Mīdē′wiwin, their native religion, say that when the first white men met them, the Chippewa were jour-neying westward to their place of origin from somewhere in the East where there are great bodies of water.   Their westward movement, in-terfered with by Fox and Sioux, was greatly aided by the use of fire-arms.   These came into their possession about 1670.   During the beginning of the eighteenth century, the Fox were driven from North-ern Wisconsin; the Sioux were driven across the Mississippi River and south of the Minnesota River.   The Chippewa then continued west-ward across what is now Minnesota and North Dakota as far as the Turtle Mountains.   While a portion of the tribe was thus moving westward, another forced the Iroquois to withdraw from the peninsula between Lake Huron and Lake Erie (Hodge, 1907, pt. 1, p. 278). Skinner notes that the territory over which the Ojibway at one time roamed "extended from the Niagara River on the east to the neighbor-hood of central Montana on the west, and from the northern part of Wisconsin and Michigan north about halfway to Hudson's Bay" (Skinner, 1911, p. 117).

Treaties between the United States Government and the Chippewa, as well as executive orders of Presidents and special acts of Congress affecting them, began as early as 1785 and continued to be made until recent times.   Twenty-two such negotiations were transacted in the 60 years between 1805 and 1864 (Kappler, 1904, pp. 13–754 passim). Until the nineties the Indians were continuously ceding lands; in more recent times the Government has been reacquiring lands for the Indians.

Today the Chippewa live on reservations within their original terri-tories in Minnesota, Michigan, Wisconsin, and North Dakota, and in Ontario, Manitoba, and Northwest Territories (fig. 1).   The entire population in the United States and Canada was estimated in 1905 to be between 30,000 and 32,000 (Hodge, 1907, pt. 1, p. 280).   The popu-lation in the United States today according to the 1940 census is nearly 30,000 (U. S. Office of Indian Affairs, 1940, pp. 9, 12, 16).

PRENATAL PERIOD

PARENTAL FACTORS

Sterility.—The cause for inherent sterility was not known.   Sterility could be produced artificially by taking a decoction, ingredients of which were known only to certain persons.[1] Sterile people were not well thought of. "Indians are proud to be able to conceive." Some informants had not heard of either partner blaming the other if their union was childless. One informant, however, knew that—

a sterile woman was suspected of having had intercourse before puberty. If a certain married couple had no children, and the man died, and his wife remarried (or if his wife left him and married another man) and if the woman then had children, everyone knew that she was not sterile. No one suspected her any longer; everybody knew then it was the man's fault.

Fertility.—Certain Indians claimed to have knowledge regarding the medicinal value of plants which, when taken in the form of a decoction, produced fertility in sterile women. On the Red Lake Reservation, "if a mother didn't have children and wanted some, they brewed two roots, ānīcīnābēkwī djībīk and básēnákwēgok and she drank it. It always worked." On the White Earth Reservation several decoctions were used. The following were two: "Use either the bark of the hazelnut brush (bágānīmīdjī nōnágek) or a sort of buttercup or waterlily found in the meadows (pákwōdīdjītēgōns)."

On the Mille Lacs Reservation both husband and wife drank the potion:

If a woman has no children and she wants some, she is given an Indian medicine and her husband drinks it too; they always have babies after that. I know of a couple who drank it; she was a relative of my husband—my husband's sister's daughter. They were getting old, drank the medicine, and had a baby; but it died when it started to creep around. No one here today has knowledge of that medicine. One old lady had it, and she died.

Another very old informant on the same reservation said: "Old Indians knew medicine which when taken by both husband and wife always caused them to have children."

On the Lac Courte Orielle Reservation, informants did not wish to name the ingredients, but said "roots and barks of certain trees." The interpreter added:

The ingredients are known only to older members of the tribe who still practice medicine. They will reveal the true recipe only when told to do so by the chief medicine man at the celebration of the Mīdē'wiwin which takes place in the fall and in the spring of every year. At the celebration certain old persons, members of the Mīdē'wiwin, are selected for promotion to higher degrees. They are then told the recipes of certain decoctions—each degree has its own particular knowledge pertaining to herb curing. When a member has completed the entire course—that is, has made all the degrees—he is a full-fledged medicine man.

Limitation of size of family.—Artificial limitation of families was not known to the Chippewa. Abstinence, however, was practiced. "Parents preached to the men and to their daughters to stay away

---

[1] Throughout this work where plants, roots, and bark are not identified, it was impossible to obtain either native names or specimens. Cf. also Preface (p. XIII). For those that were identified, see list of some plants used by the Chippewa (p. 173).

from each other. It was considered a disgrace to have children like steps and stairs." "If a man had sense, he didn't bother his wife while a child was young." "Some had many children, but none had them like steps and stairs; the men and women kept away from each other." "I didn't live with my man as husband until the baby was able to walk. I slept alone."

CONCEPTION

All informants agreed that conception is due to the collaboration of both parents. Typical remarks were such as these: "It is from the man that the child comes, as well as from the woman." "The man is responsible for the baby along with the woman. That was always believed by the Chippewa because they knew that to be true." However, it was believed that a child born with certain physical traits was not conceived in the normal way: it was considered reincarnated. Such traits were those of being born a twin; of being born with a small patch of gray hair anywhere on the head, or with teeth, or with a caul, or with "nips" out of the ears, or with birthmarks, especially ones that resembled healed wounds. It was believed that the ghost of an Indian, well advanced in years, one who showed the characteristics with which the child was born, had come near the mother's body and had entered the body of the child. This occurred either at the moment of conception or very soon afterward. "Such babies were old-time Indians. No one knew who the old-timer was, but some old Indian's spirit went up to the mother's body and entered the baby's body. This was not said as a joke; this was the truth." "My daughter was born with a patch of white hair, and I heard my grandmother say, 'There, that child is some old person come back to life.'" "Some boys and girls were born with marked ears; it was supposed that they were old Indians born again. You know in old times, Indians had their ears pierced. My grandmother had long slits in her ears." [2]

PERIOD OF GESTATION

Gestation covered a period of nine missed menstruations and was reckoned from the first one missed, birth being expected at any time after the ninth one missed. The phases of the moon served as a calendar. One informant said:

We took notice whether the first menstruation that was missed occurred at half-moon, quarter-moon, full-moon, or no moon—the old Indians reckoned everything by the moon, for we had no calendars like now. The exact time was nine moons. We made marks with charcoal somewhere to remember the moons as they passed; I used to make marks on the birchbark covering of our wigwam, in the corner, right over the place where I kept my things.

---

[2] According to Hallowell, the Saulteaux believed that a child with a few gray hairs was reincarnated. An infant that cried constantly was thought to be trying to utter the name it bore in a previous existence. (Cf. Hallowell, 1940b, vol. 70, p. 50.)

Another added:

I took notice of the phase of the moon of my first missed menstruation and counted the numbers of moons of the same phase as they passed. I kept that number in my head. I always had a good memory and didn't have to mark a stick like many women did.

Informants differed as to the exact time during gestation in which the child became a human being. Some had been told that the embryo was human from the moment of conception; others, only from the time that it gave signs of life; others had never heard any one tell. "We were taught that the child was a human being as soon as it was conceived: right from the start when we knew we were that way; from the time we didn't menstruate anymore." "After 4 months the child is completely shaped and starts to move in the mother; from then on it is a human being. Some children even hiccough at that time." "I always thought of my babies as being human beings after I had missed two menstruations." "I had an aunt who knew her baby was 2 or 3 months along when she lost it. (She lost it because she carried too heavy a load of wood on her back.) You could tell that it was beginning to form. They cleaned it just like a child that is born and wrapped it. They gave a feast just like for a dead person and buried it in the same way. They believe that a child is human when it is conceived."

Some informants had been taught that for the growth of the unborn child marital relations of the parents was necessary during the entire period of pregnancy; others noted that after conception "the mother takes care of herself and the baby grows from the mother's blood."

All informants agreed that there were no methods by which either male or female sex could be produced, either at the time of conception or during pregnancy. Sex, however, could be predicted by the contour of the mother's abdomen, by the location of the fetus, by the movements of the child, by the physical condition of the mother, or by a type of affinity. If the contour of the mother's abdomen was pointed, she carried a boy, because a boy sat in a haunched position, having knees toward front of his body; a girl sat low with knees on a level with feet thereby causing her mother's body to be rounded. "When I had my first baby my mother told me it would be a girl, because I was shaped round; and a girl it was." If the fetus was located near the sternum the mother was carrying a boy; if near the pelvic bones, a girl. Boys gave evidence of more life than did girls and they indulged in more violent and more frequent movements. Some women noted that they had to void oftener when carrying boys than when carrying girls. An affinity is said to exist between certain small children and an unborn child; a small girl will be attracted to the woman bearing a girl; a little boy, to the fetus of a boy. These children will climb on the woman's lap, throw their little arms around her neck, and wish to be where she is. They will follow her around and at every opportunity come near her.

Girls were usually born about 10 days before they were expected, but this was not so with boys. Boys were "harder on the mother when born, and labor pains took longer." "When my daughter was born, I took sick at 2 o'clock and she was born at 6." Twins could nearly always be predicted because of the movement of the two fetuses. "My sister told us right along that she would have twins for there were always two hiccoughing: sometimes they hiccoughed together; sometimes, one after the other."

Parents had no preference as to the sex of the child, except that mothers usually were glad to have a number of girls since daughters, more often than sons, cared for their aged parents.

EFFECT OF MOTHER'S PREGNANCY ON YOUNGEST CHILD

It had often been observed that during pregnancy a mother's youngest child developed an unusual thirst. This continued until the birth of the baby, at which time someone offered the child a drink of water in a small birchbark receptacle (pl. 24, 2). While the child was drinking, the person offering the drink bent the receptacle outward, thus forcing the water to spill away from the child. After this the child no longer craved water.

FOOD TABOOS AND PRESCRIPTIONS

Informants on all reservations except Mille Lacs agreed that the Chippewa husband was not hampered in his food by either taboos or prescriptions during the pregnancy of his wife. One of the oldest members on the Mille Lacs Reservation was convinced that the fathers, too, should be restricted in diet:

Both father and mother must not eat turtle. If they do the baby will stretch all the time just like the turtle stretches all the time, and that isn't good for baby. Nor must they eat catfish. I knew a baby who was born with rings of sores encircling its head; the father had eaten catfish. The sores ate into the baby's head and it finally died.

At Nett Lake the mother of a freckled-face little girl was confused and remarked that the child's father must have eaten sea-gull eggs, for she was positive that she herself had not done so.

For the pregnant wife, however, food was both restricted and prescribed. The violation of these mores at any time during pregnancy affected the physical nature and/or the personality make-up of the unborn child. The expectant mother was warned not to eat much food at any time since "it made the baby large and birth difficult," but she was to observe this rule especially immediately preceding birth—an empty stomach facilitated birth. A child's head will be large, she was told, and his limbs feeble, if a pregnant woman eats either the head or the tail of any vertebrate animal; only the parts between extremities should be eaten. Eating entrails of fish or of any other animal will cause the navel cord to wind about the child's neck, shoulders, or body, and this, too, makes birth extremely difficult. Eating lynx, also, causes the birth to be difficult, for "the lynx has a hard time giving birth to its young." Eating turtle delays birth "because the turtle is slow."

If an expectant mother would eat turtle her newborn baby would stretch continuously. Eating fat or grease or tallow caused the child's head to become large; so did eating suckers. Eating popped rice caused the baby to have difficulty in breathing. Eating sea-gulls' eggs caused the baby's face to be covered with freckles, for "sea-gulls' eggs are speckled with freckles." Chokecherries and hominy constipated the mother.

Eating porcupine caused the baby "to have a stuffy nose"; to be clumsy or crippled, clubfooted, or pigeon-toed. "I didn't heed the warnings of my mother; I ate porcupine and my boy was born clubfooted." "The teachers in our schools used to tell us not to believe these old Indian superstitions; but I believe in some of them. I can't help believing that they are true for I have seen them come true." Porcupine, too, made babies headstrong, difficult to train, hateful, and touchy, for "the needles of the porcupine are sharp."

Rabbit heads caused the child to become frightened easily. They also caused large bulging eyes. Eating the head of catfish caused the baby's eyes to be small. Eating blackbirds and robins, or any animal that makes a sound like a bird, caused the baby to be a cry-baby. Eating hell-divers made the baby moan, "a pitiful hard moan, for the hell-diver makes a peculiar sound, a kind of sickening sound." Eating duck caused the child to vomit much; eating certain fish made it bite. Siskos, a snakelike fish, caused it to have snakelike movements of the body. Eating woodchuck caused the baby to shake continuously, "for the woodchuck shakes all the time."

Eating raspberries caused red marks on the child's body; eating blueberries, little blue marks like blueberries; eating blackberries, caused black marks. "I have a blueberry mark; my mother used to say she ate blueberries while she was carrying me." "Once when I was carrying a child, we were moving camp. My mother walked behind me. I took a black raspberry and ate it. She saw me and told me what would happen; and when my baby was born, he had a black spot on his leg." Other foods that were taboo were geese, eggs of turtle, and "lash"—a fish of snakelike color. Mothers were encouraged to eat venison, wild rice, lake trout, and whitefish. (Cf. Hilger, 1936 d, 46–48.)

CONDUCT TABOOS AND PRESCRIPTIONS

Most informants had never heard that husbands of pregnant wives were in any way either restricted by conduct taboos or hampered by conduct prescriptions except that the husband was strictly forbidden to strike his wife or to speak roughly to her. A Lac Courte Orielle informant, however, related the following:

According to the Chippewa traditions, hunting was at no time and in no way ever considered to be injurious to anyone with one exception. If while an animal was being dressed that had been killed by the husband of a pregnant woman certain bad signs appeared—muscles in certain parts, say in the sides or ribs of the animal, twitched or jerked—he knew he was seeing a bad omen: stillbirth or death shortly after birth of his unborn child was in the offing. This could be averted only if great sacrifices were offered. For example, the man and his entire family and all those who lived in his household had to bring various foods—in the early days it was wild rice, berries, dried meat, etc.—to a place where all the grand-medicine men and women of the tribe were meeting. The latter were feasted and their power thereby obtained in averting the evil. The man knew, too, that from now on he had to refrain from hunting until after the birth of his child. Some violated this custom; such cases are known and the child suffered the consequences.

The expectant mother was restrained by many conduct taboos. "If she minded the old people who taught her these, she was all right; if she disobeyed them her child would have to suffer the consequences." An expectant mother was not to look at corpses of human beings if she wished her child's eyes to be bright looking and not "dazed and queer looking, or even cross-eyed." If the mother allowed her gaze to rest on a deformed person or a deformed animal, "such as a deformed calf," she knew her child would be physically deformed. It might have drooping eyelids, or have its mouth drawn to one side. In fact, expectant mothers were not to look at any unusual object and if, inadvertently, they did so "they were not to turn and look again." Nor were they to look at snakes; it was best not to look at any animal, or to torment any animal, even the smallest ones, such as a fly.

If an expectant mother stepped over a tree felled by lightning, knowingly or unknowingly, her baby was born with a rash or a queer-colored skin, and was usually subject to convulsions. Such a baby had to be bathed daily, until cured, in a decoction made by boiling bark or pulp of a tree that had likewise been felled by lightning. If notice had been taken of such a fall, the bark was then and there gathered and saved until the arrival of the baby. This taboo, however, was not known to the Lac Courte Orielle informants.

The child of a mother who had been frightened by a lizard was born with "a head shaped like that of a lizard, and with short arms and little legs like those of a lizard."

An expectant mother was told not to turn over in bed, lying down; she was either to rise on knees and turn over, or to sit up and do so. Rolling over in bed caused the umbilical cord to wind around the child's neck or body, thus causing either difficult birth or, at times, the strangling of the child at birth. "Sometimes the cord was even under the arm of the baby, because the mother had turned without sitting up." "My mother instructed me, but I never heeded her. When my children were born with their cords around their necks, she'd say, 'There, now! See, I was right.'"

Women were taught to do hard work while carrying a child and in this matter no leniency was shown them. Women who refrained from hard work might anticipate adherence of placenta after birth. "I used to saw wood and do everything; it did not hurt me, but my little girl's back was all streaked, because of the wood that I packed on my back while I was carrying her." "A pregnant woman was not permitted to lie around; she was made to do hard work, such as chopping wood, because that kept the child loosened and made birth easy." Hesitating on the threshold of a door or lying across her bed did not affect the expectant mother in any way. Such a woman was instructed, however, not to enter the wigwam of any but her immediate relatives. It was known in some cases that her enemies—jealous because of her marriage to her husband—had the favor of certain medicine men who allowed them to use their "bad medicine."[3] Some of it was of such strength that even the slightest contact with one possessing any of it was sufficient to injure the unborn child, or even to kill both mother and child. Pregnant women were not allowed to receive gifts, not even food, from anyone except immediate relatives. There was constant fear of "bad medicine." For the same reason she was not to lie on any one else's bed but her own; her clothes might come in contact with bad medicine—a thing they always feared.

Women were also advised to refrain from going to dances or from mixing with crowds. If they did so on the Red Lake Reservation, legs and feet had to be massaged previously with some medicinal preparation made from snakeroot (wīnī'sīgōns). On the Lac Courte Orielle Reservation—

there was always fear that an expectant mother might come in contact with "bad medicine" and be afflicted with pēäsīkwä'kwē (meaning she was tripped in her purpose). Therefore, any part of her body might at any time be rubbed with a mixture of a root found in swamps (mȧckwō'kāwȧc) and with sturgeon grass (nȧmēwȧc')—we now call it catnip. This would offset any "bad medicine" which was intended to harm her or her unborn child.

---

[3] When Chippewa Indians say "bad medicine" or "grand medicine" (kābē mīdē'wid) they mean a mysterious magic power, including black art, possessed by certain members of the Mīdē'wiwin, their native religion. (Cf. also pp. 71–75.)

Both induced and spontaneous abortions occurred among the Chippewa. Induced abortions, however, were not looked upon with favor on any reservation and were, therefore, of rare occurrence. Judging from the number of children born to older informants, one is led to believe that among them there were few abortions, but a rather high rate of infant mortality. One informant's story is typical of those told by many of the older women: "I had six children, all of whom are dead: One died as a mere baby; two were 1 week old; one was 3 years old; tuberculosis took one boy at 19, and my last girl at 21."

Several of the oldest informants had heard, when younger, of women who had aborted children voluntarily; these instances, however, were spoken of in whispers. Most informants had never been acquainted with such a woman. "No, I never knew any woman who did that. An Indian doesn't like to do that. My grandmother said that years ago they suspected a woman of having done that but couldn't prove it." "Mothers never induced abortions in old times; they took good care so that their babies would be born right." "Indians are proud to be able to conceive and do not think much of abortions."

Abortions, however, did occur in the olden days, and they occur today.

In old days, I heard of one woman that was not married, but that had babies; and she caused abortions. They said she used to go where there was a fallen tree and hang over that, and so cause the abortion. But after she was married, every baby died just as it was born. That was long ago. I knew of her; but I was not acquainted with her.

I know that there is medicine that women take and I know of some women way back that did that, but I don't think that is right. Sometimes the woman never gets over it, and sometimes it kills her. Some try to hurt themselves, too, and cause abortions in that way.

A very old informant knew of persons who had drunk decoctions to induce abortions: "I was brought up by my great-grandmother who had such knowledge. I never heard of abortions due to lying across a log or carrying a heavy weight. The only way I heard of was by means of tea. I don't think there was much of this since Indians liked children too well." "I do not know of any full-bloods on the reservation today who cause abortions; but some of the others do that." "I know that abortions are being committed on the reservation today, for I know several persons myself who do it. They drink Indian medicine which is made by steeping some roots or herbs; that is all they have to do. Those who know what to use do not tell." One informant had aborted seven times "because I'm not rightly married

to my man and I don't want to have his kids around. I have enough to
do to take care of two—the ones my right husband does not take care
of. Some woman here in the village gives me tea to drink. It works
every time." On the same reservation two informants told of four
old women who were dispensing decoctions to expectant mothers. A
woman 26 years of age—a mother of four small children—said she
had been told repeatedly by older women "to get medicine from 'Old
Lady So-and-So' the next time a kid was on the way." A 30-year-
old mother of 7 children had been offered information regarding
artificial limitation by a white woman on one of the reservations, and
added, "If I don't want any more children, I'll go to 'Old Lady So-
and-So' and get some drink to get rid of the baby; I don't need her,
that white woman, to advise me." Informants noted that induced
abortions, in old days, as well as today, were performed either because
husbands were mean to their wives and did not support them, or because some women did not like children. Although decoctions were
the ordinary means used, women also induced abortions by lifting or
straining themselves or by jumping off high places.

Spontaneous abortions occurred because women worked beyond their
capacity, as, for example, in splitting wood. A severe fall might also
do harm. When a woman feared an abortion she might use preventive measures, the knowledge of which was in possession of certain
persons. A 90-year-old informant possessing such knowledge demonstrated the treatment. After placing some finely crushed roots, leaves,
and flowers of certain herbs on smouldering lint on a dustpan, she
stood over it flexing her knees so that the bottom of her long skirts
rested on the ground about the dustpan. This permitted the fumes
to ascend her clothing without any of them escaping. She remarked,

> My sister and I have this knowledge. We generally use a frying pan, in place
> of the dustpan I used here, and make the woman stand over that while the herbs
> are throwing off medicine. It is done only if a woman hurts herself and is afraid
> of an abortion. Knowledge to do this came to my sister and me from my mother,
> and she received it from her grandmother. So it goes back to our great-grand-
> mother. I wanted to teach it to my daughter when she was here last week, but
> she wouldn't even listen to me; she said she didn't believe in any of it. None of
> my children believe in the old Indian ways; maybe they will when they grow
> older and wiser. Since no one but my sister and I have this knowledge, and we
> won't live much longer, it will die when we go; it belongs only to our family.

In old times the fetus of an induced abortion was buried either
under the floor of the wigwam in which the mother lived or under
the roots of the tree from which roots had been taken for making the
potion that caused the abortion, or anywhere under the ground. It
was never buried with funeral rites. Spontaneous abortions were
buried in the same manner as adults (p. 81).

BIRTH

PLACE OF BIRTH

If pregnancy ended in late fall or winter, birth usually took place in the home wigwam of the permanent camping grounds. If, however, there were preadolescent boys or girls in the family, a small wigwam was built not far from the home to which the mother retired until after the birth. "I used to erect a special wigwam so that I might be away from the children since we all lived in one-room wigwams in those days." If the birth occurred in spring or summer, the mother prepared a place in the open, some distance from the home wigwam, and gave birth there. The birth also occurred in the open if the family happened to be enroute to or encamped in a place of food gathering, such as maple-sugar making, fishing, hunting, trapping, berry picking, or wild-rice gathering. "My mother-in-law was out trapping with her husband when one of her children was born. She cut the cord herself and continued to work." "My grandmother used to tell how women at times gave birth while the families were away from home, hunting. They would stay in the same place for four days after a birth, and then go on again."

PERSONS ASSISTING AT BIRTH

Midwives (gàtā′nīwī′kwē, a term also used for any woman administering to the sick) usually attended the mother at birth. At times, however, only the woman's mother and sister, or some women who were near relatives, did. "You could have whomever you wanted: I wanted my mama and my sisters." "All women seemed to know how to assist at birth, and always there were several women present at birth." "I assist at birth even today and that without a doctor. Some of the full-bloods don't want men around; not even doctors." "I myself think it is a disgrace the way women submit themselves to strangers today when their babies are born, especially to those doctors; when I was at the hospital with pneumonia, I heard all about it. In old days not even the women looked at anyone more than necessary; a big piece of buckskin was placed over the mother to protect her modesty."

Only certain midwives, however, knew how to deliver stillbirths. This was done by means of the midwife's hands. "I know one midwife who removed three children in stillbirths." "A woman who was dying of childbirth asked me to take her child as soon as she had died. I did so and the child breathed twice and also died." "I was called to a home where the woman had died some time before. They did not want to bury her with her unborn child, so I removed it by using both of my hands. I had a hard time doing it for the baby, too, was dead."

It was not customary for any man, not even the husband, to be present at birth unless no women were available, or unless some strong person's assistance was needed. Some women objected to having their husbands anywhere near the birthplace; others tolerated them "to come in and to see how things were progressing." "Sometimes if the mother was too weak to kneel or stand, the women called upon the husband to lift his wife." "Men were not to come into the home until the baby and mother were cleaned up. A man has something inside of himself (informant insisted this was different from his soul) and if he came into the place of birth something would happen to that being in him; it might even die. The man wouldn't amount to anything after that. No; men had better stay away if they know what's good for them." There was nothing, however, by way of magic, such as walking continuously or drinking or eating a particular food, that the father could do to assist with the birth.

Medicine men or medicine women, shamans, were called in only if labor was unusually hard, and it appeared as though the mother would not survive.[4] These exercised their powers and were well paid for their services in material goods, such as cloth, buckskins, and kitchen utensils.

Other assistants who were not of the immediate family were paid in wearing apparel. Members of the immediate family did not expect pay.

POSITION OF MOTHER DURING DELIVERY

In the early days all mothers took a kneeling position when giving birth; some women do so today. "Those who are accustomed to giving birth in a kneeling position find it difficult to do so lying down in bed, like women have to do when they go to hospitals." In the early days the child was delivered on a thin layer of dry grass, which was spread either on the ground or on a bulrush mat. Today a worn blanket usually replaces the mat. "No quilts nor good blankets are used because after everything is over, all is burnt."

Mothers employed several ways of bracing during delivery. One method was to grasp a sapling that rested in the crotches of two poles that were planted firmly into the ground some few feet apart. "My children were all born while I was in a kneeling position bracing myself on a pole so that my elbows were on the opposite side of the pole; the more the arms were used the less pain there was." At the present time, the pole may extend cornerwise in a room, being nailed to the scantlings of the walls. Today, too, chairs or boxes often replace poles.

---

[4] Cf. shamanistic powers, pp. 88–90.

Some informants found pulling on a rope with all possible strength of greater benefit than bracing.   One end of the rope—either a strip of moose hide, a pack strap, or some basswood fiber—was fastened to the trunk or limb of a tree or, in more recent years, to some part of the framework of the house.   If the woman was too weak to pull the strap, a short pole was tied to the end of the strap and she supported herself by placing her elbows across it.   "I was lying in bed in great pain when my first baby was about to be born," a young woman re- marked.   "They sent for my mother.   When she came she made me get out of bed and kneel on the floor, telling me to lean against a chair. But I couldn't stand that.   Then they tied a rope—one we use for anchoring the boat—to the wall and put a stick through the end of it, and they told me to pull on it.   But I thought my end had come."

"I had an awful time when one of my babies came.   Finally, one of the two old ladies that took care of me made me stand up and put my arms around her neck like this [with face toward assistant's back] and tried to lift me.   Just as soon as she pressed her buttocks against my stomach, the baby came."   An informant on the Red Lake Reservation, in her nineties, gave the following account of the birth of her oldest child—her only surviving one of 12:

My son was born in brush like this.   I expected him because I was sick all night.   I had swept the floor of our wigwam and gotten it all cleaned so it wouldn't be dirty should anyone happen to come.   Early in the morning I took what little clothes I had for him—tanned buckskins, mostly—and a scissors and went out into the brush about as far from our home as that fence (about a rod). I told my husband to bring hay out there, and after that I was there all alone.   I knelt down and braced myself on a stick I had gotten ready the day before: I had placed a sapling in the crotches of two sticks that I had planted into the ground.   The child came, and I cut the cord and tied it.   Then I wrapped up the baby and hollered for my man to come.   He took the baby and I walked with him toward the home, and on the way I began to feel faint and my man braced me with his arm.   All that's woman's sorrow!   I fainted after I got into the wigwam.   My mother and the neighbors were all out fishing, and it all came so fast.   I drank Indian medicine and soon got well again.   The only time that I was sick at childbirth was when this child was born; he was my first child.

A middle-aged woman on the L'Anse Reservation recounted an event her grandmother told:

My grandmother, who died some years ago at the age of seventy-three, said that when she was a small girl they used to move from place to place.   Once while we were coming along the Flambeau Trail when it was cold and snow was on the ground, my grandmother, grandfather, uncle, father, and mother were traveling together.   We stopped overnight in one place, and next morning, my grandfather, grandmother, and mother stayed behind while the others moved on. When night came my father cleared away the snow in a certain place.   He built a big fire there; then removed the remnants of the fire and built over this place a wigwam covered with mats and brush, in which we slept.   We kept asking when mother was coming.   "What's wrong with mother?"   "Why doesn't she come?" After 3 days my mother and grandparents came, my mother carrying a little bundle. "Here's a new baby," she said.

In those days people picked moss in swamps. They hung this swamp-moss on bushes until it was dry and all the bugs had fallen from it, packed it in birch-bark *makuks* or sacks and saved it for new babies. The babies were covered with this moss and then wrapped in squirrel and weasel hides. Very few babies, they say, died in those early days. They were like little kittens; they lived right on. [Hilger, 1936 a, p. 21.]

AIDS AT CHILDBIRTH

At the onset of labor pains, the woman was given a decoction of herbs. "It causes the child to come at once and easily too." "Indians made their own medicine to help birth along and to make pains easy to bear. Only certain ones knew what plants to use, and you had to pay the women who made the medicine." [5] One informant used nábánānī'weōk (a root that looks like the hair of a man) ácōcwā'cōk (high weed with flowers like sunflower), and māmāskwāgā'mīsūd (root that becomes red when boiled). Another used bark of basswood (wīgōbī'mic) and slippery elm (ōcácī'gōb). A third used sweetgrass (wī'kūc). (Cf. Flannery, 1940, pp. 21–22.)

Women were encouraged, too, to move about and, if possible, to work until labor pains became very severe. "If you make them walk around or work, the baby will be loosened and birth will be easy. We were told not to overdo though." "When I began feeling sick and wanted to lie down my mother said, 'Get up, this is not a sickness!' And I had to go to work; I had to be on the move all the time." All during pregnancy expectant mothers were admonished to adhere to the prenatal food and conduct taboos if they expected easy delivery.

Most informants knew of mothers who had died at childbirth, and they attributed each death spoken of to some irregularity or difficulty in delivering the placenta. "I knew of a woman who died because a second child was born in the afterbirth." "Some mothers died of hemorrhages or neglect. The afterbirth was often hurried or pulled so that parts were left behind and caused blood poisoning." "When my boy was born, the afterbirth had grown to my side. One of the old ladies whom my mother had gotten to help with the birth washed her hands with castor oil and went around the cord and pulled the afterbirth out very easily. Not all women could do that; the ones that could also knew how to take a child from a dying mother, or a dead baby from a living mother. It seems the ones that could do that best were married women who had never borne children."

Some mothers refrained from work for 2 or 3 days after a birth; most of them, however, returned to work within a day. Several old inform-ants were much amused at the idea of being confined to bed for several

---

[5] Cf. uses of herbs, barks, roots, pp. 90–93.

days after a birth. "Some of those young women say they are Indians. They may be Indians in some things; they most certainly are not when it comes to forgetting themselves after their babies are born. Why, I have seen many an Indian woman in the old days get right up after her baby was born and help with the work—work like cooking a meal or cutting up a deer her old man had brought in." "After the baby was born, the mother got right up and walked around." "The mother was lifted up to stand on her feet and given Indian medicine to drink. After that she walked around a little, although she didn't do any work for 2 or 3 days; but she didn't lie down."

The mother drank a cupful of tea 3 or 4 times a day made by boiling the inner bark of oak, maple, or slippery elm. She did this for 10 to 14 days immediately following the birth.

THE NAVEL CORD

Usually one of the attending women cut the navel cord; at times, mothers did so themselves (cf. p. 14). In the early days a stone, chipped to a cutting edge, was used in severing the cord; in more recent years, a butcher knife or scissors.

The cord was dried and placed in a little beaded buckskin container, "about the size of my palm," the edges of which were sewed together with sinew. One such bag on the Red Lake Reservation consisted of two pieces of buckskin, each 2 inches in diameter. The bag of a 13-year-old son of an informant on the Nett Lake Reservation was made of two pieces of buckskin, 1½ by 1¼ inches each, covered with beads of no particular design and finished off at the lower end with beaded fringes. Girl's bags did not differ in appearance from those of boys. A child's bag was attached to the bow of its cradleboard so that it might play with it. This is still done (cf. p. 23).

Informants varied as to the final disposal of the cord. Densmore's informants said that the child was to keep its own cord during its entire life (Densmore, 1929, p. 51; cf. also Flannery, 1940, p. 11, and Coleman, 1929, vol. 2, p. 52). One of the writer's informants on the Vermilion Lake Reservation had saved all of her children's until they grew up; "but now they are all lost." Usually, however, the cord was disposed of early so as to be efficacious to the child. A Red Lake informant noted: "When a baby boy began to walk, his father took his bag on a hunting trip and dropped it wherever he killed the first animal. That caused the boy to become a good hunter. If it was a bear the father had killed, and the bear was in a hole, the cord was thrown into the hole after the bear was out." In the old days on the Lac Courte Orielle Reservation, after a boy was a year old his navel bag was placed in the stump of an old tree and ashes were thrown over it with the hope that a bear might find it and thereby make a lucky hunter of the boy. A girl's cord was buried under wood chips in order that she might become a diligent wood gatherer. "I placed my little boy's in the trunk of a tree. This is done all around here today," said one young mother on the same reservation.

Should a mother be careless and "put the bag anywhere," the baby, when it began to walk, might "get into things." People would then say, "He is searching for his navel cord." Placing the bag in a drawer made the child steal; throwing it into fire caused the child to play with fire, and people to say, "He is playing with his navel cord."

Some of Densmore's informants noted that the cord was saved to procure wisdom for the child, and that if it were not saved the child would become foolish. One of her informants, too, observed that if the child poked the ashes of the fire, older persons would say, "He is looking for the cord" (Densmore, 1929, p. 51).

THE CAUL

Informants on the Vermilion Lake, Nett Lake, and White Earth Reservations attached no meaning to the caul. On the L'Anse Reservation the caul was dried and put into a little buckskin bag, each child so born being given its own. Carrying it was to bring good luck. "But it doesn't always bring good luck. Two of my daughters and one of my sons were born with thin skins over their faces. One of these girls has had all sorts of bad luck; she is entirely deaf now." Another informant on the same reservation remarked:

When I assisted at a birth one time there was no doctor. I looked at the afterbirth and saw a thin piece attached to it. I was frightened, for I thought the afterbirth had been torn and the mother would get blood-poisoning. I called a neighbor. She laughed and said it meant good luck. She said, "I won't touch it; but you take it and wash it and hang it up to dry. Then give it to the boy and you'll find he'll succeed in life; he'll become a good hunter, a good fisher, etc." When it was dry I looked at it and could plainly see the impression of eyes and nose. It felt like silk. Later I helped at the birth of another boy who also had a veiled face. [Hilger, 1936 a, pp. 20–21.]

On the Red Lake Reservation "a family was highly thought of and felt honored for having such a child." Informants on the La Pointe Reservation respected the child, but not necessarily its family. On the Lac Courte Orielle Reservation an old informant—

had never heard the people around here speak of its happening except once. One old woman here remembers that it happened once when she was a child. She tells that as a little girl she was always curious to hear the conversation of older people. One time when a child was born she heard the women say that it had come into the world with its veil. She remembers how serious these women were when they talked about the new baby: they said that he was going to possess powers of a spiritual nature —that he was like manito. But this person died before he was old enough to show his powers.

THE FONTANELS

The Chippewa attached no meaning to the fontanels. Nor did they give them any treatment, except that of refraining from touching them with pressure for fear of injuring them. "Sometimes they weren't even washed; they were too soft."

THE PLACENTA

Potions which the mother was given to assist birth were usually also efficacious in bringing about the passage of the placenta. If there was difficulty, however, she was given an additional decoction made of nābā́nānīwēōk (a root that looks like the hair of a man) and nābāgōc' (a flat-leafed weed). If the decoction plus the exertion of her will power was unsuccessful, she pressed her abdomen with her hands, or stretched, or gagged herself by tickling her throat with her finger.

Informants on all reservations agreed that in the very early days the placenta was always hung in the crotch of a tree formed by the main trunk and a branch at such a height that no dogs or other animals could reach it. In later days it was buried. Informants thought that the coming of the Whites introduced the custom of burial; in the early days burying or burning it was decidedly taboo. Today, at least among the younger people, it is generally cast into the fire. "When assisting at a birth recently, I wrapped the afterbirth in a newspaper and burnt it. The grandmother of the woman grabbed into the fire for it, and exclaimed, 'Oh! you shouldn't have done that; you should have buried it,' and appeared quite angry."

THE BABY'S FIRST BATH

A baby's bathtub was a nonleakable birchbark receptacle similar to the one shown in plate 24, 2.[6] Its length was the distance from finger tips to elbow; its width, two stretches of one hand—the thumb, in measuring, gliding toward small finger. Certain plants, among them catnip, spruce boughs, and twigs of gībāīmīnā́'mīgōk, a plant that grows in swamps, were boiled in water and the baby bathed in the decoction immediately after birth or at least on the day of birth. Some used "an herb that can be found where maples grow." "Only certain Indians around here know which plants to use. They will give you the crushed herbs but will not tell you what they are. They pass the information on from generation to generation in their own family." The bath was thought to give the child a strong constitution and it might be repeated by the mother any time she desired.

---

[6] Cf. birchbark containers, pp. 134–135; and plate 24.

PURIFICATION OF MOTHER

Informants on all reservations were agreed that there was no purification ceremonial for the mother after birth, such as standing or bending over fumes of herbs and roots. "I never heard old Indians around here, nor any Indians anywhere, tell of any treatment that the mother was given after the birth."

ANNOUNCEMENT OF BIRTH AND CEREMONIAL CELEBRATION

Densmore's informants related that "if a baby was born during the night it was customary to notify the people by firing guns" (Densmore, 1929, p. 48). According to Father Pierz, a birth at any time was so made known, for as soon as a child was born the father announced its birth immediately by a "Schusz-Salve" (a greeting by gunfire) (Pierz, 1855, p. 20). An old informant on the Red Lake Reservation said that "way back they used to tell of the father firing a gun after the child was born; but that was long ago"; then added, "Yet I heard a gun fired after one of my neighbors was born, and he is forty-six now."

Another Red Lake informant remembered—

that neighbors, both men and women, as soon as they heard the gunshot, went to the home of the newborn baby, gathered at the outside of the wigwam, right near the place at which the baby was lying on the inside, shot off guns, and made diving motions as though they would take the child; they also talked to it telling it to be brave. After this they all ran into the wigwam and formed a circle around the child, each one tapping it with his hand and telling it to be strong. The mother and relatives then threw a pail of water on the persons—by this time they were running around the child—in order to protect the child. Neither the father nor any member of the family took part in this ceremonial. Nor was this done often; but whenever it was carried out the child did well: it became a warrior or some worth-while person.

Densmore recorded a similar account saying that immediately after a delivery the people were notified of the birth of a child by the firing of the gun.

The men of the father's gens and those of one other gens went to the wigwam and attempted to gain possession of the child, the father and the men of his gens defending the child against the other party. The child's relatives threw water, and sometimes a mixture of flour and water, on the attacking party, and the men fought and wrestled. It is said that "everybody was wringing wet" when the struggle was finished. The men who secured the baby took it to the leader of the gens who carried it four times around the fire while the people sang a song with words meaning "We have caught the little bird." The parents gave presents to the men to secure possession of the baby. It was said, "This was done to make the child brave from hearing so much noise as soon as it was born." [Densmore, 1929, p. 48.]

A feast—a gathering at which a meal was eaten and pipes were smoked—was given either the day following the birth or very soon thereafter. "Any number may come to the feast, either men or women. Seven men came to the feast of my son the day after his birth." "An especially big feast was given when twins were born, for they were considered sacred."

POSTNATAL INTERESTS

NOSE RINGS AND EARRINGS

Very old informants gave the names of Chippewa men and women who wore nose rings and who were old when they themselves were still children. The oldest woman on the Nett Lake Reservation remarked:

I did not have my nose pierced, but all the people that were old when I was young wore nose rings. Parents pierced the nose of a child—if they wished it to wear a nose ring—soon after birth with the point of a knife made of a moose rib. My mother wore a nose ring.

Much amused, an old Red Lake informant said: "My grandmother had a hole in her nose, but she wore her two earrings in it!" "Long ago many Chippewa wore nose rings." Densmore wrote that heavy ornaments were worn in the nose, which was pierced, some ornaments being so large that they extended down over the mouth (Densmore, 1929, p. 141). "In winter," she writes, "a little bunch of fur was sometimes substituted for the ring. An informant said that she had often seen an old Indian with bunches of white fur in his nose and ears" (Densmore, 1929, p. 36).

Although a girl's ears were usually pierced immediately after birth, "because the baby had no feeling then," or within a few days after birth, both boys and girls had their ears pierced any time while they were still small. Some had several piercings in the lobe and a number along the edge of the ear. "Some cut long holes in the ears and wore many earrings." Formerly the ears were pierced with the point of a bone knife, and consequently, the incisions were elongated; in recent times, the point of a metal knife or of a large needle was used. Any person might pierce a child's ear. The act was devoid of meaning or significance; there was no ceremonial connected with it: "It was for ornament's sake only." "In order that the piercings would grow right, mother turned our earrings once in a while." One informant pierced the ears of all her children within 4 days after birth. She molded to points both ends of lead used as weights on fish nets, brought the points together, and inserted them gently into the opposite sides of the ear lobe. Each day she pressed them a little closer together until they finally met.

Earrings were often made of coins, especially dimes. These were usually hammered out and bent into various shapes. A woman on the Lac Courte Orielle Reservation, who died in 1933 at the age of 115, wore a chain of 10 hammered dimes in each ear. The oldest woman on the Nett Lake Reservation wore earrings made of twisted wire and dimes in 1939: a Canadian dime dangled from one ear; an American, from the other. Densmore wrote: "The most common sort of earring consisted of a bunch of small, elongated metal cones, suspended at the tip. It was not uncommon for so many of these to be worn that the ear was weighted down by them" (Densmore, 1929, p. 36).

CRADLES, DIAPERS, "TALCUM POWDER," BABY HAMMOCKS, METHOD OF TRANSPORTING BABY

Cradleboards (dikinä'gŏn) (pl. 2) were being used by a few persons on all reservations except White Earth and L'Anse. In constructing them the traditional pattern had been followed. The board of one seen on the Nett Lake Reservation (1939) was of cedar wood (basswood might have been used since both are of light weight). Its length was 28 inches; its greatest width (head end of board), 11½ inches; and its narrowest width (foot end of board), 10½ inches. About 5½ inches from the head end, a bow-shaped frame was inserted, the ends of which protruded beyond the reverse side of the board where each was held in position by a small peg of wood which had been inserted through it at right angles to the protruding end and parallel to the board. The bow was double bent: the dip at the center was 11 inches from the board and each of the two outward bends 13½ inches. About 1½ inches from the foot end, a U-shaped band of cedar wood, 1½ inches wide, formed a footrest. Its ends extended nearly halfway up the board. This particular cradle had been in use for 12 years, several families using it.

A baby that was too small to be tied to the cradleboard itself was placed in a birchbark container (ōdāpī'bēwin or wīkwācīdā'cīnōwin), and then tied to the board. Containers of larger dimensions were made as the baby grew in size until it was finally big enough to be tied to the board itself.

Formerly, the cradle was prepared for the baby's occupancy by placing a piece of soft, tanned deer hide on the board, or in the container. Over this, from baby's waistline up, weasel or squirrel skins were placed—the mother had saved these in preparation for the baby's coming; from waistline down, a thick layer of dried swamp moss or rabbit skins was spread. The baby was placed on this. Weasel or squirrel skins were then drawn over the baby's chest and arms; its lower body and legs were covered with moss and rabbit skins. Next, the ends of the deer hide were brought over and tucked tightly around the baby. After this, two pieces of beaded buckskin (pl. 2, 2)—each had been securely fastened to one side of the cradle with strips of tanned buckskin—were brought together and laced over the middle of the baby, beginning at the foot end. The beaded buckskin had been replaced on the Nett Lake cradle by black velvet lined with gray outing flannel and edged in buckskin. The buckskin edges were so pierced that they could be laced together with buckskin laces.

The length of a cradleboard on Vermilion Lake Reservation in 1939 (pl. 2, *1*) was 30½ inches; its width at head end, 12 inches, and at foot end, 10 inches. The footrest, attached 1½ inches from the foot end, extended 10½ inches toward the head end. Its bow-shaped frame was 12 inches from the board at center dip and 16 inches at outer bends; it protruded 2 inches beyond the back of the board. A mother who had borrowed it—it had been made by her husband's parents for some other child—wrapped her 6-month-old baby in it in the following manner: Sitting on the ground to the right of the cradle, she folded a small blanket fourfold and four-cornered, and placed it on the board so that it reached from the foot end to the place where the baby's neck might be. Next she folded a diaper twofold and four-cornered, and placed it on the board so as to reach from feet to waistline. Over this she laid a smaller blanket, again only to waistline. She then folded the baby's dress upward so as to leave its body below waistline bare and placed it upon the folded cloths, moving it twice so as to make certain that an approximate distance of 2 inches was left between its feet and the footrest. The blanket which had been placed on the board last was then folded over the baby's body and tucked between legs and groins. After this the foot end of the outer blanket was brought over the feet. Then the portion of the outer blanket on the left side was brought over both legs and tucked under the right side; the portion on the right side was brought over and tucked under the left side. Next, the left arm was laid straight alongside the body, the blanket laid over it and held tightly until the right arm, too, was straightened. The blanket from the left side was then tucked under the right arm. Next, the portion on the right was held tightly across the body and tucked in on the left side. "He is almost too big for this cradle," she remarked. "But he likes to be in it when he is tired from moving around freely." Preventing the baby from moving by placing her left hand upon it, she brought the outer covering—the one attached to the board and in this instance of black plush—over it. She laced these from foot end to neck, leaving only the baby's head to protrude. She then set the cradle against the side of the house and went off to poke her outdoor fire for dinner. When babies in cradleboards get restless, mothers free their hands by untying the upper section of the outer cover.

A cradleboard in a Mille Lacs Reservation home in which the Mīdē'-wiwin drum was kept had been made for a baby by an old man in 1935, and it was still being used in 1940. Its length was 24 inches;

its greatest width, 11½ inches, and its narrowest width, 11 inches. The footrest, a U-shaped 2-inch strip of cedar wood, was fastened to the board 1 inch from the foot end, reaching 9 inches toward the head end; its width at the opening was 7 inches. The greatest width of the 2-inch bow-shaped frame attached at the head end was 14 inches; the narrowest, 11½ inches; its depth at dip was 11½ inches; at crest, 12 inches. Each end of the frame protruded 3 inches beyond the back of the board. It was held in position by being nailed to a 1½-inch piece of wood that had itself been securely nailed to the back of the cradleboard.

The purposes of the cradleboard are to train the baby's back to be straight, to permit the mother to carry the baby on her back when traveling, and to keep it safely in place while she is working. "The mother can set the baby up in its cradleboard anywhere, against a tree or a wigwam or any place, or she can hang it on a tree so dogs can't bother the baby while she is busy making sugar or picking berries. The baby can't get hurt if it falls over: the bow protects its head and body, and the footrest, its little feet." Gilfillan, who spent many years with the Chippewa, wrote of a Chippewa baby in its cradleboard:

It likes the firm feeling of being bound and swathed in this frame, and will cry to be put into it. The frame can be leaned against the wall at any angle, and so it can be relieved by change of position; or, best of all, the mother carries it suspended on her back, by a strap passed around her forehead, while she goes about her work. [Gilfillan, 1901, p. 86.]

Articles hung on the bow of the Nett Lake cradle were a navel-cord bag and four 3-inch strings of beads, each tipped off with the instep bone of a porcupine foot. The child in playing slid these along the bow. A Vermilion baby's cradle toy consisted of several duck craniums strung by the bills on a strip of buckskin. Other small bones of animals were often strung and used as toys. Densmore records that two articles representing spider webs were usually hung on the bow of the cradle. She was told that "they catch everything evil as a spider's web catches and holds everything that comes in contact with it" (Densmore, 1929, p. 52). She also mentions, as favorite toys, small white shells and bunches of tiny birchbark cones, one of which was occasionally filled with hard maple sugar and "hung in such a manner that the child could put it to its mouth and get a little of the sweetness" (Densmore, 1929, p. 52). Cooper records caribou teeth, the shoulder blade of the turtle, feathers from the skinned and the dried duck head, a little net to catch oncoming colds, and a beaded navel bag as cradle charms used by the Lake of the Woods and the Rainy Lake Ojibway (Cooper, 1936).

Although very often Chippewa families today have cradleboards, nearly all babies found in homes visited during this study were snugly and tightly wrapped up in small blankets or in cloth of some sort. One method of thus wrapping the baby was like that used by the Vermilion mother in wrapping her baby for the cradleboard (p. 22); the blanket, however, was held in place by safety pins. A mother on the Mille Lacs Reservation placed her baby to her right on a square piece of blanket resting on the ground in diamond position, with the head corner turned over toward the inside. She straightened the baby's legs and held them in position by placing her left hand on its knees. She then brought the foot end corner of the cloth over the feet and well up over the abdomen. Then holding the baby in position with her right hand, she straightened its right arm and laid it snugly against its body. She next brought the corner of the cloth at the right of the baby across its body, laid the baby's left arm snugly against its side, and tucked the cloth tightly under the baby's left side. The remaining corner was next brought tautly around the baby and fastened in the back with three safety pins, one each at chest, back, and feet. "Babies get so used to being tied up this way that they will not rest any other way," remarked the young mother (pl. 2, *3*). Densmore notes this custom arose "after the Chippewa attained cotton cloth" (Densmore, 1929, p. 48). One very old informant on the White Earth Reservation was heard to say regarding a crying baby, "Pin him up tightly in his blanket. You know, I used to hear my old grandmother say that babies like best to be wrapped tightly in deer hide for then they feel like they did in their mother's womb." Babies so wrapped were usually placed in hammocks.

Babies' hammocks or swings (wēwēbē'sīkin) were seen on all reservations (pl. 3, *3, 4*). They were made by stretching two ropes and fastening the ends to opposite stable objects, such as poles of a sun shelter, trees, or scantlings of walls in a house. A blanket was folded over the ropes and the ends were so placed as to overlap well underneath the baby, thus preventing the baby from falling through. The ropes were held apart at the head end by a small stick, crotched at the ends; on hot days one was also placed at the foot end. A baby was seen resting in a hammock under a sun shelter where a mother was making birchbark trays used in winnowing wild rice; under trees near a home where a mother was braiding rugs; under trees in the woods where a mother was picking berries; fastened cornerwise in a home where a mother was doing her kitchen work; or fastened cornerwise over a bed on which a grandmother was sewing while tending the baby. In the early days hammocks were made of cords of basswood fiber and tanned hides.

Very small babies, as indicated before, were transported on their mothers' backs in cradleboards. A baby, however, that was able to stand the strain was carried on its mother's back seated in its mother's blanket or shawl. This baby was said to be bēmōmȧkwȧ′sō (pl. 4). On the La Pointe Reservation, a mother stooped so deeply that her back was nearly horizontal, took the hands of her 4-month-old baby, swung the baby gently to her back over her left shoulder, brought its little arms about her neck, flung her blanket over her head, pulled it tightly about her waistline, and then knotted the two ends that met there. She raised herself while pulling the upper section of the blanket tightly around her own shoulders, thus holding the baby snugly in position. She then tied the upper corners into a knot also. Caring for the baby in this way left her hands free to hold things. Mothers on all reservations tied their babies similarly and carried them long distances.

On Vermilion Lake Reservation a young mother returned from a visit to friends living a few miles away. She packed her 8-month-old baby on her back and carried a package of groceries and two winnowing baskets in her hands. She dropped the latter upon arrival, stooped so deeply that her back formed a horizontal plane, untied the knot of her blanket (all four corners formed one knot), pulled the blanket off with her left hand, and with her right hand slid the baby off her back, to the right.

Although rabbitskins were used as diapers, being washed and re-used, or more often thrown away, swamp moss (āsȧ′kȧmik) alone, or mixed with well-dried down of cattail, was most generally used. Moss was gathered from swamps and marshes in summer, hung on bushes until dry, and then shaken and pulled apart so as to rid it of all insects and dry weeds. Mothers kept supplies of it on hand, storing it in mākōk′ (pl. 24, 3b). "When moss was used for diapers the baby seldom became chafed, and when it was unwrapped you could smell only sweet moss."

Several types of "talcum powder" were used for babies. Some informants had used ashes of cedar bark, or finely powdered rotten stump, or decayed wood of cedar or of Norway pine; others preferred charcoal of cedar wood rubbed to powder between palms of hands. "This was put wherever the child was chafed and healing set in at once." Some used cattail that had grown old and gone into powder; others used finely crushed dried leaves and flowers of mŭckēgō′bōk, "a plant that grows in swamps." Some used deer fat.

LULLABIES

The Chippewa lullabies are conventional songs of nonsense syllables. Upon insistence that an informant sing a lullaby with words, she answered, "The Whites have words but we Indians don't; the Indians just sing: 'Bā! bā! bā!' and 'Wē! wē! wē!'" While an interpreter transmitted information, an aged informant rocked her great-grandchild in her arms singing to it in a friendly, talking manner, but merely saying, "Bā, bā! Bā, bā! Wī, wī! Wī, wī! Bā, bā! Bā, bā!" Another lullaby consisted of a repetition of the syllables, "Wā, wā! Wē, wē!" [7]

A CHILD'S FIRST CLOTHES

The rabbitskins and weaselskins in which a baby was wrapped when in its cradleboard (cf. p. 21) were its first clothes. In cold weather these not only covered the upper part of its body but were often wrapped about its feet. When a child was old enough to creep about the wigwam, it wore a little slip of soft, tanned deer hide—fawn hide if available—in cold weather; it wore no clothing whatsoever in warm weather.

When about a year old, a child wore its first moccasins. These followed the pattern of those worn by adults except that each had a small hole "about the size of a blueberry" cut in either the heel or the ball of the sole. This was done hoping that the child when grown to maturity would work so hard hunting, if a boy, or gathering wood, and berries, if a girl, as to wear out his or her moccasins. Neglecting to do this would cause the child to grow up to be lazy—"so lazy that he would not even wear out the soles of his moccasins."

At night babies were wrapped in rabbitskin blankets (wā'bōs swā'yākī). One such on the Vermilion Lake Reservation measured about 50 inches square. The maternal grandmother of the baby for whom it was made had used from 60 to 70 rabbitskins. Her daughter, her assistant in making such blankets, described the process as follows: Skins were stripped off rabbits from the back toward the head, hung up to dry, then rolled together and stored until a sufficient number was at hand. They were neither tanned nor salted. On the evening preceding the day of weaving, the inner side was sprinkled with water, "just like you sprinkle wash." In the morning the skins were cut in strips an inch wide, beginning at the head end and cutting round and round the body circumference. When all was ready for weaving, a framework of poles was set up and a strip of fur stretched taut across the top. Next, a strip of fur was attached to the upper left corner of the frame, and moving toward the right was tied in loops to the taut strip of fur, each loop being fastened by means of a knot. When the weaver had reached the right-hand corner, she moved leftward, again forming loops by tying a knot to each loop of the first tying. Looping and tying was continued back and forth until the blanket was of the desired size.

---

[7] Cf. Densmore, 1910, p. 163, and 1913, p. 241, for music to lullabies; 1913, pp. 138–139 and 302–305 for songs for entertainment of children. For other Chippewa songs, see Burton, 1909.

One informant and her mother assisted each other simultaneously on the same blanket. The informant worked from left to right, and her mother, from right to left. Both met halfway, knotted their strands together, and each returned to her starting point with her own strand. It took an entire day to weave one large blanket.

Rabbitskin blankets were sometimes worn as coverings by adults, the number of skins required ranging from 150 to 200. The number of skins needed also depended on the looseness of the loops: the looser the loops the fewer skins were needed. Some workers made loops so small "that one was unable to poke one's fingers through them."

Blankets if stored in mothproof boxes or trunks or hung up so as to be completely exposed to air lasted for many years. One was so exposed on the wall of the kitchen of a Vermilion Lake informant in August 1939.

A CHILD'S FIRST ACTIONS, FIRST WORD, FIRST STEP, FIRST PORTAGE, AND FIRST TOOTH

No significance was attached to a newborn infant's clenching its fists during the first days of life. However, on the Mille Lacs Reservation its elders would not allow it to touch the fingers of one hand with those of the other, for "that is not a good sign; it's like counting the number of days it has still to live." All informants were agreed that no significance was attached to a child's first word. "People simply said, 'Now he is talking.'" Since, however, early speech was considered a sign of intelligence, a child was often given raw brains of any small bird as food in the belief that it would thereby be aided in developing early speech.

When a child took its first steps (cīgāwē′cīkwē)—"more than one or two, for it has to take a little walk, at least half the length of the wigwam"—a feast was given. If the steps were taken at home, the parents gave the feast; if it walked to neighbors, the latter gave it. Sometimes small children in the neighborhood were invited; sometimes "everybody that was near." "No feast was given when the baby made its first step. But when it took its first short walk alone (3 yards would be sufficient) its parents gave a feast." "When the baby walks alone to the neighbors for the first time, the neighbors give a feast because the baby has been on its first visit. Always the ones to whom it goes give the feast."

Nett Lake and Vermilion Lake informants gave a feast on the day that a child made its first portage on foot. The parents of the child provided the feast and all those portaging were invited. "My brother made his first portage on foot when he was three years old."

The advent of the first tooth was not celebrated by Chippewa on any reservation. Nor was any significance attached to the loss of the first tooth.   But on the Mille Lacs Reservation at the loss of each tooth, the loser blackened the tooth with charcoal and then threw the tooth toward the west saying, "Nōkå' [Grandma], let another tooth grow immediately!"   The charcoal was thrown to the east, the person saying, "Nīmi'cō [Grandpa], let my tooth grow right away!"   "I have lost all my teeth," said an informant older than 90 years, "and I threw all of them over there [to the west]."   According to Flannery's informants, the milk teeth were thrown toward the east with the same belief that new teeth will grow faster and stronger (Flannery, 1940, p. 12).

NURSING AND WEANING

NURSING

In most instances a mother nursed her baby immediately after birth. An old Lac Courte Orielle informant, however, said that a child should not be nursed until 2 days after birth, because "mother's milk is not considered healthy until then.   If the baby cries the first two days, it is to be given water; if it sleeps, it is not given anything."   If the condition of the mother's breasts did not permit nursing or if the mother died, the child was given either wild-rice or corn-meal porridge boiled with meat or fish broth.   The baby sucked this from a small hole punched in a thoroughly cleaned and dried bladder of an animal—"moose or rabbit or some animal like that."

There was no set time for nursing; babies were nursed whenever they cried.   Nor was there any custom as to which breast was to serve the feeding at any particular time.

Children were commonly nursed until they were 2 years of age. All informants, however, knew children that nursed when they were 4, or even 5 years old.   "Children used to play around and come running to their mothers to be nursed."   "One woman in the village is nursing her boy now, four years old.   My youngest brother used to be playing with a bow and arrow and, with them in his hands, come running up to mother to nurse.   Mother weaned him by going off on a trip, leaving him at home."   "I knew a boy who nursed when he was five years old.   I have seen him pull his mother's sleeve while she was visiting, wanting her to leave the company so he might nurse."

Densmore's informants knew of instances in which a mother nursed two children, 3 and 4 years of age, at the same time (Densmore, 1929, p. 51).   Gilfillan, too, observed this: "Then it gets hungry and goes and takes a pull at its mother's breast, and this it keeps up till three or four years of age; even after a younger baby has come, the mother nurses both together" (Gilfillan, 1901, p. 64).   A child, however, was not nursed while the mother was pregnant.

Mothers nursed babies either holding them in their arms or holding them tied to the cradleboard, the cradleboard being held as would be the baby. The bow-shaped frame extended backward beyond the arm. One young Lac Courte Orielle mother was seen repeatedly nursing her small baby in a cradleboard. Older children stood while nursing.

In order to increase milk secretion, mothers were advised to eat porridge of fish or meat broth and corn meal or wild rice. "Corn soups and such thick soups made the baby strong." "The mother was always given the best kind of food, such as venison and soups; that made the milk flow, and helped the baby grow."

Eating hominy or chokecherries "dried up the milk"; so did potatoes and bread. One very old Red Lake informant blamed younger mothers for violating these customs:

In old days they gave the mother only soups for a week after birth. Babies today don't become strong because mothers eat everything; they eat choke-cherries and wild fruits of all kinds and soon their milk flow is blocked. Then they come to old people whose advice they wouldn't follow and ask for help. Some old man or woman who has the proper knowledge for such cases, brews tea for them. The women drink it, and their milk comes back.

When asked if magic played a part in this she replied:

This has nothing to do with magic. It's common sense! It's the only cure we had!

A decoction of raspberry roots (miskēgē'mi nākā'wic) was especially potent in producing milk secretion.

WEANING

A mother wishing to wean her child separated it from herself by placing it with relatives or neighbors, or by leaving it at home while she herself went away on a visit. Some mothers tried to prevent the secretion of milk by tying muskrat hides or similar soft hides across the breasts.

Formerly, some mothers frightened children by blackening the nipples with charcoal; today some treat the nipples with peppered grease or with peppery salad dressing. One informant said: "While I was weaning my four-year-old girl she used to climb on this bed whenever I'd take a rest, wanting to nurse. I'd scare her by saying, 'You'd better not; a mouse might climb on the bed!' She was afraid of mice."

Often the child was given the rind of bacon to suck. Densmore noted that babies were weaned by being given fish broth or wild rice well boiled (Densmore, 1929, p. 51).

ATYPICAL CONDITIONS

TWINS AND TRIPLETS

Informants were certain that twins (nicō′dē) were born to Chippewa before they intermarried with Whites. Twins are born today to those who consider themselves, and who are considered, full-blood Indians; several such families have two sets of twins and one has three sets. Some twins were both of one sex and others each of a different sex.

Mothers predicted twins during gestation because of simultaneous or successive hiccoughing in two distinct parts of the uterus. All members of a family having twins were respected and well thought of in the community. "The Indians felt a reverence toward twins and considered them one." The oldest Red Lake informant said, "We didn't tease nor touch twins like we did other children. All their lives twins were treated better than other people: they were held more sacred. They were given no extra food nor were they petted; but it was a crime to mistreat them or talk badly about them." "People honor twins and feel they are something special," said an old medicine woman on the La Pointe Reservation. "Sometimes a twin is mistreated and dies, and soon the other twin is dissatisfied and also dies."

Informants had not only heard twins spoken of as related to the spirit world, but themselves believed they were. "Twins are said to have come from the thunders (ānīmīkī′)." "You know the Indians were scared when twins were born; they honored them as spirits." "I remember the first set of twins born on this reservation [Vermilion]. Everybody respected the mother, and thought it was wonderful; they thought much of them; they spoke of them in connection with manito." No supernatural powers, however, were ascribed to them.

Informants knew of only three sets of triplets among the Chippewa: one in Canada, one on the Red Cliff Reservation (Wisconsin), and one on the Red Lake Reservation. The Canadian triplets were two boys and one girl. "They were quite big when we left Canada," said the informant. "All three used to hop out of their wigwam and play together." Two sisters on the Red Lake Reservation, in their seventies in 1939, said Indians honored twins as spirits but were frightened when triplets arrived. They related:

When we were real small, a woman gave birth to triplets. The mother's grandmother helped with the birth. The babies came one right after the other. The grandmother got very frightened and killed the three babies—three little boys—and dropped one on top of the other in a heap. We were too young to remember seeing it, but we remember the commotion that existed, and people crying, and everybody being sad. When we were older, we were told that the old lady cut the cords, and then cut the babies' heads off. We were related to them, and this is the truth.

A very old Mille Lacs informant knew quadruplets—four boys—who grew to maturity. "All four were respected by the people and seemed related to manito. They possessed supernatural powers: all four were sometimes called to a sick person and were always able to tell whether that person would live or die."

SICK BABIES

Decoctions in which sick or weakly babies were bathed might be made of catnip (nȧmēwȧc′) and cedar boughs (gī′cīk kwȧbȧk), or of an herb that grows "where there are maples." Plants were gathered at appropriate times during the year, and dried and stored. In nearly all Chippewa homes, bunches of herbs and roots can be seen hanging from rafters or from joints of rafters and walls (cf. pp. 90–93).

Sick babies were given purgatives. One of these was made by boiling "roots of various kinds" with maple sugar and storing these as maple sugar cakes. When needed they were melted in a little water and given the baby to drink. Nursing mothers chewed the root or bark of cābō′cīgōn (literally, "a little purgative"), the baby in drinking its mother's milk deriving the benefit of it. Sometimes a buckskin sack of the same root or bark was heated and placed on the baby's abdomen, the belief being that the medicinal effects penetrating the intestines relieved constipation. An older baby was given a piece to chew.

Densmore noted that an ailing child "was held in the warmth of the fire and its body rubbed with grease, goose oil being approved for this purpose" (Densmore, 1929, p. 51).

Although very soon after birth a child was given a name by some elderly person who had been in continuous good health during life and who had received power in a dream to give a name (p. 38), a sickly child—one that cried a great deal—might be given a second name by another old person for the restoration of health. "The sick child was given to some old person so that it would live as long as that old person had already lived. This person gave a name to the child at a feast and named the child in the same way as it was given its first name." Should a child take ill a second time and continue in its illness after medicinal remedies had been applied, it was given a third name by a third old person with all the ceremonials used when receiving its first name. A child might therefore have several names, receiving all but one for the restoration of health. "Other names than its first one are given when a child is sick so it will live long and become an old person. As long as it is a child, it can be given a namesake for health's sake." [8] "Sometimes a child who was critically ill

---

[8] Hallowell found that among the Saulteaux an infant that cried constantly was thought to be trying to utter the name it bore in a previous existence, and that if it was given this name, it stopped crying (Hallowell, 1940, p. 50).

was given to another person as namesake and he gave it another name according to his dream. And the child usually got well."

Sickly children, too, were admitted into the Mīdē′wiwin with the hope that health would be restored. Two sickly children between 4 and 5 years old were admitted at the Ponsford celebration on the White Earth Reservation in June 1938 (pl. 6); one a little over a year old, at the Nett Lake Reservation in August 1939 (p. 64).

DEFORMED BABIES

Neither head nor body deformation was practiced by the Chippewa. If a child was born deformed, it was said that the mother had been frightened while pregnant. "Twelve years ago a woman in this village had a baby whose head was shaped like a lizard's: it had short arms and little legs, just like a lizard's. The woman had been frightened by a lizard after being pregnant a short time." "A boy born here had a mouth like a rabbit and elbows at the shoulders; his rump and backbone were hairy and he had a tail. People said that the mother must have been frightened by a rabbit while she was carrying the boy." "My mother told me of a baby that was born with a tail, and of another that had ears near the temples."

INCEST

Informants on the Nett Lake, Lac Courte Orielle, Red Lake, White Earth, Vermilion Lake, and Mille Lacs Reservations were questioned as to incest between parent and child and between siblings. The facial expression, the tone of voice which dwindled to a whisper, and the firmness of the "No! No!" (Kâ′in! Kâ′in!) lead one to believe that incest was decidedly an unusual event. "No, I never heard of that. It couldn't have happened in old days, for parents took care of their children then." "I never heard anyone say anything like that to have happened in old times. I heard of a man, who is still living, who was the father of his daughter's child; the daughter is dead now. That could never have happened in old days. Everything was very strict then."

ILLEGITIMACY

Illegitimacy occurred among the early Chippewa. One old informant remarked,

Yes, there were some illegitimate children in the early days, but not many. It is different now; it is quite common now. It was a scandal then; now it is nothing. We didn't like that to happen. Such girls were not respected after it occurred, but we did not send them away. Girls in families were always treated better than boys, but when that happened the girl was no longer well liked. No, nothing was ever said to the father of an illegitimate child. Long ago when an unmarried girl was pregnant, her father was waiting to kill her child. I heard of one girl, when I was a child, who gave birth to her baby in the woods and killed it there; at least no one ever saw the child and everybody knew she gave birth to it in the woods. I remember people talking in a whisper about that girl whenever she came around.

Kēmī'cēgōn, the Chippewa word for illegitimate child, means "a stolen child," or "a child conceived through sneaky ways."

The unmarried Chippewa mother did not desert her child formerly, nor does she do so today; "that's a law of the people." She usually cared for it in her parental home. The child was not well liked until after it grew up; "it was considered lower than the rest of the people, but it was cared for." "Grandparents of the child (paternal and maternal) quarreled with each other, telling each other to take care of the child." Parents of both the unmarried mother and the unmarried father felt disgraced; "both were always in hopes that the man would marry the girl." If the mother married a man, other than the father of the child, she gave the child to her own mother.

Infanticide of either illegitimate children or other children had not been heard of by any informants, other than the two accounts given above (pp. 30, 33).

SLAVES, SERVANTS, AND ADOPTED PERSONS

The Chippewa at no time enslaved people, nor did they treat anyone as a servant. Adoption of persons, however, was very prevalent in the old days, and is so today: nearly all homes visited while making this study housed nonmembers of families. Small children were, and are, adopted not only by relatives, but also by friends. Older children and adult persons either chose a home and asked to be adopted or they were invited to do so.

There were no adoption ceremonials. All that was necessary was a clear understanding by the parties concerned. In the case of small children, the parents' consent was required. One informant said she was present when her dying mother arranged for the placing and adoption of her children; she was old enough to remember the occasion well:

Today, people have to arrange with the Agency [local U. S. Indian Service] if they wish to adopt a child. It wasn't that way some years ago. Before my mother died, she selected the relatives with whom she wanted all of us children to stay; she might have selected friends or anyone else instead of relatives. All of my mother's people talked with my mother and they decided among themselves who would take each child; we were five. If my father had been of the Chippewa Tribe, he would have had something to say and could have kept all of us if he had thought he could care for us; but since he is a Winnebago, he was not consulted. However, if mother had had no brothers nor sisters, my father could then have taken us. [She mentioned the names of three widowed Chippewa fathers on the reservation who were caring for their children.] But as things turned out, my oldest sister was given to my grandmother, my mother's mother; my brother was given to one of my mother's sisters; my two youngest sisters, to another sister; and another aunt raised me. I was treated just like the rest of my aunt's family; there was no discrimination shown as to food or work. At times, however, that is done; my brother was badly treated and the old lady with whom he was living struck him with a poker so that it penetrated his foot; she also hid bread from him. That is why he is now neglecting her.

An informant who had been willed a grandchild by her daughter said: "When mothers are certain of dying, they will their children to someone—to relatives, or to the missionary, or to someone; the husband has nothing to say about it." Another informant noted: "The grandmother, if she lived, always took the children after the mother's death."

A 50-year-old woman told of her plans to adopt a grandchild whose parents were still living:

When my son's wife goes to the hospital, he will bring their 2-year-old girl to us to keep. My son himself will probably bring her, and she will stay here all the time. And I am willing to take her! I can't wait until she comes! My husband plans on it too, and is more than anxious to rear her. He and I had discussed taking her before her father ever spoke about it. That's just the way it happens that you find these children in Indian homes!

The following accounts describe the adoption of mature persons:

A family in Ponema [Red Lake Reservation] had a son who died; he was about the age of my boy. Six years ago, the man and his wife came over here [Red Lake] on a special trip to ask me if they could have my boy as their son. I thanked them for asking me, I was certainly glad somebody thought so much of my son as to adopt him. He spends much time with them now, and they treat him as their son. Two years ago he stayed there all winter. No, there is no jealousy on my part. I feel flattered!

A 50-year-old man at Reserve (Lac Courte Orielle Reservation), the father of three children in their teens, related this experience:

An old couple in the village lost a son by death a year ago. Shortly after the old lady met me on the road between their home and mine, and said, "I had a son as big as you and I lost him, and now I'll adopt you as my son." Both of the old people call me their son; I remind them of their own son because I am so large. I go up there once in a while to see if they are all right, and I get their wood for them. They bring us something once in a while too—fish or bear meat, usually. We really feel related now.

Warren, a native, relates that at intervals when the Sioux and the Chippewa were not at war,

a Dakota chief or warrior taking a fancy to an Ojibway would exchange presents with him, and adopt him as a brother. This the Ojibways would also do. These adopted ties of relationship were most generally contracted by such as had lost relations in the course of their feud, and who, in a manner, sought to fill the void which death had made in the ranks of his dearest friends. [Warren, 1885, pp. 268–269.]

A 12-year-old girl on the Red Lake Reservation whose mother had died asked a woman with a family if she would adopt her as her own mother: "She looks on me now as though I were her mother, and I treat her like a daughter. She comes over here and tells me things, and I give her advice. I also give her things, like dresses."

NAMING THE CHILD

VARIOUS NAMES

Although a Chippewa had no family name, he might have several surnames. Shortly after birth he was given his Indian name, the name which he retained during life and which for him had a very real significance because it had spiritual value; its origin lay in a dream. If he was a crying child or an ailing one, he might be given several additional dream names (cf. pp. 31–32).

Pet names were given to most small children, and as they grew older they received a nickname also. These were usually humorous: they might indicate a resemblance to some object or animal or be associated with an event that occurred during the first day of life. "I heard a little girl who was very spry called Grasshopper. Another was called Little Twig until she was old enough to know that it was not her real name." The first born of twins was called Oldest One; the latter born, Small One or Younger One.

Children were not given names at puberty. Many, however, were given American names when they first attended boarding schools, this being true particularly of those whose Indian names were difficult to remember or which, in translation, were long names compounded of several words. Old Indians who did not attend school speak of their American names as "my Agency name" or "my name at the Agency." In the schools and at the United States Indian Agencies, little, if any, attention seems to have been given in assigning names to members of the same family, for it is not uncommon to find several siblings each having a different name and all names being different from that of the father.

ORIGIN OF NAMES

All informants agreed that Chippewa Indian names had their origin in dreams. They differed, however, as to the period in life during which dreams had value in naming children. Some maintained only prepuberty dreams were significant; others told of names that came to them in dreams of later life, even when quite old (cf. pp. 39–48). "Only dreams that we had when young and innocent counted in giving names to children. Dreams a boy had once his voice began to change were of no value." "When I was still innocent, that is before I menstruated for the first time, I dreamed of a rainbow several times, and I have since named a child after it." "Before persons think of anything impure, that's the time dreams count." One informant, in her eighties, told of a child, less than a year old, whom she had named, but "I never named it until it was three years old. What I should call the child didn't come to me before that time; I waited until I dreamed a name for the child. After I dreamed it, I told the parents who then gave a feast at which I named the child." Jones speaks of "a man in his youth and during a fast" who dreamed of the sky, for instance, and, having occasion "to believe that the sky was the source of his life and the cause of bountiful gifts," later named a child in accordance with the dream and thereby placed it under the same being that had been benevolent to him (Jones, 1906, pp. 136–137). Good dreams and one useful in naming children were those in which birds, thunder, sun, lightning, persons, and all animals, except snakes were involved. Bad dreams and ones to be forgotten were those dealing with dogs, water, and snakes.

Pierz accounts in the following way for the origin of names among the Chippewa and the Ottawa:

> The name is usually taken from things of earth or air. The man shoots an arrow into the air and notices what is found near the place at which it lands. If this be an animal, insect, stone, grass, tree, or something else his child will be named after it. Some have a habit of simply looking into the air and taking a name from wind, weather, clouds, thunder, or lightning or whatever appeals to them. That is why Indian children have names taken from nature, and never carry their father's name. No one may ever change the name. When it happens that the old fellow who is naming the child is not on good terms with the mother it may happen that he gives the child a nasty nickname, such as snake or turtle, bear paws or fox tongue, or wolf's teeth.[9]

Pierz' information was checked on the Lac Courte Orielle, La Pointe, Red Lake, White Earth, and Mille Lacs Reservations, but the writer was unable to verify it. Informants listened attentively to his account and then uttered such remarks as these: "I never heard anyone of our people tell that." "That must have been the way with some other tribe." "We never heard of that before. No, we dreamed our names." It is possible that Father Pierz never heard the Chippewa tell the true origin of their names, for several of the very old Indians were quite reticent in speaking of it to the writer even today. One remarked, "Long ago, Indians did not speak to each other of their dreams. Now they tell everything; therefore, much is dying out." Gilfillan speaks of this reticence also:

> One of the things about the Ojibways that seems strange to us is the mystical importance attached to a name, and the concealment of names. No Ojibway man or woman will tell his name, unless he has become very much Americanized. If a name has to be given, say to be put in some document, and the man is asked his name, he will not give it; but, after a long period of hesitation and embarrassment, he will indicate some other man who will tell his name. That man, finally, after prolonged consideration, mentions it, and when it comes out, a

⁹ Pierz, 1855, pp. 20–21 (writer's unpublished translation).

sensation lies over the assembly as if some great secret had been let out.
So in a store, if the name of the intending debtor be not known to the storekeeper,
and he has to know it to charge the goods, he asks, with a manner indicating
profound secrecy, some one else to tell him the man's name, and it is given to
him in a whisper, as a great secret. Often I have asked a man his wife's name,
and after a long hesitation he would confess that he had never heard it. On
questioning, he would admit that he had been married to her fifteen or twenty
years. This secrecy is about their Ojibway name; about their English name, if
they have any, they have no such feeling.

The reason for this reticence, which seems so queer to us, is that by them
great importance is attached, as in the Old Testament, to a name; that the names
all mean something, as Abraham, father of a multitude, Isaac, laughter, Jacob,
supplanter, and that the name is given as a religious act. So a father says to his
son, "My son, I give you this name; it has a spiritual signification; it is to you a
sacred thing; the spirits give it to you, if you make light of it, or mock it, or dis-
close it, I do not say that the Great Spirit will kill you, but you will have disgraced yourself." Hence is the concealment of the names, the reverence with
which names are regarded. [Gilfillan, 1901, p. 111.]

The following are names of informants: Coming-over-the-hill (the
namer, a woman, repeatedly dreamed of cows coming up to her over a
hill) ; Morning or Dawn; One-that-can-walk; Ice-feathered-woman;
Round-old-woman; One-that-can-climb (namesake dreamt of a bear
"and a bear is one that can climb"). William Jones mentions Flood-
of-light-pouring-from-the-sky (Jones, 1906, p. 137).

THE NAMESAKE

Parents usually selected the namesake (wādāwā′sōk) of their child;
occasionally an old person asked to name it or announced that he would
do so. The namer might be chosen on the day of birth or as soon as
the parents desired to have the child named. An unfailing rule, however, was that he be an old person and one that had not been sickly
during his life, "the belief being that the child would then be healthy."
A 53-year-old informant was not old enough to name a child, but was
old enough to be invited to the feast at which a child was named. "My
son was 3 months old when he was named; he has only one Indian
name. He never needed another for he has always been a healthy
child." "Each one of my children was given its Indian name a few
days after baptism." "When a child is born an old lady might say to
the parents, 'Now, you give me that child for my namesake.' Another
would say, 'Let it be my namesake.' Parents select one then and give
a feast at which the child is named."

A retention of this old custom survives on the L'Anse Reservation
where many others no longer exist. An old Indian will announce
himself as the namer of a child, and will name it; but no feast is given.
A L'Anse interpreter related two instances: "When my sister was a
mere baby, a very old man from the neighborhood came into our
house and said, 'I want the baby for a namesake.' Mother didn't know

what to think of it. He took a red ribbon from his pocket, pinned it to the baby's pillow, and started to smoke. 'Your little girl's name is going to be Bâtâwâ'sāgōkwē, meaning Two-clouds-and-a-sunshine-between-the-clouds,' he said. That's how my sister got her name. Another old man who was at a certain home where a child was born asked the mother if he might have the child for a namesake. He called her Bōgānōgē'cīkwē, which means A-hole-in-the-sky. After he named her this he hit the ground with his cane as many times as the years of his age, saying he wanted the child to live that long."

The term "namesake" is reciprocated by the child and the namer. A man might name a girl; a woman, a boy: there are no fixed rules as to the sex of the namer (windâwâs'sōwīnīnī—man namer; windâwâs'-sōkwē—woman namer). Nor was there a limited number of children that any one person might name. No namer gave the same name twice. "I have named about 20 children and all have different names. I dreamed each name: dreamed them as I needed them," said an informant on the Vermilion Lake Reservation.

CEREMONIAL

The naming of the child was done at a feast (windâwâs'sōwin) of venison and wild rice prepared by the parents of the child—"a real feast, a big feast of moose or deer!" Only invited guests attended. The namer held the baby in his arms, talked to it about Kīcē' Man'itō (Supreme Being), asked a blessing on the child, said that he wished the child to become as old as he was, gave it its name, and then handed it back to its mother.

At one such feast in 1930 the maternal granduncle (60 years of age), the maternal grandmother (52), an old man, nonrelative (80), and a maternal aunt (49) were the invited guests. The feast was given in the maternal grandmother's house. Oilcloth was placed on the floor and on this, at each guest's place, a small piece of plug tobacco. American food was served. The guests, after taking their places and smoking, talked about God and their dreams, and expressed hopes that the child would have long life. Then the namer, the 60-year-old granduncle, took the baby girl in his arms, talked to it, and named it Hole-in-the-ground. After this the baby was passed from one person to another and finally handed back to the mother. "This namesake feast," the mother added, "took place right after they brought the baby back from baptism."

In 1935 a young Chippewa mother and her 13-month-old baby returned to the reservation from Chicago for a visit. The 90-year-old great-grandmother of the baby invited the wife of a medicine man to name the baby. "Before they ate anything, this woman, holding the baby in her arms, put a handful of tobacco in the stove," remarked the young mother, "told her dream, and then named my baby, Hole-in-the-sky. She didn't give the baby any sermon; she simply told her dream. Then we all sat down and ate; the baby sat at table too."

A 21-year-old Mille Lacs mother and her husband gave a feast at which their 2-month-old baby was named (1940). "We invited six old persons from around here. I don't like to give their names since they might not like it; they consider this sacred and so do we.—I don't know why.—They all sat in a circle on the floor; a dish of tobacco was in the center. After they all took some of this, I handed the baby to the leader—you choose one person as leader—and I said, 'I give you this child as your namesake.' He took the baby, kissed it, talked to it, telling it to live long, gave it a name, and then passed it on to the next one. This one talked to it and passed it on and so on to the last one, each one kissing it, and telling it to live long. Then my husband and I served meat boiled with wild rice, cake, cookies, and coffee."

Jenness, in recording the naming of the Chippewa, wrote: "A pleasing ceremony accompanied the naming of each child; when the relatives and friends had gathered for the feast, the grandfather (or another elderly kinsman) took the child in his arms and called on all the great powers in the spiritual world to impart their blessing to its name" (Jenness, 1932, p. 280).

PREPUBERTY FASTS

AGE OF BOY AND GIRL

In primitive days most Chippewa boys and girls spent some days in silent commune with the spirit world, abstaining from food and drink. The number of days varied from 1 to 10; the length of the time as well as the number of times of fasting depended on the age of the child and on its endurance. Some children fasted for the first time before they reached the age of reason, that is at 4 or 5 years of age, or "when so high" (about 3 feet). Children of such early ages fasted but 1 day; those from 6 to 8 years old, 1 to 4 days; and those from 10 to 12 years old, from 4 to 10 days. A 10-day fast was usually rewarded with supernatural or shamanistic powers. No particular child, however, was selected for a 10-day fast. The significant power that came through fasting was impressed upon older children more than upon younger ones, and, because of this, informants thought, certain children made attempts to fast many successive days.

SELECTION OF FASTERS

Parents decided upon the time that the child was to fast. The time chosen usually depended on the dream that the child related some morning on rising, either of his own accord or upon request. The parent would not necessarily have done so but might have directed the child when retiring the previous evening to dream and to remember its dream.   One old Red Lake informant, however, knew of fathers who had dreamed that it was time to send a child to fast.   "When a child is about 5 years old and it tells its mother a dream which the mother considers good, the mother takes charcoal, blackens the cheeks of the child, and sends it out to fast, even without water, for 1 day." "After children reported a good dream, their faces were blackened with charcoal before breakfast and they were not given anything to eat until sundown."   "A mother might any morning call one of her children—it didn't make any difference which one—and ask it what it had dreamt last night.   If the dream was considered a good one, the child's face was blackened and it was made to fast."

An informant on the Lac Courte Orielle Reservation gave the following account:

Among the old pagans when a boy was 10 or 12 years old, his father said to him, "Tonight I want you to remember your dream."   Next morning his father would ask him whether he had had a dream.   If he had not dreamed, his father would tell him the next night to dream.   When, finally, he had a dream which satisfied the father, the father took charcoal from the fire, rubbed it between the palms of his hands, then rubbed the face of the boy, blackening it, and saying to the boy, "No breakfast this day."   He is going to make something out of the boy through his dreams.   He may abstain from food, though not from water, for 5 to 10 days.   I have known boys to fast until they could scarcely stand. Later in life they may exercise their dream power by finding something which is lost.   One might dream one night, and the next day find the lost article.   If a man's dream comes true, he is a person of importance among his people; if he lies, he is nothing.   [Hilger, 1936 c, p. 34.]

SIGNIFICANT DREAMS

On the Lac du Flambeau Reservation significant dreams were "those related to the thunderbird or to any bird; to the sun, thunder, lightning, in fact to anything in nature; to persons and all animals, except snakes."   On the Lac Courte Orielle Reservation dreaming of dogs or water predicted ill: "It was an indication of a short life; these dreams were to be forgotten at once."   A L'Anse woman was told by her mother "never to dream of black horses, for such a dream would be followed by a death in the family; dreaming of a white horse brought good luck.   Dreaming of clear water was a good sign; muddy waters brought heartaches."   On the Mille Lacs Reservation dreaming of water or of anything in the water was a bad dream; it indicated that a child would die.

MANNER OF FASTING

After a parent had decided that the child had had a good dream, he took charcoal from the fireplace—or in more recent times soot from

the bottom of a kettle or a pot—blackened the palms of his hands, and
then rubbed the child's cheeks, leaving them well blackened but without decorative design. Older children blackened their own faces in
the same manner and without design.

Small children—4, 5, or 6 years old—after having had their faces
blackened were merely sent out into the woods to spend the day
there. "In the early days both boys and girls were sent out alone
to wander around in the woods. Each one was sent alone; never were
two sent together. Here the spirits were to talk to them, and they
to the spirits." "Children were usually sent out in the spring or fall.
While wandering around they would probably see someone in the
woods, someone like manito, for example. They might see things,
too, in the shape of trees, etc., these things being spirits would have
pity on them and give them more power or longer life. This is done
before the girl becomes a woman or the boy a man. The person must
still be a child."

Fasting, if done for only 1 day, consisted of abstinence from food
and drink from sunrise to sundown.

They waited, in those old days, for the sun to peep up—the sun had to be
looking at us when we got our faces blackened. And just as the sun went down
we had our faces washed—the sun was supposed to see us get washed. I fasted
one day when I was about 5 years old: I got no bread nor water nor any
food all day. Those who fasted more than 1 day were usually permitted to
drink, but not to eat.

As children grew older, greater significance was attached to fasting.
The number of days was increased so that many children, especially
boys, spent 4 or more days without food, consequently sleeping and
dreaming. A child that did not return after 4 days of fasting was
thought to be receiving extraordinary powers—that he was being
given the "power" to be a medicine man or medicine woman. "Such
a child was learning how to cure certain diseases and how to combine
certain herbs for certain medicines, etc." "Some received such powerful 'medicine' that they could pull someone's mouth to one side, cripple
him, make him crazy, or even cause him to die." [10]

Hoffman in his study of the Grand Medicine Society of the Ojibway
makes the following statement:

The first important event in the life of an Ojibway youth is his first fast.
For this purpose he will leave his home for some secluded spot in the forest
where he will continue to fast for an indefinite number of days; when reduced
by abstinence from food he enters a hysterical or ecstatic state in which he
may have visions and hallucinations. The spirits which the Ojibway most
desire to see in these dreams are those of mammals and birds, though any
object, whether animate or inanimate, is considered a good omen. The object
which first appears is adopted as the personal mystery, guardian spirit, or

[10] Cf. "Grand Medicine," pp. 71-75 ; "Tipi shaking," pp. 75-78.

tutelary daimon of the entranced, and is never mentioned by him without first making a sacrifice. A small effigy of this man'idō is made, or its outline drawn upon a small piece of birchbark, which is carried suspended by a string around the neck, or if the wearer be a Midē' he carries it in his "medicine bag" or pinjígosân. The future course of life of the faster is governed by his dream; and it sometimes occurs that because of giving an imaginary importance to the occurrence, such as beholding, during the trance some powerful man'idō or other object held in great reverence by the members of the Midē' Society, the faster first becomes impressed with the idea of becoming a Midē'. [Hoffman, 1891, p. 163.]

"One old man here told how he fasted 10 days in the woods by himself. His only sustenance was water that had collected in the pitcher plant. Fasters were not allowed to dip water out of lakes for drinking." Of children who fasted several days, boys were subjected to more rigorous fasts than girls. "I have known boys to fast until they could hardly stand on their legs." Informants had not heard of any one dying from fasting, "although some had fasted for 10 days and were hardly able to walk after that." All boys were expected to fast; those who did not were considered cowards.

Boys usually fasted and slept in trees, on platforms or in "nests" (wâdisswâ'nī gīīkgī'cīmō—he fasted in a tree). Each boy built his own in the tree of his choice; but birch, white oak, or hardwood trees of any kind were favorites. "Nests" described by informants, who had either fasted in them or who had seen them, were of two kinds. The platform type was built by resting poles—trunks of saplings—on the limbs of a tree and covering these with straw. "We slept up there and fasted without food and water, fasting and dreaming in order to get a helper." A "nest," or basketlike type (wâ'dissân—bird's nest), was built of twigs, lined with hay, and attached to the lowest strong limbs of a tree. "Each was really a nest of twigs and hay, deep enough so the boy could lie down or sit up in it. These nests were always built in a lonely place." "In the fall after all the leaves had fallen, one could see nests here and there all through the wilderness; they were up where the strong limbs began."

Nearly all girls fasted, but few fasted longer than 4 days. Those who wished to obtain the powers of medicine women fasted 10 days. One woman had fasted 6 days at 10 years of age. On the first day she abstained from water and ate only a small piece of bread; on the remaining 5 days, she partook of a small piece of bread and a sip of water. "I was hungry but I didn't mind it very much, for I slept nearly all the time," she added.

It was not customary for girls to fast in trees: they fasted walking about the woods. "I was sent out to fast one time early in the spring to a dry place where there was no snow." An old Red Lake informant, however, said she had tried to fast in a tree after hearing her grandmother tell the following story:

When you look across the lake (Red Lake) you see a big hill on the sand bar near Ponema. At one time four girls built four nests for fasting over there—each built one for herself. They were very close to each other in one tree. The girls were up there and some one began to throw stones at them. So the girls whispered to each other asking if the stones were hitting any of them. Three didn't know what it was; the fourth knew and said, "Some men are throwing stones at us." So the third one wanted to know who these men were, and the fourth one said, "We'll see them," and sure enough, a boat came with four men in it. It was hard to see them at a distance. But soon they sounded like doors slamming. And these were water gods, like mermaids. That happened long ago.

"After hearing this," the informant added, "I tried once to fast in a tree, but my mother wouldn't let me do it."

Fasting in most cases was done before puberty. Most informants were emphatic in saying that girls, after their first menstruation, and boys, after their voices began to change, were no longer eligible for fasting. "They are impure after that." "No, the old people ('old men' and 'old women' were those past puberty) never fasted. After puberty they couldn't fast; it was considered a disgrace to fast then." "Before persons think of anything impure, that's the time that fasts and dreams count." "Only girls who are pure and innocent—that is before first menstruation—have dreams for powers." "This is done before the girl becomes a woman and the boy a man; the person must be a child still. Their dreams are of no significance once they are old enough to beget children." "I fasted twice a year while I was a child, from the time I was 6 or 7 years old: once in the fall before the snow began to fall and once in the spring when the birds began to come." "No man fasted after his voice began to change; he was considered impure after that. No woman fasted after her first menstrual isolation for she was considered impure from that time on. No one with sense would have attempted to fast after that; everybody would have laughed at him." On the Mille Lacs Reservation, however, a girl who was being subjected to her puberty isolation and fast might have a dream in which supernatural power was granted.

When a faster—boy or girl—returned home, the mother or, if she were dead, the grandmother or aunts prepared a feast and invited friends. The faster was advised to eat slowly and not to satiety. His food was served in a birchbark dish (pl. 24, 2), which was later hung upon a small twig on the lower trunk of a tree near the home. "The tree near one house was loaded with these little dishes, indicating that there had been many days of fasting in that family." "My grandmother told of a boy who, on the tenth day of his fast, told his father—his father had come each day to see if he was all right— that he was coming home and that his mother should prepare the feast." At the feast both faster and guests told their dreams.

PURPOSE OF FASTING

Parents obliged their children to fast because they were desirous of having them contact the spiritual world and obtain a medium in it in the form of a guardian spirit. "You call him guardian spirit; we call him the spirit of a vision or ōbȧwȧgē′kgōn. We use the same word for a girl's helper as for a boy's." Fasts in very early childhood were less significant in this regard than the ones that were prolonged enough to produce sleep and consequent dreams. It was during dreams, or in visions during the waking hours of a prolonged fast, that the guardian spirit, the helper for all times, communicated with the faster. Gīïkkwī′cīmōd is the word used to describe the fast no matter how old the child, how prolonged the fast, or how significant, shamanistically, the results. Occasionally, a faster was not favored with a dream or vision. When this occurred he could receive power only by joining the Mīdē′wiwin (cf. pp. 63–71). "I never dreamed of a guardian spirit although I fasted 6 successive days on one occasion," remarked a Lac Courte Orielle woman.

The guardian spirit usually took the form of a person, an animal, an inanimate object, or an activity of nature. His prerogatives were to give advice, knowledge, and power to the faster. Powers received were of various kinds, such as producing rain or winds, bringing success in war, discovering healing properties of plant life, predicting future events, or finding causes for past events. "Sometimes children fasted 10 days. If children did this and grew up they became powerful. It was during the dreams they had while fasting that people received their guardian spirits and the powers they used in later life. Today, for instance, if a storm comes up and a person with power related to the storms talks to it, the storm will subside. Or should a person be walking around without a home and have nothing to eat and will talk to the sun or stars or whatever he dreamed of as a child, he will receive what he needs. It is said that old Indians always had clouds or the sun or moon or stars but not any animals as their power." "A certain boy went out to fast. On the eighth day he heard someone singing. Soon he uncovered his face and looked out and saw a flock of geese that now sounded like men speaking.—The boy had not had anything to eat nor drink for these eight days.—The head one—there is always a head goose—spoke to the boy telling him never to have fear in any war and should he be in danger in any war to think of this flock of geese and he would always come out unhurt." "The old Indians believed that thunder and lightning were caused by thunderbirds. The ones who had dreamt of these birds when fasting while they were still innocent had power to stop storms. Here is what they would do: When a storm arose they went out-of-doors, motioned with their hands for the storm to move away, saying, 'Go slowly; go around;

go away !' " "One time the Ottawa and Chippewa from Marquette and La Pointe [Wisconsin] joined our bands here and all met the Sioux at Portage Lake.—We were at war with the Sioux then.—The sun was going down just when our side began to win. One of our men who had power over the sun asked it to continue shining. The sun stayed right in the sky and the war was won !" "My husband's mother's helper was thunder. She used to make us very angry during blueberry-picking time for she would talk to her helper, light her pipe and smoke it, and cause thunderstorms. And all that while we were all right out there in the blueberry patch !"

Tanner tells of hunting trip which he made with some Objibway. He quotes an old man in the group as saying :

> When I was yet a little boy, the Great Spirit came to me, after I had been fasting for 3 days, and told me he had heard me crying, and had come to tell me that he did not wish to hear me cry and complain so often, but that if ever I was reduced to the danger of immediately perishing of hunger, then I should call upon him, and he would hear and give me something. I have never called before, but last night I spent in prayer and singing, and I have assurance that I shall this day be fed by the bounty of the Great God. I have never asked before, and I know that he will not forget his promise."

Tanner continues :

> We all started at the same time in the morning, but went to hunt in different directions. I hunted all day without finding anything, and so weak was I, that I could traverse but a very small extent of ground. It was late when I came in ; the two young men were in before me ; all began to despair ; but old Gitch-e-weesh was still absent. At a very late hour he arrived, bending under a heavy load of meat. [Tanner, 1830, p. 154.]

After a successful fast, the faster invariably carried with him, usually tucked in a small buckskin bag or wrapped in a piece of cloth, some token of esteem that would either resemble his guardian or be a reminder of him. The contents might be a feather, a claw, a piece of cloth, or a bird's head. The contents plus the wrapping were spoken of as "medicine bundles" (pīcēgō′sān), "medicine" indicating magic power, and were held in great reverence. "It was at the time that a boy slept in a tree and thought of manito that he received the power that he kept in his 'medicine bundle.' If such a boy grew up to be a man and did not have good luck when hunting, for instance, he returned home, gave a feast at which he opened the bundle and prayed for success and success would be his." "My grandfather fasted ten days and received a wolf as guardian spirit. In his dream he saw a man coming along with fresh deer meat on his back. The man dropped the meat and said, 'This is what I give you !' and then ran away in the form of a wolf. That is why my grandfather always fastened the tail of a wolf to the side of his belt when he went hunting." "Supposing a robin would be a boy's dream object—a ribbon had been

the person who spoke to the boy when he dreamed or had a vision—
well, then, every robin living would be sacred to that boy for he depended on the robin for help and advice. And that boy would always
carry with him some part of a robin, probably some feathers."

In Old Indian Village on the Lac du Flambeau Reservation a piece
of cloth with a thunderbird painted on it had been placed in a small
wooden frame and attached to the top of a pole twice the height of the
house near which it was erected. The thunderbird represented the
dream power which one of the parents had received while fasting when
about 5 or 6 years old. Small pieces of clothing of each member of
the family were hanging near the picture. "A piece of tobacco, about
one inch square, must also be tied on up there near the picture," said
the interpreter, peering to see it. Similar poles were seen in several
places on the reservation and were erected to protect homes nearby.

Beltrami tells of a hunting expedition in 1823 in company with the
Ojibway at Red Lake:

We searched for the animal I had fired at, which it seems retained strength
sufficient to drag itself to a few paces distance among the brushwood, to which
traces of blood had guided us; it proved to be a wolf. My companion refused to
strip the animal of its skin, a superb one, viewing it at the same time with an
air of respect, and murmuring within himself some words, the meaning of which
will probably surprise you. In fact, the wolf was his *Manitou*. He expressed
to it the sincerity of his regret for what had happened, and informed it that he
was not the person who had destroyed it. [Beltrami, 1828, vol. 2, pp. 390–391.]

A Red Lake informant told the following in the presence of two
persons who collaborated:

A young fellow, probably 20 years old now, a 'Cross Laker [resident of Pone-
mah] about 6 years ago [1926] dreamed for power. He climbed up a tree and
sat in it for 4 days and 4 nights without anything to eat. Since then he claims
to have a special knowledge. One day when payments [U. S. annuities] were
made, a woman, who held her baby in one arm and many bundles in the other,
found upon arriving home that her 90-dollar payment had been taken from her.
(All this happened 'Cross Lake.) Her old man went to the dreamer and asked
him if he knew who took it. The fellow went away and sang and pounded a
small drum, and when he returned he told the man that a certain woman (naming
her) had the money and had not yet used any of it. "Go to her and tell her that
she has your money and that you want it." He went to the woman and in a
gracious manner said to her, "You must have taken my wife's money by mistake."
She admitted that she had the money and handed it right over to him and said
she had not spent any of it. Not long ago that same dreamer came across the
lake with some young men. These fellows thought they'd try him out and bet
with him that he didn't know who the first Indian would be whom they would
meet at Redby. He remarked that he did (naming the man), and sure enough
it was he. He is the only one 'Cross Lake or in this vicinity who can do that.
This young man often goes to the Point and stays there for days. He doesn't
eat, and no one knows what he does there. My neighbor's youngest brother went
to dream for power, some 20 years ago. There was an old man near here, too,
who had the same power; but he died last winter.

PERSONAL ACCOUNTS OF DREAMS

Some informants were quite willing to relate details regarding incidents of their guardian-spirit dream, but they were reticent to tell the dream itself. There were several reasons for this. Relating the dream was like communing with the helper, and this is not done except in case of necessity, and then only after ceremonial smoking and singing and, at times, fasting. No "necessity" seemed involved in merely satisfying the request of a visitor. A Red Lake informant preferred not to tell of her helper, "for I'm afraid he won't help me any more if I tell my dream and talk about him when there is no need of doing so."

Another reason for reticence was possibly that the informant feared that relating his dream would produce some visible effects, something he did not desire. Several of the oldest informants had never told their dreams to any person. A member of the Mīdē'wiwin of the Lac Courte Orielle Reservation considered his helper so sacred that he "couldn't really talk lightly about him"; his dream was too sacred to be told. The interpreter, his daughter-in-law, explained that "while he would be telling it to us and smoking his pipe, it would be thundering: that is if his helper is the thunder. If he would do this unnecessarily, something would go wrong. Lighting a pipe is the same as praying, for when he lights his pipe he asks his helper to help him."

Some were unwilling to tell their dreams because they might reveal secret information involving medicinally valuable herbs and roots, unusual powers for finding objects, or powers of revenge. These powers were "copyrighted" and sold (by being told) only upon the payment of a good price in cloth, hunting implements, etc. One old informant said: "Long ago Indians did not even tell each other their dreams; now they tell everyone. Therefore, much is dying out."

One aged Lac Courte Orielle woman remarked: "That's a great thing they want to know!" And then lapsed into silence. After some moments she remarked, "It's too great a thing to tell them my own dream. My old man's was about thunder, and he used it too." One of the oldest women on the same reservation, however, related the following two dreams:

I fasted when I was about 5 years old; men fasted long, but women did not. I dreamt about a big house. I saw green stairs leading to the sky and when I looked again they seemed to be of green velvet. While I was still looking, I saw four women in veils coming down to meet me; they told me to follow them. My hair too seemed all white like a veil. I followed them a short distance up the stairs. Here they sang a song which I did not recognize. One woman told me that I might go no farther on the stairway, and by this she meant that I had lived a part of my life and that I still had a part to live. When I told my mother this dream, she blackened my cheeks, and I fasted one day. It was too cold to go out-of-doors, so I stayed around the house. I was not allowed any bread or water all day. Of the dreams I had when I was six years old I remember only one. I dreamed that same dream several times at intervals when I was small, and I have used it several times. Only those dreams count that persons have before they think of anything impure; that's the time the dreams count. Well, I used to dream that I was swinging in a swing to Shogytown. Someone called from the sky telling me that what was below was mine: "Why don't you take it?" When I looked down I saw a deer which I took with me. And that was my dream; and it was a good one. One time my two sons brought a Sioux along and the three went out with my old man deer hunting. They were gone for a long time and came back without anything. So I told them of my deer dream. One of my sons laughed at me but the other didn't. Then they went out hunting again. The son that didn't laugh came back with two big deer; the other had none.

The following account of a Red Lake woman includes a dream and several preliminary factors:

I, too, fasted, but only for one day at a time. I tried once to fast in a tree but my mother made me come down and wouldn't let me do it; she said it was too hard for girls to do that. But one day I fasted; I was about so high [3 feet]. I knew of a girl who had fasted, and so I wanted to fast too. I asked my father if I might. He told me I was too young; I'd get hungry. But I insisted, and so he let me try it. I blackened my face and went into the woods. When girls fasted they had to work all day and were not to sit down; even when girls fasted in nests they had to do some work. So when my father found out that I was really going to fast, he went hunting and said he'd bring something for me to eat by supper time. By noon I got lonesome and was thirsty and felt uneasy— I had been out in the woods all forenoon—and so I came home. But my mother said, "You wanted to fast; so now go out and fast for today." This was my first fast. My father killed two moose that day and he brought home only the best meat. They made a feast for me and invited old people—not any young people. I wasn't served with a plate like the rest; my food was put in a birchbark dish. I asked for a second helping, but I was refused because I had fasted. After I had finished my meal, they made me take my dish and hang it on the limb of a tree so the opening faced the sun. Indians believed the sun would smile on this. After this I fasted twice a year for a day; once in spring when the birds began to come and once in the fall before the snow began to fall. I quit fasting after my first menstruation. The Indians fasted in order to learn something for themselves just like white men study to learn things.

In response to the question what things she had learned by fasting, she told the following story, assuming a quiet and reverent attitude—there had been much gesticulating at other times.

At one of my fastings I saw some animal in the clouds. It appeared to be floating in the clouds and it was coming toward me. And this animal showed me his long hair, holding it away from his body. Since then I have always had a sacred feeling toward this little animal. And that little animal was a porcupine. When I was a young woman I could take my hair in my hands and hold it out the length of my arms and even then it hung about a foot beyond my hands; it was so long.—The old Indians on the reservation can tell you about my long hair.—The old Indians told me that my hair would be as you see it today, a mixture of white and black like the back of a porcupine. Yes, the porcupine formerly granted me favors; they were like the favors I now get from God. Whenever I wanted a favor, or was in need, not knowing where to look for help, I just thought of him and wished that he'd help me. I thought of him the same as I now think of God. My chums fasted too.

PUBERTY CUSTOMS

BOY'S PUBERTY CUSTOM

Densmore follows her account of a girl's puberty custom with the following statement regarding a boy's:

At about the same age a boy was required to undergo a fast in which he hoped and expected to obtain a dream or vision. The father taught the boy to prepare for this and insisted that he persevere until he secured the dream. The boy blackened his face with charcoal and usually went away from home for his fast. Sometimes the father took the boy a considerable distance and made a nest for him in a tree. He left the boy there several days, going occasionally "to see if he was all right." It was not unusual for a boy to make several attempts before he secured a dream, but complete failures were very rare. [Densmore, 1929, p. 71.]

Jenness notes that among the Parry Islanders an adolescent boy "fasted and prayed in solitude to gain the protection of some supernatural power throughout the rest of his days" (Jenness, 1935, p. 96).

Landes not only records puberty fasts for boys of the Ojibway of western Ontario, but notes that every few years the parents of all pubescent boys in the village decided to send the boys out to fast. Boys did not fast alone but were near enough to each other to be able to talk together (Landes, 1938 b, p. 4).

Chippewa informants who contributed to this work were agreed that there was no puberty custom for boys.[11] Some said that a boy was considered to be an "old man" as soon as his voice began to change, and "it was a disgrace to go out to fast then." Others said that boys could fast at any time; that some fasted for power even at 20 years of age. An old Mille Lacs informant was certain that no more than two boys ever fasted together:

Boys fasted alone for 10 days, drinking only a birchbark dish of water a day (one-half cupful). When boys fasted they learned in their dreams how to become warriors, as was necessary for fighting the Sioux, or how their lives would turn out, or whether they would die soon or live long. The father decided when the boy should go; never did all the men get together and decide when their sons should go. The boys were sent about the time their voices were expected to change, and they stayed 10 days. Usually two boys went together—never three or four—and these were generally related, like cousins, or were good friends. Many liked it best to go out alone. In one of the trees on a big hill on Murray Beach near here there was a big nest for many years in which a boy fasted. That man is still living. He built the nest himself. The nest was still there 25 years ago. Nothing was done for a boy when his voice changed except that he had to learn to do a man's work in earnest: all the things that he should know before he married.

---

[11] Cf. also Kohl, (1859, pp. 233–242) for account of old Chippewa man's fast when the man was a "half-grown lad."

GIRL'S PUBERTY RITE

Although well-defined customs ushered a girl into her maturity, few
girls received any instructions regarding the occurrence or the significance of menstruation before it occurred. "I was taking care of someone's children when I was that way the first time. It was in the fall
at the time when people were fishing for whitefish. I ran away into
the woods. My grandmother found me and explained things to me.
Nobody had told me before then." "I began to be that way while I
was away at school. I was dreadfully scared and ran home and hid.
When my mother found me, she explained my condition to me and
built a wigwam for me." An interpreter was certain that "girls today
were bad because mothers gave them full instructions about all these
things." Several informants were convinced "that girls learnt too
much in the American schools: there they learn everything long before
they should know it!" Puberty of informants or their daughters had
occurred between the ages of 12 and 15 years. Mothers worried about
their daughters when menses had not occurred at the age of 15.

A girl during her first menstruation was isolated continuously
both days and nights in a small wigwam called bākānēd'jē (a tent
made by herself). Some informants had been so isolated for 4 or 5
days; others for as many as 10. "But some mothers were afraid to
leave their daughters alone in the woods, they brought them home
before the ten days were up." A girl living in her menstrual wigwam
is called bākānē'gȧ (living by herself); the period of isolation, is
called mȧkwȧ' or mȧkwȧ'wē (turning into a bear; the bear lives alone
all winter).

The wigwam, usually located several rods from the home wigwam,
was built either by the girl alone, by her mother, or by the girl with
the assistance of her mother or grandmother. Wigwams varied in
type, but were never larger in size than to permit the girl to stand
or to lie down. If isolation occurred in summer when cooking was
done out-of-doors, the wigwam was dome-shaped but if it was being
used in cold weather when indoor fire was a necessity, it was more or
less peaked and open roofed, so as to emit smoke. The framework
consisted of saplings; the coverings were of either branches or twigs
and of birchbark, or, if cold weather required a warmer shelter, of
hides or cloth. One informant's wigwam was covered with mosquito
netting "for that was all that was needed; it was about this time of the
year (early June)." The floor of the wigwam was either partially
or entirely covered with cedar boughs. "My mother built a little
birchbark wigwam for me high enough so I could stand up. I was
that way the first time when I was 12 years old." "Formerly they
built a little wigwam for such a girl, a real small one just big enough
so a girl could lie down or stand up in it."

The girl was prepared for entering the wigwam by having either cheeks alone or cheeks and forehead blackened with charcoal or soot that had been rubbed between the palms of hands. No design was made; palms of hands were merely rubbed on cheeks in circular fashion, movements being ear-chin-nose-temple-wise. "I used to see young girls that I had played with blacken their faces and live alone and everybody shunning them. I wondered why they were doing this. Everybody seemed to be afraid of these girls, too."

The girl's hair was either tied back or completely covered with buckskin or cloth. While in isolation her mother combed it; if the girl touched her hair, she ran the risk of having it fall out. In fact, she was not allowed to touch herself in any way. If she wished to relieve an itching feeling, she was to use a little stick which had been given to her for that purpose.[12] Neither face nor hands were washed until she left isolation.

The mother of a very old Red Lake informant had prepared a substantial meal for her daughter as soon as she was aware of her condition. Since the girl was not allowed to touch food herself, she was fed by her mother. After the meal, the wigwam was built. "Yes, that's exactly the way it was done. My sister was treated the same way. We know, for we went through it ourselves."

While in isolation the girl was required to cook her own food and to use none but her own dishes. In some groups the custom of using and caring for separate dishes continued during the entire first year following puberty, the year being completed when the season presented the same appearance as at first menses. In years intervening between puberty and marriage, girls were required to use and wash their own dishes only during menses. Food was brought to the girl at sundown. "In the evening my mother brought me rice and water; during the rest of the day, I had nothing to eat." Densmore's informants said in the old days the girl "was allowed absolutely no food during this period," but that in later days "an older sister or other relative brought a little food to the girl" (Densmore, 1929, p. 70). Under no circumstances was food in season, however, to be given to such a girl. "When I was that way, they were fishing. My mother brought me my food, but they wouldn't think of giving me any fish then for that was the time for getting them. If they had given me fish, all the tribe would have had bad luck fishing. If a girl happened to be that way for the first time in the spring, say at sugar-making time, and her people had given her sugar to eat, there would have been no sugar worth while that season. Or if they had been picking berries or other fruit and given her some, the rest of the berries would have withered; and possibly

---

[12] The above is in agreement with the findings of Densmore (1929, p. 70). Cf. also Flannery (1940, p. 12).

there would have been few or none the next season." "Such girls were given dried meat, dried fruit and wild rice. Years ago the Indians saw to it that they had all these prepared if they had girls of that age; they kept them on hand then."

If a girl at puberty touched plants, it withered them; if she went into lakes or rivers, "she was liable to kill the fish, or at least all fish would go away from there." By looking at a person, touching a child, or crossing the path of any person, she paralyzed that person. In fact during the entire year following first menses, she was not to touch babies, or clothes of her father, or brothers, or of any man, for it would cripple them.

Idleness during isolation was taboo. The girl was required to sew or do beadwork. "You couldn't do much else; the space was too small." Time spent out-of-doors was devoted to gathering and chopping wood. One informant under the direction of her mother mended birchbark cups used in gathering maple sugar (pl. 24, 2) by plugging cracks in the bark with pitch heated in a little pan over a small fire in her wigwam. Mothers also instructed their girls at this time how to lead both good and useful lives. They were taught "that now they were 'old women' and must learn to do the work expected of women, such as chopping wood, sewing buckskin, building wigwams; in fact, everything a woman had to do later."

After isolation, the girl bathed herself and washed her clothes. In the meantime her mother prepared a meal of the father's hunting to which old women were invited. When all was ready, the girl walked from the small wigwam to the home wigwam on a path of cedar boughs or of bark of some tree. This was done to keep the girl from stepping on the ground, thus making it impossible for a man to walk the same path later or to walk across her path, thereby paralyzing himself. There was no purification or fumigation ceremony, such as standing over hot coals covered with herbs.

After the feast the girl was free to mingle with the people, but she was not yet permitted to participate in gathering and preparing food in season. Customs differed as to the manner of removing this taboo. On the Lac Courte Orielle Reservation the girl was freed if someone fed a small portion of it to her. If she handled any of it before that time, she ruined the growth of that particular kind. "Something happened to it: either the birds or worms got it or hail or drought destroyed it; or if animals were involved, they died out. People have firm faith in this around here today and ascribe the droughts of the past year to it." Another informant on the same reservation said that it was customary for people to gather at a feast and partake of the food they were then gathering. This might be fresh berries in berrying time, maple sugar in maple-sugar-making time, or fish, if it were fishing time. After the people had eaten, some of the food in season was handed to the girl. After eating it, she was permitted to participate in whatever seasonal occupation the people were then engaged in.

A 75-year-old Vermilion informant described the removal of the taboo as follows: "Before picking any fruit or berries, or doing whatever the Indians were then doing, an old man made a speech. After this the girl gathered a small quantity of whatever was being gathered then (if berries, about 2 quarts), ate some charcoal, and after that, some fruit or berries, or whatever they were gathering. If she didn't carry out this custom she spoilt whatever the people were doing at the time." A 32-year-old interpreter on the same reservation said that in her day a girl was not allowed to pick strawberries, raspberries, blueberries, or any fruit until she had eaten one mouthful of them mixed with charcoal. After this a feast was given for her. "I know it, for when I was that way for the first time, I was not allowed to go any place; I had to sit around and sew. But they needed me for blueberry picking; so they had me eat blueberries and charcoal, and gave a feast of blueberries. After that I was permitted to pick berries but I was not supposed to look at anything else."

During the years of this study puberty customs for girls were found in some modified form on all reservations covered in the study, except L'Anse. In some instances girls were isolated by being kept upstairs; in others, they were made to stay by themselves "around the house and were not allowed to look at anyone or to touch anything." Many were obliged to eat off dishes reserved exclusively for them, washing them as well. Many were told not to eat foods in season such as berries, fish, etc. until they had been served to them by someone else. Two puberty wigwams were seen near homes in which grandmothers were rearing grandchildren. Informants and interpreters had seen others in recent times but thought that they had been burnt, since the old custom required that the wigwam and all things used in connection with isolation, such as cedar boughs, scratching stick, dishes, etc. be burnt.

After puberty a girl was never allowed out of sight of her mother, or of some older woman designated by the mother. "This was usually the grandmother, since grandmothers advised girls and watched over them like mothers did." Nor were girls allowed to sleep away from home, "like in the home of a neighbor." An aged Red Lake informant after lamenting the present lack of morals among her people remarked, "I was never allowed to go out alone after I was that way the first time. That was the custom. And that's why in old days no girl had a baby unless she was married; now every little girl has one. All has changed since the Whites have come. In old days a girl never went away without her mother or some older woman. I had a chum. One day we two went out to pick berries with our mothers. My chum asked me to come to her house and sleep with her that night. I asked my mother, and she said, 'No!! You have a place to sleep at home.' In those days parents were obeyed; things are different now. Mothers are different now, too."

Isolation during menstruations following puberty was not required. Freedom, however, was restricted: girls were "to stay around alone" and not mingle with others. Until married—on the Mille Lacs Reservation, even after marriage—they were expected to use dishes reserved for them and were not to touch food that was to be eaten by others. "The dishes were tied together after her days were over, and laid aside until the next period." They were not to touch or step over clothing since it might paralyze the owner.

A Red Lake informant gave the following account typical of many others:

My mother had sent me to get a knife and I noticed that there was something wrong with me; so I ran away. I was so scared. I stayed away until towards evening and when I came back my mother asked me what was wrong. I told her and she told me it was about time, for I was old enough. "You are now a 'big woman' (kitcīkwē', meaning both big woman and first menstruation). You cannot go into our wigwam for it will make it bad for your brothers and sisters." I believe she knew all that day what was wrong with me for while I hid in the woods, she had built a little wigwam of balsam boughs for me. The floor and my bed she had covered with cedar boughs. My grandmother spent most of her time with me while I was in the little wigwam; she even slept with me. However, girls were not afraid to stay alone, for no one would come near them then; men were afraid of girls during that time. (I remember this occasion well, for many of our people were dying of smallpox at the time.) I stayed in my little hut for 5 days and nights. They brought me food from the regular meals: mostly bread and potatoes baked out-of-doors. They would not let me touch their dishes for that would have made them all sick. Nor was I allowed to step over anything. The Indians consider this an important event. They made me work, too; I had to cut wood. After 5 days they brought me clean clothes, and burnt the small wigwam and everything I had used. It was sugar-making time; but before they gave me any sugar to eat, I had to eat charcoal, about the size of a pea, taken from among the coals.

A Mille Lacs informant, older than 90 years, related the following:

When I knew I was that way, I put charcoal on my face and went into the little wigwam that my mother had built for me way out in the woods about a mile from home. The girls had to be there by themselves and couldn't be near anyone else. Indians believe that at this time nobody is to see them and that they were not to look at anybody. If a man came near them or crossed their path he might die from this. I didn't eat anything and wasn't hungry during that time. Every evening my mother brought me a birchbark dish of water (about half a cupful). The little birchbark cup was hung on the outside of my wigwam; I couldn't use any other and nobody could use it. During that time I had a dream that told me I would live a long time and would have white hair like you see I have now. I dreamed this; I did not have a vision. I consider the dream I had too sacred to tell to anyone. I tell it only when I am given a namesake or when I have to talk at ceremonies. I have often been offered money to tell it, but I wouldn't tell it.

The oldest woman on the Mille Lacs Reservation also obtained power during her puberty isolation:

Every girl was isolated in the woods at first menstruation. I fasted 10 days and my three sisters also did. Only those who wished to fast fasted. (I don't know of any girl who did not fast; but we did not live near other people.) During this time I had a dream which gave me power. I saw myself as I am today, an old lady. I again isolated myself at second menstruation and dreamed again, and this made my dream power stronger. This is the dream that I use in naming children and I relate at feasts, but I don't relate it without a good reason.

After puberty then, the Chippewa girl, although only 12, 13, 14, or 15 years of age, had reached maturity; she was now an "old woman." Play life had ended. Mats had to be made; hides tanned; birchbark receptacles prepared; beadwork designed; wigwams built; meat, fish, berries, and fruit dried. Life was now to center about obtaining all knowledge which was necessary in the life of a good housewife.

TRAINING CHILDREN

TYPE OF EDUCATION

A Chippewa child was not subjected to formal education, such as we conceive it, but it was taught in an informal way to conform to the moral standards, as well as to the religious, the economic, and the political pattern of his tribe. It learnt, too, the mental content of the culture pattern of its people and participated in their diversions. Much of this knowledge was learned by boys and girls before they reached puberty; all of it was expected to be theirs before marriage.

METHODS

Methods employed in training children were those of lecturing and counciling, of listening-in, and of having ideals presented; of imitation of elders in play or of participation with them in serious work and ceremonials.

Some instructions were of a formal type; some followed a most informal procedure. "Little girls, so high [about 6 years of age] were made to do work that they were able to do, such as carrying water or washing birchbark dishes." "Children did the same things fathers and mothers did, but on a small scale: a little girl made a small net but used the same knots her mother used, and she set that net just like her parents did." "If a woman had a reputation for tanning hides a

mother said to her young daughter, 'Go, learn from her.' Girls
followed their mother's ways. They started early making little wigwams and small buckskin clothes."

Densmore also observed that small girls imitated their mothers at
work: "A little girl was trained in what might be termed the accom-
plishments of feminine life, as well as in its household tasks. Her first
lessons in applied beadwork were the decoration of her doll's clothing,
straight lines, either continuous or interrupted, being the easiest
patterns from which she progressed to diagonal patterns and the
familiar 'otter-tail pattern' " (Densmore, 1929, p. 62). A girl, she
noted, also participated in her mother's work: "The companionship
of a Chippewa girl and her mother was very close and the child learned
many household tasks by watching and helping her mother. Thus a
little girl was early taught to chop wood and carry it on her back, and
as she grew older she carried larger and larger bundles of wood until
she could carry enough in to the wigwam for the night's use. A girl
was taught to make little birchbark rolls like those which covered the
wigwam, her mother saying 'You must not grow up to live outdoors
and be made fun of because you do not know how to make a good wigwam.' She was also taught to make maple sugar, gather wild rice,
and do all a woman's tasks" (Densmore, 1929, p. 61).

Children were taught the value of plants as Densmore points out,
by being encouraged to gather every flower they saw in the fields,
drying and pulverizing them and using them in the making of bever-
ages. At the same time the child was also taught that some plants
had medicinal value "while all were placed on the earth for the good
of mankind" (Densmore, 1929, p. 61). Boys were told not to destroy
birds' nests for birds too were here "for the good of the earth" (Densmore, 1929, p. 61). She continues, "As soon as a boy was able to hold
anything in his hands he was given something resembling a bow and
arrow, and taught to go through the motions of shooting. A bow and
arrows were first given a boy when he was 5 or 6 years of age, and
with this he took his first lessons in the craft that was most necessary
to a hunter or warrior in the old days" (Densmore, 1929, p. 65).

Children were taught good behavior by object lessons as occasions
arose: evil deeds were pointed out to them as undesirable; good ones,
as worthy of imitation. "Certain persons that had done wrong were
pointed out to us and we were told, 'That's what happened to them.' "
"If a man displayed anger in presence of children, parents later discussed the occasion with their children, and told them what to do and
what not to do in such instances."

INSTRUCTORS

Although parents did much toward training their own children,
they were quite willing that grandparents should take upon them-

selves a goodly share of the responsibility of doing so. Grandparents not only instructed children by word of mouth, but taught them by demonstrating to them or by interesting them in participating in the daily routine of work.

Both parents and grandparents constrained children to listen to lectures given by elders, and obliged them to learn from those skilled in the arts. "My mother never told us anything, but my grandmother did." "Grandmothers advised girls and watched over them like mothers did." "My mother used to tell us stories that taught us to do right; my father, when he was old, told stories only occasionally to his grandchildren." "Years ago when we were young, we often sat around in a circle while an old person in the group talked, telling us what was ahead of us; what we should do to live good lives." "Boys, as young as seven, were made to go where old men were talking to listen to them; parents made the children go. Old men usually talked to boys, and old women to girls." "One day my old grandmother asked me if I was menstruating. I said, 'No, not for five moons.' Then she told me what condition I was in. I didn't know before then. No one told me before I was married. I trusted my grandmother more than my mother. She was older and had had more experience." "My father told me things; my mother never said anything to me for I was a boy; grandfather told me things too." "A grandfather often took a grandson when his voice began to change and preached to him. This was done especially in the evening but at any time of the year." "My mother never called us all together to instruct us, but my father did." Densmore's informant at Ponemah (Red Lake Reservation) had four brothers and four sisters. His "father gave counsel to the boys and taught them the best way to live," and his "mother told the girls how to conduct themselves" (Densmore, 1929, p. 60).

TIME OF INSTRUCTIONS

The time of instructions was often an occasion; frequently it was a planned affair. However, legends were never told in the summertime because "people were afraid that toads would gather in their place if they did." The first ones were told in the fall when the reptiles began to crawl into the ground; the last ones, in the spring when the leaves began to appear. Some legends were told for entertainment only; others taught young children the things in nature which they were to respect. Legends were taught to each generation by grandparents, chiefly grandmothers, and usually to children from 5 to 10 years of age. Children were often sent to grandparents for that purpose, mothers giving them tobacco to be presented as a gift to the old person.

Copway, a native, in discussing legends says:

These legends have an important bearing on the character of the children of
our Nation. The fire-blaze is endeared to them in after years by a thousand
happy recollections. By mingling thus, social habits are formed and strengthened. When the hour for this recreation arrives, they lay down the bow and
the arrow and joyously repair to the wigwam of the aged man of the village,
who is always ready to accommodate the young.

Legends are of three distinct classes, namely, the Amusing, the Historical, and
the Moral. In the Fall we have one class, in the Winter another, and in the
Spring a third. . . .

Some of these stories are most exciting, and so intensely interesting, that I
have seen children during their relation, whose tears would flow quite plenti-
fully, and their breasts heave with thoughts too big for utterance.

Night after night for weeks have I sat and eagerly listened to these stories.
The days following, the characters would haunt me at every step, and every
moving leaf would seem to be a voice of a spirit. To those days I look back
with pleasurable emotions. [Copway, 1851, pp. 98–99.]

REWARD AND PUNISHMENT

Although reward and punishment, scolding, and frightening played
a part in the training of many Chippewa children, no great emphasis
was laid upon them. Every attempt was made to make children mind
by speaking to them as occasion arose or by teaching them to do so at
times of formal instruction.

The child was usually not given much praise; occasionally it was
given a reward, such as maple sugar, a toy carved out of wood, or a
doll of grass, for work well done.

Sensible parents, informants agreed, never ridiculed their children
for failures. Children were scolded, but "too much scolding often
made them worse." At times a child was frightened by some masked
person; more often by expressions such as these: "The Sioux will get
you." "You lazy old thing: you don't know anything, and you'll
never have anything either." "The owl will put you in his ears!"
"The owl will put you in his ears, and fly away with your little feet
sticking out of his ears!" "The owl will come and stick you in his
ears if you don't stop crying!" If children refused to go to sleep at
night, mothers poked their heads out of wigwams and called the owl,
saying "Kō-kō-kō! Now, hear the owl!" On the Lac Courte Orielle
Reservation some parents hesitated to threaten children with the owl,
for "long ago an owl did come and get a child."

An expression that was very hurtful and brought immediate conformity was that of "Gā!" accompanied by a gesture of the right
hand. In inflicting it the mother brought all finger tips to the tip
of her thumb, stretched her arm full length toward the child, released
the fingers, spreading them out completely, and at the same time said,

"Gā!" Mothers used this gesture mostly when they were busy and children became annoying. Both children and dogs were seen to mind at once when thus corrected.

For mere annoyances children were punished at times by being sent to bed early, but never without food. For more serious offenses, such as lying, quarreling, being gone all day without permission, refusing to obey, or taking things that did not belong to them, children older than five years—"but never babies, one, two, or three years old"— were switched or slapped. Either parent administered the punishment by switching the legs or buttocks with a little stick, once or twice, while the child was standing, or by slapping it with the hand across the shoulders; it was never taken across the knee. "Parents made us mind by striking us a little across the shoulders and slightly pushing us. My mother once asked for salt—the salt was in the house and we were out of doors. No one fetched it; all five of us continued running around and playing. So our father slapped each one of us across the shoulders with his hand, and said, 'Can't you hear? Can't you hear?' Our mother herself often struck us across the shoulders when we didn't mind but never whipped us. She would say, 'I'll tell your father!' and then we minded, because we were afraid of him." A Mille Lacs informant was "spanked on legs and hands with a little switch. I got spanked by my father once because my little sister fell into the lake. I was supposed to be watching her. The ones who got spanked turned out to be good; the others did not."

Not all parents, however, approved of whipping children. "Real Indians don't believe in striking children; they say, 'You'll knock the spirit out of the child'." "My father never, never, switched us! He talked to us every evening, telling us how we should conduct ourselves the next day." A young Vermilion mother noticed that her grandmother invariably showed by her demeanor that she disliked seeing her daughter, the informant's mother, switch any of the children. "She doesn't want me to whip mine either. She often takes the children and talks to them; she holds other people up to them as good or bad examples."

A child that persisted in crying was never punished by having a cloth tied about its face, or by being tied to a tree or to the wigwam, as is the custom among some Plains Indians.

DISCOVERING RIGHTEOUS CHILDREN

If parents had convictions that a child was giving promise of "becoming something special" they tested it by sending it to bed without food. "In the morning such a child would be hungry and would be handed both food and charcoal. If it chose the charcoal and merely held it without eating it, it gave promise of becoming something; if it walked around nibbling the coal, it would most certainly be something; if he took the food first, it would be only ordinary."

If a child walked away from a group that was being instructed by a parent or an older person "say in the evening when all were together, everyone knew that it would not lead a good life. My deceased mother's sister had a daughter that used to do that, and this one didn't lead a good life; she drank, and the life she led is not worth telling. The girl's mother tried to talk to her alone, but she would not listen even then. Today hardly anyone listens to parents."

RELIGION AND SUPERNATURAL POWERS

THE SUPREME BEING

Belief in a Supreme Being was firmly rooted in the Chippewa culture. This Being, called Kī′cĕ Măn′itō or Great Spirit, was far away from them. He was seldom addressed directly or alone in prayers, and offerings were made to Him only at the Mīdē′wiwin celebration. Informants spoke of Him in subdued tones and with much reverence; they spoke of Him as the giver of life who protected and cared for them. "He put everything on the earth and takes care of everything," added an old man, the most powerful medicine man on the Lac Courte Orielle Reservation. An old woman on the same reservation said that when praying the old Indians addressed themselves to Kī′cĕ Măn′itō first, and then "to the other great spirits, the kit′cī măn′itō, those that dwelt in winds, snow, thunder, storm, trees, and everything." An old Vermilion shaman was certain that "all the first Indians around here knew there was a God long before the Whites came; only they didn't go to God for things as they do now as Christians. They got their favors from their special helpers then." Three L'Anse informants agreed that "Kī′cĕ Măn′itō was always thought of as being up in the heavens somewhere; He was never thought of as being near or around the people." Prayers of the Mīdē′wiwin were addressed to Him. These were vocal prayers, a type of prayer seldom addressed to minor deities; prayers to them, and at times to Kī′cĕ Măn′itō, were those of meditation.

MINOR DEITIES [13]

Deities of lesser power than Kī′cĕ Măn′itō were both those that dwelt in nature and those that formed the individual's helpers, namely the guardian spirits. Guardian spirits, the intermediaries between Kī′cĕ Măn′itō and the Chippewa man or woman, were obtained when fasting

---

[13] See also Hilger (1936 b, p. 2). Cf. Coleman's excellent article on Chippewa religion (1937, pp. 33–57). Her informants, however, differed from the present writer's in the meaning of Kī′cĕ Măn′itō and kit′cī măn′itō.

as a child (cf. pp. 39–48). An appeal to the guardian spirit by his client when he was in need was always heard. Several informants told of helpers that appeared to them in dreams or visions in later life but not while fasting. A Red Lake informant received such a helper when in dire distress. She said,

My place was struck by lightning and everything was burnt. The government then built this house in which I now live, but I had very little furniture and practically no utensils when I moved in. After dark on the first day I was to sleep here, I walked to the north door. Just as I looked up at the sky, I saw 12 girls (bust size) in the air, looking at me; they were all white girls with heads drooping. I knew that they had come to be my helpers. After that I was given things by different people on the reservation; one day by this person and another day by that one. This happened 22 years ago; but even today when I am in need or lonely, I think of those 12 girls and things brighten up.

A L'Anse woman told of a helper that came to her husband's first wife while asleep. She dreamed "that she was sick with tuberculosis, and while walking along the beach saw two sisters who said to her, 'Don't be scared. We are the Thunder. Whatever you will ask, we will give you.' She asked for health, and got it from the Thunder" (Hilger, 1936 a, p. 23). Her father when about 18 years old dreamed—

that he was like a white cloud and could fly like a bird over mountains and lakes; that he was a prisoner of two women in a wigwam near the Sault. It seemed he couldn't move; he felt paralyzed. The wigwam opened; a little weasel entered, took him by the head, and he could again fly. He dreamed this same dream two or four times. Then he went to an Indian in Canada and told his dream. This Indian said, "You'll cover a lot of land, and because the little white animal got you by the head, you'll get as white as the weasel." He became captain at the Sault Locks. Later he was land surveyor, mail carrier, transporter of minerals to Detroit, Chicago, Buffalo, and Canadian shores. He was never sick and died at the age of 76. [Hilger, 1936 a, p. 23.]

Other minor deities were those that resided in things of nature, such as lakes, rivers, and hills; rocks of uncommon shapes or magnitude; trees of unusual size or formation; birds, fish, animals of all kinds, and vegetables; thunder, wind, storms, and lightning. "We were taught to show respect for the thunder; we were told to sit down and to be quiet until the storm had passed over. It was just like God going by." "Old Indians think that stones have spirits, especially large stones. That is why they place tobacco as offerings on stones." "I often saw an old man who lived near here—he is dead now—put tobacco on the big stone that you saw on the side of the road on your way out here."

The Chippewa also believed in evil spirits (ma'cī măn'itō). They were personal and individual and not tribal and general. Their origin lay in dreams. Racoons, fish, and turtle were possessed of evil spirits for some informants. "In old days evil spirits were spoken of as doing harm, but no one ever spoke of a leader among them. The belief in the devil came with the Whites."

Tobacco, the usual ceremonial offering (pindākō'cīgē—he offers tobacco), was seldom offered to Kī'cē Măn'itō. It was, however, offered to all other deities by anyone inclined to do so: to guardian spirits to obtain favors; to evil spirits to ward off harm. Tobacco was offered as a ceremonial gift either in its natural form or by being smoked. "I burn tobacco in our stove whenever it thunders for the first time in the spring." "Whenever there is a thunderstorm we put tobacco near a tree or near the house or in any clean place (a place that cannot be stepped on by human beings) so the lightning won't strike us." "Long ago when a thunderstorm was gathering, we threw tobacco outside and said to the thunder: 'Take this tobacco and go your way; there are lots of other Indians on your way.'"

A Lac Courte Orielle interpreter knew an old Indian, "a very old Indian," who placed pinches of tobacco on a big boulder found between Reserve and Chief Lake. Many informants were certain that offering tobacco to the deities associated with bodies of water was an old custom. "My aunt always strews tobacco on the water, all around the boat, before leaving the shore in order to drive away the evil spirits." "Early in the spring when we make our first trip on the water, we throw a pinch of tobacco into the lake." An 87-year-old Red Lake informant had seen Indians fill a miniature birchbark canoe with tobacco and "offer it to the spirit of the water by throwing it into the lake." His son had caught three dead dogs in his fish net (1939). Since each had a small bag of tobacco tied to its neck, he "supposed that someone had drowned the dogs in the lake as an offering for good luck."

An old Mille Lacs informant noted: "Some white men drowned here in the lake, and that did not happen for nothing. Some things are sacred to Indians and white people who make fun of it can expect to be punished. Whites have laughed at Indians putting tobacco in the lake. We put tobacco into the lake whenever we go swimming, or when we want to cross the lake. One time, long ago, we were crossing the lake in a steamboat called 'Queen Anne.' Many Indians were on the boat. We were coming from Waukon and going to the Point. The waves were so high that we thought we were going to drown. My great-grandfather threw three or four sacks of tobacco into the water and soon the waves took us back to Waukon. We were all saved." "If a person dies the surviving members of his family must throw tobacco into the lake before they take their first swim. My husband and his brothers did so this spring; their brother died in the winter (1940)." "Yes, we boys put about a handful of smoking tobacco into the lake," added the husband.

Tobacco was smoked as an offering to Kĭ′cē Măn′itō at the Mīdē′-wiwin, and to the deities appealed to when exercising shamanistic powers. It was also smoked when invoking a guardian spirit, naming a child, treating sickness, making use of medicinal knowledge, averting danger, or petitioning for a favor. "Lighting a pipe is the same as praying, for we light our pipes and ask our helper to help us." The head nurse at an Indian hospital neglected to awaken an old Indian when a thunderstorm arose. "I wanted to smoke my pipe and ask protection on all the people of the reservation, as well as those at the hospital. That nurse didn't awaken me after I asked her twice to do so; so now I smoke for all, but not for her!"

Tobacco used in the early day consisted of the inner bark of red dogwood—Indians on all reservations called it "red willow."[14] An informant removed the outside bark of a twig with her thumbnail and noted that the remaining layer of bark when carefully shaven off served as tobacco, so-called kinnikinnick. Today kinnikinnick is a mixture of finely crushed inner bark of the red dogwood and shavings of plug tobacco. The mixture is worked in a mortar with pestle, both mortar and pestle being of wood. This mixture, too, is used today for ceremonial smoking.

THE MĪDĒ′WIWIN [15]

Warren defined the Mīdē′wiwin as the Chippewa "mode of worshiping the Great Spirit, and securing life in this and a future world, and of conciliating the lesser spirits, who in their belief, people earth, sky, and waters . . ." (Warren, 1885, p. 100.) All reservations included in this study except L'Anse had held Mīdē′wiwin celebrations within the year preceding the writer's visit. Interested persons on the L'Anse Reservation usually partook in the Lac Vieux Desert celebration (Wisconsin).

Traditionally the Mīdē′wiwin was held regularly in the spring after warm weather set in, and in the fall before cold weather began; it could be given in addition at any time of the year as a thanksgiving offering for favors received or as a petition for the restoration of health. These traditions have been retained on most reservations.

Persons of any age were received at any celebration, membership being by acceptance and initiation, and not by inheritance.[16] An old Lac Courte Orielle medicine man remarked: "In the old days not all Indians were members of the Mīdē′wiwin, nor was there an age limit. Sometimes children and old people joined at the same celebration. In

---

[14] Densmore (1929, p. 145) classified the "red willow" as *Cornus stolonifera* Michx.

[15] Cf. also Hoffman (1889, 1891); Hallowell (1936 b); and Lafleur (1940).

[16] Cf. Kohl (1859, pp. 40–52) for description of ceremonial at which child in cradleboard was adopted.

fact, anyone could join who wished to derive benefits by being a member." One informant having been a sickly child had been initiated when very young. She remarked: "Some old man performed the duties which I should have done had I been full grown when initiated. It did me much good; that's why I'm living today." A person wishing to join announced his intention "ahead of time and had to keep that promise; if he didn't, he could expect bad luck. For instance, a person announcing now that he will join next fall must join next fall, and not at any other time."

At the spring celebration (June 1938) at Ponsford on the White Earth Reservation, two children between 4 and 5 years of age were admitted (pl. 6, *1* and *2*). The mother of one had promised during the previous winter that she would have her child that had been restored to health initiated in the spring celebration; the mother of the other had asked for its admission hoping that thereby the child would regain health and strength and reach old age. On the Nett Lake Reservation in August 1939, a mother asked that a special celebration of the Mīdē′wiwin be given in order that her child, not yet a year old, might be admitted and thereby be cured of swollen glands in neck and chin; it had suffered from them for months. On the Lac Courte Orielle Reservation in the spring of 1935, two small children and one adult married woman were admitted. An informant on the same reservation had been admitted as a child, but had not gone beyond the first degree. He said persons joined the first degree in order to obtain long life; he preferred not to comment on the other degrees.

Informants, whether members, ex-members, or those who had never been members, on all reservations were hesitant to discuss matters pertaining to the Mīdē′wiwin. Hesitancy was possibly due to loyalty to their beliefs, to respect for the beliefs of others, or to a fear that revenge might be visited upon persons divulging secrets. Some information, however, was collected.

Degrees and ceremonials differed somewhat in the various groups. Informants believed these differences had a historical background in that in the early day each band held its separate Mīdē′wiwin. At the present time persons still travel distances to participate in the ceremonial of the group that admitted them. An old couple on the White Earth Reservation had traveled to the Mille Lacs Reservation to participate in the celebration in June 1939, and had in mind to continue to do so each year. If ever the time arrived when they had no one to take them or when they were no longer able to travel so far, they intended to celebrate the Mīdē′wiwin on the White Earth Reservation either with the Mille Lacs group at Elbow Lake or with the group of the White Earth band that celebrates at Ponsford.

A Lac Courte Orielle informant contributed the following:

There were usually four degrees or stages in the Mǐdē'wiwin; in a very few cases there were five or six. The following are the degrees: ōǒ'gě mǐdē'wid, initiation or 1st degree or 1st stage; nǐ'cō mǐdē'wid, 2d stage; mǐs'sō mǐdē'wid, 3d stage; nǐ'o mǐdē'wid, 4th stage; nä'nō mǐdē'wid, 5th stage; käbē' mǐdē'wid, 6th stage or final or last stage or finishing stage. Making the first four degrees is the normal or average attainment. Only in exceptional cases are the 5th and 6th degrees granted. The 5th degree is granted if one loses a loved one and in consequence of the bereavement his health is jeopardized—he becomes so sick that people think he will die of a broken heart. The spirit is asked in this degree for greater power to endure sacrifice; the person is willing to exchange what powers he has for a prolonged life. The 6th degree is very, very seldom granted. The degrees differ slightly on the various reservations. Ours are about the same as those on the Lac du Flambeau Reservation. The following are the degrees on the Lac du Flambeau Reservation and again in order of importance: 1st, weasel or its family, mink, beaver, etc.; 2d, some kind of water fowl, such as hawk, owl, etc.; 3d, fox and its family; 4th, the bear; 5th, an exceptionally large snake, copperhead, pine, etc.; 6th, a bear hand with claws, etc.

When a person has completed the fourth degree, he has attained the highest degree of the Mǐdē'wiwin; he is then considered as having completed the entire course of Indian religion. There is nothing more beyond this stage, except, as stated before, in exceptional cases when certain persons for very special reasons are granted special degrees. But the powers of these persons in no way exceed those that were attained in the 4th degree. The skins of animals which the dancers or participants in the Mǐdē'wiwin carry are symbols of achievement in the Mǐdē'wiwin course. Each type of skin represents a certain degree. (These skins do not represent any power that the carrier attained through his fasts or dreams.) Names of skins are the following, each corresponding to the degree: 1st degree, weasel (cingō'sīwā'yàn); 2d degree, fowl of any kind (binē'sīwā'yàn); 3d degree, fox (wā'gōcsīwā'yàn); 4th degree, small bear (mākwā'sīwā'yàn); 5th degree, large snake (kēnē'bǐksīwā'yàn); 6th degree, bear claw or paw (mākwā'nindjsīwā'yàn).

A White Earth informant contributed the following:

The degree of the Mǐdē'wiwin, or rather the method of procedure, differs somewhat from locality to locality. Those of the members of the Mille Lacs band living at Elbow Lakes on this reservation differ considerably from those of the Ponsfordians on this reservation and both of these differ from those at Ponemah on the Red Lake Reservation. At Ponsford there are eight degrees but the last four reiterate the first four. The first four degrees are called ábàding' mǐdē'wid (once "grand-medicined"), nǐdjō mǐdē'wid (twice "grand-medicined"), nǐsō' mǐdēwid (three times "grand-medicined"), nēō'mǐdē' wid (four times "grand-medicined"). The "medicine bag" of each degree is distinct. That of the first is the cingō' sǐwā'yàn (weasel hide); of the second, cànkwē'sīwā'yàn (mink hide); of the third, mākwā sīwāy'wàn (bear's foot); of the fourth, gǐcik' (cedar). The third degree might also be signified by the hide of the owl or the hawk; formerly also by that of the otter. The cedar of the fourth degree is whittled out in four places and mǐgis (shells) are placed in these four holes; ribbons are tied to both ends. The "medicine bundles"—dream badges—are distinct and are not the same as these used at the Mǐdē'wiwin.

The badge of the first degree on the Lac du Flambeau Reservation is the weaselskin; the second, the skin of the owl or some fowl; the third, the foxskin; and the fourth, the highest degree, the bearskin.

The ceremonial was held in an elongated wigwam.[17] Frameworks of the Mīdē'wiwin wigwam were seen on all reservations covered in this study, except L'Anse. They were always found near the home of a member (pl. 26, 1), and were in his care. One such wigwam on the Lac Courte Orielle Reservation (June 1935) measured 125 feet in length and 13 feet in width. Two entrances, one at each end, had been barred with two saplings tied to the framework in the form of an X; the height was, therefore, not measured, but it appeared to be that of wigwams scattered about the place—wigwams occupied by participants during celebrations. One of these was 6½ feet in height. The framework consisted of 2 rows of 11 saplings each. The heavier ends of the saplings were planted securely in the ground about 12 feet apart; the slender ends of opposite ones, bent over and fastened to each other to form an arch, thus forming a rounded ceiling. Pine and cedar twigs had been intertwined between saplings for about 2 feet above the ground. The upper section of the wigwam was uncovered. The Mīdē'wiwin member who cared for the wigwam noted that during the days of ceremonial this section was covered with hides, birchbark rolls, and canvas. Down the middle in the interior was a row of 20 stones, each about 6 inches in diameter, set about 4 feet apart. The entire row was skirted by a path. Outside the wigwam and a little distance to the side of one end was a circle of twigs about 5 feet in diameter. In the center of this was a stone of unusual contour and bordering it, a thin outline of red clay resembling a turtle. Wherever the contour of the stone permitted, a pinch of smoking tobacco had been placed. The Mīdē'wiwin had been celebrated in this wigwam in May 1935.

The Mīdē'wiwin wigwam on the White Earth Reservation differed little from the above in construction, except that the upper section was not covered during the ceremonial, nor did the cedar and pine twigs reach much beyond a foot above the ground. Within the enclosure, not far from the east entrance, were two poles, each of which was topped with a carved wooden representation of a bird (pl. 6, 1 and 2). The Mīdē'wiwin was celebrated in this wigwam in June 1938. The framework of a Mīdē'wiwin wigwam on the Mille Lacs Reservation consisted of two rows of nine saplings each. Poles were tied horizontally to these, encircling the wigwam about 2 feet from the ground. Four rows of poles rested on top and were tied to the framework, the entire upper weight being supported by three poles planted in the ground along the center. Basswood fiber had been used in all tying. The spring celebration which had been delayed was to be held there about July 4 (1940), remarked a member of the hawk degree.

---

[17] Cf. pl. 6. All Mīdē'wiwin lodges were formerly covered with birchbark and bulrush mats, like the home wigwams (cf. pp. 137-141).

At that time the lower section, extending a little beyond the encircling poles, was to be covered with long grass, twigs, and branches.

The Mīdē′wiwin ceremonial celebration lasted 4 days. It consisted of gesticulated dancing and singing to the accompaniment of a drum; of fasting, feasting, and smoking; and of sacrificial offerings. The songs of the Mīdē′wiwin were used exclusively during the ceremonials.[18] Members had them recorded in pictographs on birchbark rolls and frequently rehearsed them before celebrations. Only members were able to interpret the pictographs. The meal served to members at the Nett Lake and at the White Earth celebrations consisted primarily of wild rice, beef, and meat of dogs—dog meat being considered essential to the feast. At Nett Lake dogs were described by nonparticipant observers as "just about the size of this little black dog; they are about eight weeks old." The one used at the final meal at the White Earth ceremonial was larger and older. He was kept within the enclosure of the Mīdē′wiwin wigwam, being tied to its framework with a rope. He was quieted and petted by one of the members, and never left alone.

Members partook in the ceremonial feast only upon invitation. A young man extended such invitations on the Nett Lake Reservation by handing a small stick to each person invited. One of these, handed to an informant during an interview, invited her to partake of the feast given during the ceremonial held for the cure of the child with the swollen glands, earlier referred to in this work (p. 64). The surface of the stick of wood, about 6 inches in length and in thickness that of a lead pencil, was cut hexagonally, and was encircled with a groove about one-quarter of an inch from one end. A young man delivered this invitation about 4 o'clock in the afternoon. He and another young man had already extended several invitations and had yet a handful to deliver—"at least eight more." Only the very old members were being invited. The informant called her grandchild from play and sent it into the house to fetch her grandmother's gray enameled dish (6 inches in diameter) and her red flannel bag (8 by 6 inches) containing her pipe and tobacco. In the meantime, an old man carrying a similar dish, a buckskin bag with pipe and tobacco, and a washed-out pink cotton blanket, stopped to say a few words to our informant and then walked down the path to the Mīdē′wiwin wigwam. Soon she, too, carrying her pipe bag and dish followed the path. Her daughter remarked that although she herself was 50 years old and a member of the Mīdē′wiwin, she could not help in this case and was therefore not invited. "Only the old people can help in this case; the chief and five old men have carried on the ceremonial since yesterday."

---

[18] Cf. Densmore (1910, pp. 11–118) for songs sung at the Mīdē′wiwin celebration. These pages also contain a rather detailed description of the ceremonial.

Offerings at the White Earth celebration consisted of four cotton blankets, three 2-gallon tin water pails, several small cooking dishes, several pieces of calico cloth, and some packages of wild rice and groceries (pl. 6, 2). Observations of offerings could not be made at Nett Lake, the wigwam being a closed one. They were described by one informant who had seen them as similar to the above, including, in addition, two hides which the mother had tanned. A member on the Lac Courte Orielle Reservation thought that providing the offerings—an absolutely necessary thing—was the condition hardest to fulfill.

If one can get together the offerings, [he added] one can make all the degrees. In the old days offerings consisted of buckskins and blankets. Parents make the offerings when their children are admitted. All offerings are really made to Kǐ'cē Măn'itō, but the persons that dance and take part in the ceremonials receive them. These ceremonies can't be changed; they are exactly the same as in old days. They are the same as when the Indians first came on this earth. They are just the same!

Each degree possessed its own design of facial and body decoration. An old Mīdē'woman on the White Earth Reservation when prepared for burial (September 1938) had two stripes, one blue and one red, painted diagonally across each cheek from bridge of nose toward lobe of ear, and a disk of blue on the center of the forehead. The red paint was made of soil; the blue, from the lead of an indelible pencil. Many Wisconsin Chippewa obtained red paint from L'Anse Indians, soil for red paint being found on the shores of Keweenaw Point on Lake Superior:

On the rock just beneath the water, there will be found little cup-shaped formations in which there is a jelly-like substance of dark red color. This may be scooped out and dried in the sun; it will seem like clay when dry. When red paint is desired, it may be mixed with any grease, preferably bear grease—bear grease was always used in old days. Some men also made clay pipe bowls of this material.

A very old Mille Lacs informant, member of the hawk degree, said designs for all degrees in life and at burial consisted of lines and disks. Colors differed: the first or weasel degree, used white paint; the second or mink, brown; the third or hawk, yellow and vermilion; and the fourth or bear, black.

Each member kept "power" or "medicine" in the skin of the animal distinctive of his degree (cf. p. 65). This formed his badge. Each member was buried with his own skin. The White Earth woman was clasping the skin of a weasel in her hands when ready for burial. An old informant on the same reservation was saving the skin of a weasel that had inadvertently wandered into his garden (July 1938); he wished to have it on hand when the adopted child by his daughter would be admitted to the Mīdē'wiwin. He was a member of the owl-skin degree; his wife, of the weasel degree.

These skins containing "power" were carried by members during
the ceremonial dances of the Mīdē′wiwin. At the White Earth celebration, the two mothers sat in the center line each holding her child
in her lap, while the participating members (eight in this instance)
danced along the path, the full length of the wigwam, singing and
carrying in their hands the skins of their degree. As each member
approached the child, he or she, with a quick motion of the hand,
pointed the head of the animal at each child, bringing it very near its
face. The child invariably cried with surpise and fear. Nonparticipant observers were unwilling to comment on the significance of these
gestures.

A former Mīdē′wiwin member on the L'Anse Reservation described
her uncle's initiation thus:

My uncle sat in the middle of the long wigwam. The medicine men, four or
five of them, came dancing in, carrying pouches. The pouches were made of the
skins of beaver, otter, white martin or weasel—all elongated like snake skins.
The dancers danced along the path of the wigwam and when they came near my
uncle they threw their pouches at him. The "medicine" in them was so strong
that he fell over and fainted. Each man then picked up his pouch and laid
it on him, and he came to. From then on my uncle had powers to punish his
enemies.

A 70-year-old Vermilion informant had joined the Mīdē′wiwin at
the age of 16, having been chosen by his parents to do so. He owned
two books (ledger-ruled, about 9 by 6 inches in size) which contained
information that he had obtained as a member of the Mīdē′wiwin. A
number of pages contained names of roots and herbs of both medicinal
and magic value written in Chippewa. Each line of such information
was followed by several explanatory lines of pictorial writings, the
drawings being mainly animals and men. One page contained the
sketch of a front view of a person. Lines led from dots on various
parts of the body to numbered circles drawn in the margin of the page,
the numbers referring to information on succeeding pages. Each dot
indicated the place on the body into which magic power was infused
during the Mīdē′wiwin ceremonials. "A weasel member, for example, will motion toward this point of the body with his weasel,"
remarked the informant.

The Mīdē′wiwin drum is called mītikkwākōk′ (wooden pail);
when in actual use it is called nīmicōmis (my grandfather). The
drumsticks for this drum are called bāgākōk′kwān. The drum used
at the White Earth celebration was about 18 inches long and 8 inches
in diameter. It was made by hollowing out a log cylinderically, leaving one end closed. When in use it contained several cups of water,
the open end being covered with a piece of scraped but untanned fresh
rawhide. As the hide dried, it shrunk, thus forming an airtight taut
covering. The water caused the sound of the drumbeats to carry a

long distance. Both men and women members beat the drum during the ceremonial, this being the only occasion at which women beat a drum.

A larger drum, the so-called "big drum" (dēwē īgōn) "one as large as a washtub with rawhide stretched on both ends," is also considered sacred. Formerly it was used at the sacred dances other than the Mīdē′wiwin, such as the War Dance. The Mīdē′ drum is the older, but both drums were held equally sacred. It is believed that both had their origin in dreams: the small one, among the Chippewa; the larger one, among the Sioux. An old Lac Courte Orielle man had heard a Sioux describe the origin of the big drum thus:

Long ago there was a war. A young girl found herself trapped under much grass that was hanging over the side of a river. The enemy was camped right near by. Four days she was imprisoned there. On the fourth day the Great Spirit appeared to her and asked if she were hungry, and she said, "Yes." The Great Spirit then told her to follow Him and He led her right into the enemy's camp where they both sat down and ate. The enemy couldn't see them. After they had eaten, the Great Spirit told her that she was entitled to have a drum in her possession; that this drum would bring peace between the people; and this was a Sioux girl. The Chippewa got their drum from the Sioux, and this is its origin. We consider the big drum sacred, and place offerings of tobacco and clothes near it.

Today the large drums are still held sacred but are used at social dances, such as pow-wows.

Drums were seen or heard during this study on all reservations except L'Anse; none had been used at L'Anse for some years. In 1935 five large sacred drums were extant on the Lac Courte Orielle Reservation. One was owned by each of five groups: the Chief Lake group, the Barber Town people, Reserve village, the Round Lake group, and the Whitefish people, and cared for by men in each group.

When the United States Government moved the Indians from the village of Old Post to the village of New Post on the same reservation (the land at Old Post having been flooded by a newly built dam), the Indians of the reservation presented the New Post group with a sacred drum. After we had moved to New Post, some Indians came over with the drum. That morning everybody went out into an open space, a field. Those who brought the drum lined up on one side and our Indians opposite to them. They started drumming, and soon everybody joined in and danced Indian dances. Then the drum was given into the safekeeping of two of our men, and from then on it belonged to New Post. Indians consider the drum very sacred and will never leave it alone for long; somebody is always in the room with it. He might step outside for a few minutes and leave it alone, but he won't be gone long.

In Indian Village on the Mille Lacs Reservation a large drum, well decorated with bands of beadwork and copper medals about the size of 25-cent pieces, rested on a shelf in the corner of one of the homes. On the La Pointe Reservation, "the Martin group owned one, and one was owned by the group across the river (Bad River)."

Drumsticks (bāgākōk′kwān) were about 1 foot long with the end, used in beating, well padded with buckskin.

"GRAND MEDICINE," OR POWERS OF MEMBERS OF THE MĪDĒ′WIWIN

The supernatural power ascribed to members of the Mīdē′wiwin included black art, generally spoken of as "grand medicine" or "bad medicine" (kābē′ mīdēwid).[19] In exercising it, it was believed that Mīdē′ members, (mīdē′wininī—medicine men and medicine women), could bring great misfortune upon people, even causing them to become ill or insane or to die. Powers could be exercised by personal contact, by being in the presence of persons to be influenced, or by being at great distances from them. The medium used was acquired in the various degrees of the Mīdē′wiwin. "Persons who had completed the entire four degrees of the Mīdō′wiwin were given an insignia, usually a thimble-shaped article wherein was carried 'dope.' He wore this on his person; not in a conspicuous place, however. The 'dope' is 'bad medicine.' As he is advanced in the degrees, more damaging medicines are revealed to him. The medium is sometimes carried in small doll-like men and women made of unbeaded buckskins called ōdēcēnō′win." Influence could be exerted on Indians and Whites, but was seldom exercised on the latter. Expressions used in describing these shamanistic activities are mīkē′cī mīdē′wid (being "grand medicined").

Members used various methods when exercising evil powers, the commonest probably being that of the "fireball" (cinkwānē′nōk or mā′djī ic′kōtē). On all reservations informants either had experienced the effects of the "fireball" in their own lives or had observed it in the lives of others. To the eye the "fireball" appears like a ball of glowing, flameless material. Young informants, as well as Whites intermarried with Indians, who had investigated "fireballs," were convinced that they are merely marsh gas or "will-o'-the-wisp." Chippewa who conceded that they were marsh gas still persisted, however, that they were used by the Mīdē′ to transmit "bad medicine" or "grand medicine," even great distances, the effects being ill health, death, or "bad luck of some sort."

The following are personal experiences of informants:

An old Indian told me that he once saw three "fireballs" the first one larger than the others, rise one after the other east of here and travel far over to the west, sailing about a half mile above the earth. The Indians called these balls cinkwānē′nōk. They are omens of sickness or bad luck.

---

[19] Hallowell (1936 b, vol. 38, pp. 48–49) tells of a favor bestowed on some young men by a Saulteaux through the exercise of his "medicine." Cooper (1936, pp. 8–13) records several types of divination and six types of medicine men for the Lake of the Woods and Rainy Lake Ojibway.

When I was young I rose very early one morning while the rushes were yet damp with dew, to make a bulrush mat. It was still dark. I saw a light, like a flash, pass across the river. It passed among the trees and over toward Green's meadow. I whispered this to my brother William who was with me. He took a pitchfork and hit at it. It disappeared in the woods, and we never saw it again. There was a sick girl nearby, and we think the "fireball" went for her. At least she died soon after.

Indians are afraid of "fireballs." They were afraid, also, of certain light that used to appear in the woods near the Convent. One evening a little girl visited here. It was dark when she was ready to go home and she was afraid to pass those woods. My girl offered to go with her, but I was afraid to have her come home alone. Finally my husband said he would go with them. On the way back he saw the light, and went up to it, and it was a rotten fungus on some old tree stump. He brought part of it home and said to me, "Here is what the people have been talking about." My husband has no Indian blood in him. [Hilger, 1936 a, p. 19.]

A "fireball is an ill omen for Indians. When one is seen, it is believed that a medicine man has been hired by someone to injure a particular person. Some time ago, during the night, a "fireball" was seen to leave the swamp near here and go eastward.—The direction which the "fireball" takes will tell where the evil effects will show up.—Several weeks later, during maple-sugar-making time, one of the men was tired from walking back and forth for sap, and he laid down in the open. The ground was damp and he contracted pneumonia and died after several days. It was said that that "fireball" had been "bad medicine" and caused his death. His wife has been sick too since that time. Every spring one hears things about "fireballs." My brother-in-law had a stroke a year ago, and claims it was caused by means of Indian "medicine."

Late in the afternoon on the day when my son William and some men had exhumed six graves—one being that of a chief—in the new roadbed between Redby and Red Lake (Red Lake Reservation) a deadful storm arose. It was the worst one, the old people said, that had visited the reservation in 40 years. Upon his return home William found the neighbors gathered about his house and much excited. They insisted that before it began to rain a "fireball" had come out of his house. My daughter, too, had seen it. He found many of the tall pines near his home broken down. The neighbors insisted that the dead chief was avenging the exhuming of his remains; the terrible storm was a punishment to all the village, while the "fireball" gave evidence of special disfavor to William. One old man insisted on placing tobacco on William's doorstep hoping thereby to pacify the dead chief.

Not being certain who had injured her husband, a Lac Courte Orielle informant engaged a medicine man to discover the culprit:

I once hired a medicine man. It happened like this: About 2 years ago, in the fall, while I, my old man, and an old neighbor woman were sitting on our front porch facing the lake, a stone in the shape of a "fireball" hit my old man's leg. Soon his leg broke out with sores, even to his waist line. So, in the spring we hired a medicine man to discover the source of the "fireball." He went away and upon his return said that an Indian enemy had done it, and advised us to save the stone. [The stone, about 3 x 2 x 2 inches, was stored in a Mason fruit jar.] We paid the medicine man half a pound of tobacco for his services. One can pay them anything.

Black art could also be exercised as "grand medicine" on figurines of wood made to represent persons (mǎckī′kī māsīnīgō′cīkŏn). An interpreter at L'Anse related the following:

A few years ago I was asked to clean out an old house. In it I found a bundle which contained two figures carved out of wood, one representing a man, the other a woman. At about the position of the heart was a little red spot and an arrow. An old woman who looked at them said, "That's bad. The Indian who moved from here must have killed these two people by 'medicine'." She examined them and said they represented a man and a woman who had been done away with some time ago. [Hilger, 1936 a, p. 18.]

Another method of exercising evil power required contact with an enemy's person. "They tell of an Indian here who, pretending to be in good faith, distributed tobacco to several persons. While doing so to one of the men, he dropped 'poison' which he had stored between his fingers along with the tobacco, thus causing this man's mouth to be drawn to one side." A young man was similarly afflicted for laughing at a medicine man who was relating an incident. "The medicine man gave him one look, and everybody knew that something would happen to this fellow. And sure enough, after some time his mouth was pulled to one side." A L'Anse interpreter when afflicted with a swollen ankle was told by her aunt, "That is just what I expected would happen. I notice people want you to work for them in preference to other Indians. Somebody is jealous of you. You are getting along too well; that's the reason."

Members of the Mĭdē′wiwin could also cause death. On the L'Anse Reservation this story prevails: "Years ago an old medicine man came nearly drowning in Keweenaw Bay, but the mermaids (mǎmā′kwǎsā) saved him; whereupon he promised them a person every year, for 10 years. This man lived on an island near Pequaming. Every year after that until the medicine man's death—he died bereft of his mind—a person was drowned in the Bay." An old Lac Courte Orielle informant had been told by his father that Bagawas, a medicine man, had killed many children by merely beating his drum. "In old days," he added, "the Indians were scared of each other, especially of old fellows."

Insanity was often the result of being "grand-medicined." "They put that 'grand medicine' in a bearskin bag, and do such powerful things with it as to make a man crazy; I have seen it!" said a Red Lake informant. "Years ago a woman across the Lake from here (at Red Lake) ate her own children.—The one who does that must be crazy; she can't be right!—She claimed she was eating bear meat, or porcupine meat. But she had killed her child, and cooked it. The Indians said some one had 'grand-medicined' her for she was doing the will of another and not her own. So they had her 'grand-medicined' by a stronger medicine man and she became sane again." The following was related on the L'Anse Reservation:

A surveyor whom I knew very well robbed the Indians of much property. He surveyed lands for Indians at Watersmeet, Lac Vieux Desert, Granville, and Iron Mountain. He was given money to buy lands. He might be given $400 for the purchase of a piece of land and obtain from the Indian owner a deed and a receipt for $400, when in reality he had given only $200 and retained the other $200. The seller expected the balance of the money. Many were tricked in this way and finally the culprit was discovered. One day when he came home he fell and stretched out about six feet; his body seemed to become that much elongated. He jumped up and said, "Hard game!" He had these spells during a period of six months. He would foam at the mouth, but nobody could do anything for him. We tried everything, even rubbing him with vinegar. Every time he came out of a spell he would say, "Hard game!" The old chief had found him out and had sent bad medicine to him. After awhile he became foolish. One time he wore my shoes to town. He finally confessed he wronged the Indians. Now he knew they had punished him. [Hilger, 1936, p. 19.]

Upon the refusal of parents on the Red Lake Reservation to allow a daughter to marry a medicine man, the latter "grand-medicined" the girl causing her nose to bleed for 2 days and 2 nights. Upon the advice of another medicine man, an old one, the former was recalled to fumigate the girl. This he did by placing herbs on two hot stones over which the girl held her head, head and stones being covered with a blanket.

A woman on the Red Lake Reservation told of her plight:

Yes, twice I was "grand-medicined." I almost died; even my hair came out. It happened like this: One fall when we had caught a great many fish, a young man wanted to buy some; but we had already sold all we could spare. Since I couldn't give him any, he became angry and had me "grand-medicined." I was going to sleep when I saw him; his mouth was bloody. People said I was asleep; but I saw the man come. He tried to throw me into a hole in the ground from which I knew I should never have escaped, had he succeeded. I was out of my mind for a long time. When I came to, a man, a near relative said, "Don't you think there is somebody doing something to you?" I knew very well who was doing it; it was an old man. I knew the old man who was doing this to me; but that young man had paid him to do it. This old relative said, "I am going to that old man and ask whether he feels justified in doing that to you just because somebody else hired him to do it!" He went; and everything came out all right. They gave me medicine to fumigate my head and after that I was well. When anyone is fumigated, herbs are placed on heated stones in a little wigwam. The person then crawls into this hut. Sometimes herbs are put on hot stones in the house and a blanket thrown over the head, allowing the fumes to be inhaled. The old medicine man later came and gave me a shawl and said, "You will be all right from now on." That same fall that old man died.

A L'Anse informant had heard of medicine men who charmed a fly, identified themselves with it, and traveled in the form of a fly.

A long time ago [he said] one party at war with another put up a defense of brush and lined it with hides. A medicine man cut a hole about 3 inches in diameter into the hide, and then by means of his "medicine" gradually made himself into a fly with feet so small that they were only 1½ inches long. He crawled through the hole to the enemy's side, discovered their location and plans, returned through the hole, and gradually took over the form and size of a man again.

It is firmly believed that injury done by a medicine man or medicine woman can be undone by one with greater power. A L'Anse informant had had the following experience:

Some years ago I landed a boat full of fish every morning. One morning some fellow came along and talked about my good luck. While we were taking fish out of our nets—I had 30 nets—he saw a big whitefish and asked if he might have it. I let him take it. That fellow spoiled my fishing! I couldn't get any more fish after that. Well, one day when we were out on the lake we pulled up to the shore where some of my wife's relatives lived, and went there for something to eat. The man said, "I suppose you get plenty fish." "No", I said, "not any more." And I told him the story of the whitefish. "Never mind," he said, "we'll fix him." And he took a half pailful of lukewarm water, washed the "bad medicine" off my nets, and hung them up. When they were dry he said, "Set out one net and you'll catch one whitefish, an unusual whitefish. Clean it very carefully, put the scales into some water, and then wash your nets in that water. Take the big whitefish and eat all of it with your family." I took the net and set it. We caught the big whitefish, only it looked somewhat red. My wife baked it in the oven, and she and I, the old man, and my two children ate all of that big whitefish! [His wife interjected: "It was a pretty hard thing to do, it was such a big fish."] "Never mind; we'll get that fellow yet," said the old man. He told me to sink 3 nets the next day, 6 the following day, and keep doubling the number each day until all the 30 nets had been sunk. And now I began catching fish again, and lots of them. It was all due to this medicine man's power being stronger than that other man's.

"TIPI SHAKING"

Certain medicine men have shamanistic powers to discover factors involved in past, present, or future events. Since the shaman's investigations are connected with the tremor, or, at times, violent shaking of a small dome-shaped wigwam (cīsāgī'kan), the name "tipi shaking" (cīsāgī'kwin) has been applied to it. The shaking may be in two opposing or in all four directions. Medicine men possessed of this power were still extant on the reservations of Lac du Flambeau, La Pointe, Vermilion, Red Lake, Lac Courte Orielle, Mille Lacs, and Nett Lake in the summers of ethnological studies covered in this work; there were none on the L'Anse nor on the White Earth reservations, but persons on both reservations had engaged shamans so endowed from other reservations to make discoveries for them.

The shaman with "tipi-shaking" powers was invariably an old man. His communications with the spiritual world were carried on only when in a small wigwam and when alone, after having smoked and mediated. A Lac Courte Orielle informant had not only observed "tipi shaking" but had helped to build a wigwam for his granduncle:

My grandfather's brother was a fake medicine man. He was asked to discover whether a sick child was going to live or die. His sons and nephews were told to build a tipi; we built a regular one of light poles 7 feet high and 4 feet in diameter. We tied the poles together and covered the tipi with blankets. Some 12 feet from the tipi was a bonfire. Some men sat near it and beat the drum. Halfway between the acting medicine man—in this case my grandfather's brother—sat down and smoked his long pipe. He sat on the ground with the bowl of his pipe resting on the ground. His hands clutched the pipe stem, his arms rested on his bent knees. He continued smoking his pipe and staring before him at the ground, continually staring, while the others beat the drum. Finally he said, "Everything is all right!" meaning, he was ready to go into the small tipi. He goes in, and in a few minutes things begin to rattle. Often there are bells at the top of the tipi, and these begin to rattle. My great uncle went in and, as soon as things began to shake, the tipi went to pieces. We had purposely constructed it carelessly, so as to annoy the old man. He was cross and said, "Come, now, make a good one." Next day we built one of poles so strong that we were hardly able to bend the poles in order to tie them together. Now the old fellow couldn't make things go; things only quivered. He came out and said, "Spirits won't come." So another man who sat nearby was asked to go in. He didn't want to, but finally he did; he was middle-aged. He made the thing go because he was a powerful medicine man. He nearly shook it to the ground. I knew that fellow; he wasn't so strong physically that he could shake that tipi! We fellows who had made it, tried our level best to make it shake, but couldn't move it. This fellow made it shake! My grandfather's brother had failed, for he was a fake. This fellow said the girl would live, and in 2 days she was up and around.

Another time I saw a medicine man work. Two medicine tipis were built not far apart. The same strong man that acted in the case of the sick girl was to occupy one, and another man, the other. The first one refused to act. The second man came and said he would try. They beat the drum, and he smoked, and thought, and studied, gazing on the ground. Then, raising himself up, "It is all right; we can start." He crept on hands and feet for 5 feet to the tipis. He took off his shirt, tucked it in one tipi, and went into the other. Both tipis began to shake and sway from side to side. The purpose was to find out whether a certain person was going to live or die, and what medicine should be used. [Hilger, 1936 c, pp. 46–47.] [20]

A Mīdē'wiwin woman on the same reservation, approved of the above account, and added, "The wigwam in which a medicine man talks with the spirits is open at the top. The spirits enter and leave through this opening."

An old L'Anse informant remembered well the days when there were powerful medicine men. When still young he assisted in the building of a shaman's wigwam:

One winter in January we heard my mother's father was sick. My mother was greatly worried, but she couldn't go to see him for it was cold; the snow was deep and there was no trail. We lived where the road comes down to Rabbit's Bay. An old medicine man said to my mother, "You give me tobacco, and I'll find out how your father is getting along." He ordered five or six of us boys to build

[20] Cf. Hallowell (1942 b) for an over-all account of conjuring among the Saulteaux of Berens River, Manitoba, a branch of the Ojibwa-speaking peoples. Cf. also Hallowell (1940 b).

a wigwam. We built a solid one! We took 12 poles, set them in a circle about 2 feet into the ground, tied other poles solidly around these and covered all with canvas. The medicine man went in and took with him a buckskin drum. The older people sat close to the wigwam; but we boys had to go about 5 feet away. About 9 o'clock at night the old man began to sing. (We laughed; but mother said, "Be quiet!") Soon the tipi began to shake, first slowly, and then faster and faster, swinging from one side to the other; suddenly it stopped with a thump. The spirit, Owācàgàbō′wis, had come to talk to the medicine man. We could hear different voices. One asked the old man, "Why do you want me?" "I want his soul." (He meant my grandpa's soul.) In a moment the tipi began to shake again, just like before, and again it stopped with a thump. Then we could hear my grandfather talk; his voice was weak and it sounded hungry. Some boys in our crowd said, "There is your grandfather." Then the tipi shook again like before, and that's when the spirit left.[21]

A Lac du Flambeau interpreter had been an observer of several "tipi shakings." She told of two:

About 10 years ago, a woman gave a hide and some tobacco to a medicine man asking him to make inquiries about her daughter in Oklahoma. He did so. Suddenly the tipi began to shake; we could hear various noises and several voices! The fellow must have changed his voice! He came out of his tipi and said: "Your daughter is all right; in a few days you will see her." And sure enough, in two days the girl came home! I saw another "tipi shaking," about 8 years ago, while I was interpreter for a Winnebago woman who wanted to talk to a Chippewa medicine man but couldn't speak our language. I told the medicine man that she would give him three ponies, two boxes of maple sugar, four pairs of blankets, two beautiful shawls, and a man's suit, if he would discover for her whether or not she'd be cured of her illness. He did all the necessary things and went into his little wigwam. When he came out he told her that she'd be cured. But that was a big "fib" for she died a few years after!

On the White Earth Reservation two small children had died within a brief period of time in 1938. "So the father got a medicine man from Mille Lacs Reservation to shake his tipi and was told that the fault lay in his not having joined the Mĭdē′wiwin." A young woman on the Red Lake Reservation had seen her grandfather, a grand medicine man and "tipi shaker," "crawl into a small tent into which he called the spirit of a man upon whom he was exercising revenge for another man. This other man had hired him to do so. My grandfather had powers to cause the man on whom he was exercising revenge either not to wake up again some morning or to make his mouth crooked. He had power, too, to make white men's mouths crooked but he never used it."

A Lac Courte Orielle interpreter contributed the following:

A medicine man may be called on, day or night, to discover the cause and the cure of some internal disease. The sick man is placed on a mat outside the small wigwam in which the medicine man is exercising his powers. All during the ceremony some one on the outside beats the drum. It is absolutely necessary that the wigwam sway back and forth, for, without it, the procedure is ineffective. As soon as the tipi shakes—which indicates that the spirits are in the wigwam—

---

[21] Cf. also Flannery (1940, pp. 14–18) for good account on beliefs related to conjuring.

the medicine man asks the persons on the outside who are interested in the sick man what they wish to know. The spirits on the inside answer. One can hear them talking but only the man in the wigwam usually understands the language, for only occasionally do the spirits speak Chippewa. The voices sound like those of a large crowd. It's these spirits that make the wigwam sway. We call this "tipi shakes." Long ago the swaying was so violent that the wigwam touched the ground from side to side. If many spirits come into the wigwam, the medicine man comes out tired and weak. In the early days the medicine man performed ceremonies similar to the ones above to discover whether it was safe to break camp.

BELIEF IN LIFE AFTER DEATH

LIFE AFTER DEATH [22]

Not only is the Chippewa belief in life after death evidenced in their burial and mourning customs, but there exists a tradition among them that after death their spirits go westward "to where the sun sets," "to the camping grounds of eternal bliss and happiness," to cībī′odēnȧ (spirit town or happy home). Nonmembers of the Mīdē′wiwin live outside cībī′odēnȧ and have only bark as food. At a burial, as the body of a Mīdē′wiwin is lowered, the attending medicine man says: "Do not look back. Keep going until you arrive at the camping grounds of our fathers and grandfathers and parents, where you will enjoy everlasting happiness."

DEATH

Formerly when death was imminent, the dying person—adult or child—was clothed in his best buckskin clothes including moccasins, and his body decorated with Indian paint. Some were known to have been buried with trophies and war awards hung about the neck. Today, death usually, but not always, has occurred before the body is dressed for burial. When ready for burial both hat and shoes are worn. In 1930 an old Red Lake man was dressed for burial "in his dancing clothes, feather bonnet, and moccasins."

Immediately following the death of a Mīdē′ relative at which a Lac du Flambeau interpreter was present in 1935, the Mīdē drum was brought in. It was placed close to the dead woman, all women present dancing around the body in step with the beat of the drum.

If it had been a man, the men should have done so. After the women had danced awhile, they talked to the body saying, "We will now let you go, because your body has changed. Always take the right road; don't let the devil tempt you. You will come to a river where you'll see a log; don't cross it.—The log is a snake.—Some one there will speak to you; but keep to the right-hand side. On the opposite side there will be another person. He will reach out his hand across to you. Give this person some tobacco."—With a person are buried a little sack of tobacco, four matches, and four small pieces of bread which are to last for 4 days, that is until the end of the journey to eternity. Fire is also built for

---

[22] Cf. also Hallowell (1940 b).

the dead at the grave during the first 4 nights after death, the first night being that following the day of death; persons must be buried before sundown after death.—"Then you will come to a hill," these women continued. "You will hear beautiful sounds of dancing and singing. You will see your dead relatives. They will inquire about the people who are still living. Tell them we are not ready to come." And the women repeated this until burial time.

Informants recalled hearing death announced by the shooting of a gun. They were unable, however, to tell the manner of doing so before guns were introduced. "If anyone died in our band," said a Lac Courte Orielle informant "a gun was shot three times. At Odanah (La Pointe Reservation) guns were shot five or six times. This idea originated with the Chippewa; they didn't get it from the white people." An interpreter, while still a child living on Leech Lake (Minnesota), related that one morning her family heard repeated gunshots.

Soon a man came into my father's trading store. His forehead and his body which was naked to the waistline had been blackened. Each arm was pierced with a stick, about the size of an all-day sucker. Rope had been passed between the protruding ends of the sticks and the arms, tied together in a knot, and allowed to hang down. I was much frightened and ran into my mother's room, but she assured me that the man was only mourning; that his little boy had died during the night.

Body mutilation as an expression of sorrow at death is not traditional among the Chippewa. Most informants on all reservations seemed surprised when asked this question. However, several Red Lake women had legs well scarred with slashes made while mourning. Chippewa were taught not to weep at death, not even at the death of nearest relatives. "Old Indians advised women not to weep even at the loss of a child, for this action might be visited on the next child." "Indians were told not to weep in presence of others when death occurred in the family. Their weeping was to be done while sitting near a tree or a rock: its manito would soothe them and console them."

In order to ward off the spirit of a person just departed, not only relatives but other persons also blackened their faces with charcoal or soot, but without design. "When anyone died my mother put charcoal marks on my face so that the spirit of the dead person would not come near me." A L'Anse interpreter told the following:

One time I was called to a young woman dying of blood poisoning. The woman said, "I am going soon. I won't stay long. I am sorry I can't take my baby." Toward midnight I wanted to go home. I was very tired and other women were there. But I was afraid to go, for when I told her I was going and that I would return in the morning, she said, "When you go, I am going with you." At about three o'clock in the morning she died. I went to tell an old woman who was in the kitchen and she at once went to the teakettle, rubbed her hand across the bottom of the teakettle, and blackened the forehead of the dying woman's child and of two other small children who belonged to two of

the women present. One of the women noted that the old Indians believed that
when an Indian dies two others will soon follow him; now it wouldn't be any
of these three children, for they had their faces blackened. [Hilger, 1936 a, pp.
23–24.]

INTERMENT

The remains of a departed one were kept in the home until burial,
which took place before sunset on the day of death. Immediately
preceding the removal of the body relatives spoke to it. This custom
maintains today. "My deceased daughter's pagan husband leaned
over my deceased daughter just before we closed the coffin and talked
so feelingly to her, and promised her that he would have their daughter raised a Catholic."

In old days bodies were flexed "with knees pulled up toward chest."
It seemed befitting that persons should leave this earth in the position
in which they were when they came into it, "the position they were in
when in their mother's body." Arms were extended lengthwise on
either side. Food and cooking utensils were then placed near the
body and all was wrapped into birchbark and held in position by being
tied with cords of basswood fiber. The body was placed in the grave
in a sitting position, the top of the birchbark "casket" being from
5 to 10 inches below the surface of the earth. At times the bottom
of the grave was lined with a bulrush mat. Often useful implements
were also placed around the wrappings after the body had been placed
in the grave, the belief being that the spirit of all objects enclosed
in the grave would travel with the dead person on his journey to the
hereafter. Since there is great difficulty in obtaining large pieces
of birchbark today the Red Lake man buried in 1930 (p. 78) was not
wrapped in birchbark but was placed in a sitting position in a box
made of lumber. His burial faced north. With him were buried
dried meat, berries, bread, wild rice, and a frying pan. An old woman
informant in the same area had buried five of her family near her
home, all in flexed positions, "with knees near chest and arms straight
down the sides." All of her burials faced north. She had not heard
why Indians should be buried facing north. "But all do," she added.[23]

On the Lac Courte Orielle Reservation burials faced all directions,
informants there being unaware that burials anywhere among the
Chippewa faced only one direction. In one of the Mīdē'wiwin cemeteries on their reservation, all bodies faced east (pl. 7, *3*).

On the Lac du Flambeau and Lac Courte Orielle Reservations immediately after the body of a wife or husband had been lowered into
the grave, the living partner walked across a plank of wood—or if

---

[23] Hallowell's informants said of Saulteaux burials: "The head is placed to the north,
but the body is said to be 'facing the south'." It was thought that life after death was
spent somewhere in the south. (Hallowell, 1940 b, p. 34.)

none was available, a planed tree trunk—that had been placed over the grave, signifying thereby "that they were letting the dead partner go, but that they were not yet ready to go." An interpreter was told at a funeral of a man that his widow meant to show thereby "that she had gone as far as she could go with her husband. I have often seen this done by women but never by men," she added. Before the grave was closed, those attending the funeral danced around it three times giving the spirit a start on its way to the hereafter. A very old Mille Lacs informant said that "the burial ceremony was the same for children as for adults. Food was given to both. The belief was that the dead person was going on some journey or trip, and had to have clothes and food. He was buried in new or clean clothes. Two little bags made of flour sacks or muslin were laid near the body while it was laid out, and were later put into the grave. One contained tools, like a jackknife, and other things that a person carries; the other, food, like wild rice, etc. There was no ceremony in the cemetery. The wife did not walk around the grave nor across a plank laid over the grave of her husband. For four nights after the burial, no matter how cold it was, relatives had to keep fires burning at the head end of the grave. I don't know the reason for burning it at the head end. The hole in the grave cover is also always at the head end."

An induced aborted fetus was buried under the floor of the wigwam in which the woman lived (p. 11). A spontaneously aborted one or a child stillborn was buried in the same manner as a mature person. "I know of a fetus that was only 2 months old. We gave a feast, wrapped it in birchbark, and buried it a little below the surface of the earth. Then we covered it over with earth, put birchbark on top of this, and weighted it down with poles and rocks. I remember two other burials, one of a fetus 3 months old and the other 4 months old."

Jenness records the following:

Whether or not death occurred naturally made no difference in the manner of burial. Only for a still-born babe were there special rites, because its failure to live was attributed either to sorcery, or to some wrongdoing on the part of the mother, and the latter, being always suspect, had to seek forgiveness from the Great Spirit and from her kinsfolk. The corpse was, therefore, deposited in the hollow of a stump for 9 days, and each day at the hour of birth the mother walked nine times around its resting place. At the end of 9 days the grave was opened. If the corpse had disappeared, as sometimes happened, the Indians believed that it had perished completely, body, soul, and shadow; but if it had not disappeared they interred it without ceremony in the woods. [Jenness, 1935, p. 105.]

There were no wills, but a woman might indicate before death persons to whom she wished her personal belongings to be given. If she had not expressed her wish, all her belongings were placed in a container and at the end of a year distributed either to her children, near women relatives, or particular friends. Occasionally, today, immediately after the funeral, personal belongings of the deceased are burnt, but always in an open fire outdoors. Traditionally, the family of the deceased gave a feast soon after burial. This custom still survives in some families. An interpreter's aunt had given "a big feast after every death in her family, a feast of doughnuts, cake and everything good to eat."

Three old women who had been present at burials between Redby and Red Lake (villages on Red Lake Reservation) and who were also present when the remains were removed (removals were made to permit the building of a highway), identified the graves as those of a chief, of two other men, of a little girl, of an old and of a young woman. All skeletons were found wrapped and tied in birchbark in sitting positions with knees drawn to chest and hands extending straight downward on sides. All bodies faced Red Lake (north). The graves were 4 feet in length and were covered with 1½ feet of earth; over each rested a small wooden house. Among the remains were found pails, parts of forks, knives and spoons, two pipes, a tomahawk, beads, a mirror, and a large silver medal. One of the old women, the wife of the exhumed chief, remarked that a big dance had been held when he was buried and that with his remains would be found a medal given to his father by a United States President, his father having been one of the first Chippewa who in a body went to see the President. The medal was found as she predicted (Hilger, 1935 c, pp. 321–323).

GRAVES

The old custom of covering graves with small mounds of dirt overlaid with poles, brushes, birchbark, or rush mats, survived on several reservations covered in this study. Substitutes for coverings on other graves were pieces of cotton cloth, oilcloth, or tar paper weighted down on corners and edges with small stones. "I can't bear to see my graves uncovered; they seem so naked and cold." (Cf. pl. 9, 2, and 4.)

On every reservation except L'Anse graves were also covered with small wooden houses. Some consisted of four sides and a gabled roof, or of four sides and a flat roof (pls. 7, 8, 9); others of only a gabled roof. A gable-roofed cover located 50 feet from a home on Vermilion Lake (1939) was 50 inches long and 24 inches high. The roof was covered with tin; the front and back, painted white. A small box, 10 by 4½ inches and 6½ inches high, was attached to the end facing the lake and served as a deposit box for food for the dead. The front of the box served as a door which could be closed by means of a latch made by fastening a bent nail over a tack. The house was enclosed, on all but the lake side, with a fence made of 3-foot posts crossed by poles. A 9-foot pole was planted to the front and right of the grave, facing it. "A small rag is sometimes attached to the top of it so that people may know that it is a new grave." The grave was that of an 8-month-old baby buried in 1934. On the Lac Courte Orielle Reservation clothes of one recently buried were often hung on the top of a pole near the grave. "The dress you saw hanging from the top of the 20-foot pole near a grave on the Couderay River belonged to my 12-year-old deceased sister," said an informant.

Each grave house in a Mīdě'wiwin cemetery on the Lac Courte Orielle Reservation had a 3 x 5-inch opening at the foot end or east end of the grave (pl. 7, 3). On a ledge nailed directly below the opening on many of these houses rested empty dishes, small vases, or sandwich-spread jars. Dilapidation of two houses permitted birch-bark coverings weighted down with stones to be seen.

A grave marker (ōdēmīwå'tik) made of a small piece of wood with representation of the dō'dåm of the buried person either drawn or carved upon it was seen at either the foot or the head end of several graves. The dō'dåm emblem was often inverted. One such marker of cedar wood on the Lac Courte Orielle Reservation had an outline of a bear carved into it, with head toward ground and tail toward sky. The portion showing above the ground was 3 x 8 inches. All graves in a cemetery on Mille Lacs Reservation were marked, markers ranging in size from 2 x 6 to 4 x 12 inches (pl. 9, 4). Two of these markers, one engraved with an eagle in flight and another with a bird at rest, were not inverted; the following were inverted (head toward earth and tail toward sky): bullhead, beaver, weasel, bear, fox, and elk. One group of graves in this cemetery contained the remains of a man, his wife, and their two sons, all of whom had been killed in automobile accidents in 1939 and 1940. At the head end of the graves of the father and the two boys, a bullhead dō'dåm marker had been placed; at the mother's, a beaver. "My father makes dō'dåm markers without being asked and does not charge for them. He merely makes them and puts them at the graves. There are others around here who make them also."

OFFERINGS FOR THE DEAD (CĪBĒNĀKĪ'WIN)

For several days after a burial relatives offered food at the grave and kept a fire burning there, the belief being that the spirit of the fire was being used by the deceased in the preparation of the food while the soul was on its journey. In some communities on the Red Lake Reservation the fire was kept burning for 3 successive days and nights: "When a man dies his wife keeps a fire burning near his grave for 3 days and 3 nights; it takes that long to reach the hereafter.   When a woman dies her husband does the same for her.   When a child dies, both father and mother keep the fire burning."   In other communities on the same reservation the fire was kept lighted only during the first three successive nights after burial and not during daytime: "I often saw relatives build a fire near their new grave the first three nights after burial.   They believed that the food that had been buried with the dead person was being cooked by him on his way to the resting place; it took three nights to go there."   On the Lac Courte Orielle Reservation the fire was kept burning four successive nights, "for it takes four days and four nights to go to the other world."   Charcoal remains, 1½ feet in diameter, were seen near a recent grave on the Mille Lacs Reservation.

Offerings for the dead consist today as formerly of maple sugar, wild rice, wearing apparel, or anything that is treasured.   These are not only placed on graves immediately after burial but at any time of the year, and for many years after death.   "It's the best food, or the best of anything they have that they put on the graves of their dead."   Food thus offered is never eaten by persons depositing it.   It may be eaten by persons who find it or by persons who are invited to do so. "When we were children we used to run around to different graves in search of maple-sugar cakes."[24]   On the Lac du Flambeau Reservation, in midsummer of 1935, an old woman, her daughter, and two small children, entered a cemetery, plucked weeds off the grave of the old woman's son, a war veteran, and also from the path surrounding it, sat down near the grave, unpacked food, placed some on the grave, and ate the remainder.   At the end of the repast they shot off several fire-crackers, and then left in their automobile.   After a half hour they returned, dropped three boys, about 10 years of age, waited in their car until they were certain that the boys had gathered the food left on the grave, and then drove off.   The boys returned leisurely, two eating an orange each and the third an individual pie; cracker-jack boxes filled their pockets.   "Those people picked us up near the store and brought us over here to get the food," they said.   "We are cousins of those kids in the car, that's why they picked us up; but they could have picked up anybody."

BURIALS

Cemeteries with many burials were found near permanent village sites and also near Mīdē′wiwin wigwams.   Burials of smaller groups, five to eight graves, were often seen near homes in various parts of the reservations (pls. 8, *2*; 7, *1*).

---

[24] According to Hallowell (1940 b, pp. 36–37) the Saulteaux made offerings to the dead and later collected them in order to maintain a certain relationship with deceased relatives and to enable the dead to continue the tradition of hospitality and of sharing with others something they had been accustomed to do in life.

About 100 feet from a group of homes of related families, among them the home of the interpreter, on the Mille Lacs Reservation, were 13 graves. Burials included the maternal great-grandparents, brothers and sisters, and children of the interpreter. Flat-topped boxes made of lumber rested on 11 of the graves; 2 were encircled with stones about the size of a man's fist. All boxes faced south of Mille Lacs Lake. A 2 x 4-inch hole had been cut in the south end of each box. Several boxes were so dilapidated that birchbark coverings could be seen resting upon the burials.

No scaffold or tree burials (ōgàdō′ cībā′mik), traditional modes of disposal of bodies, were seen on any reservation, nor were any recent burials of this type known to either informants or interpreters. Informants remembered well, however, when bodies were thus disposed of. In the early days remains so deposited were wrapped in birchbark; in more recent days they rested in home-made coffins. A scaffold consisted of a rectangular framework of saplings resting on four upright poles that had been securely planted in the ground. A Red Lake interpreter remembered well as a child playing near places "where bodies in coffins of boards lay up high on stilts or in trees. The bodies were never removed from these places and the smell was terrible, terrible!" Parents of informants on the same reservation "used to speak of painting dead persons as though they were preparing to go to a dance, and then wrapping them, first in a blanket and then in birchbark, and putting them up in trees, half lying and half sitting down. They hung an entire cooking outfit and something to eat on the tree for the first 3 nights. It was their belief that a person had to make three stops on his way to the other side, to the place the Whites call "the Indians' happy hunting ground." "I saw rough boxes with dead bodies on four poles and kettles hanging on the poles, when I was a child," said a White Earth informant. An old Mille Lacs woman remembered seeing burials on scaffolds: Bodies were wrapped in birchbark or blankets and placed on four poles erected close together and about one foot from the ground. "An island in Sandy Lake was the burial ground for all the Indians in this area," she added. "My mother used to say that you could go over there and see bones on the ground in many, many places. And we know these things to be true, because people saw them."

Mounds on the Lac Courte Orielle Reservation are considered burial places of very early times. Old Indians had repeatedly heard their elders say that the Odāwà′, sometimes called the Dāwāsā′gōn, built them "long, long ago. We always believed that these mounds were their wigwams, that they lived in them, and died in them during starvation times. At Old Post some mounds were opened some years ago when a cellar was dug. The bones found in them were those of large

people. At Old Post, too, a white pine, a yard in diameter, is growing
on a mound; that must tell something about its age." Erosion of the
hind leg of a bear effigy mound takes place in heavy rainfalls, often
causing arrowheads to be washed out. To the northeast of this mound
is an oval-shaped pit about 12 feet deep; in the center of it is a bed of
charcoal.

MOURNING

The period of mourning lasted for a year or less (nētȧkī′win). It
was customary for all in mourning to dress carelessly and allow the
hair to hang loose and disheveled. On the Lac Courte Orielle, the
Lac du Flambeau, and the Mille Lacs Reservations mourners had been
seen carrying a doll-like bundle of cloth, or merely a bundle formed
by rolling cloth around a dish (wīwȧpī′djigȧn). At times a few hairs
of the deceased person were enclosed. Such a bundle was seen at Flambeau (Lac du Flambeau Reservation) in 1935; on the Mille Lacs Reservation in 1939. A Lac Courte Orielle informant related the
following:

> If a pagan (Mīdē′) man's wife dies, he carries on his back a dish wrapped in
> a bundle shaped like a person; but if his child dies, he carries a dish without a
> bundle (ōnȧ′kȧn) anywhere on his person. Should he be eating a meal when
> visitors arrive, he will place food on the dish and offer it to one of the visitors.
> A year after death, he'll give a feast at which he will present some article to
> each guest. This custom releases him from mourning. My aunt who is a pagan
> carried a bundle with a dish, after her husband died. I told her that in these
> days she didn't have to carry that dish, but she replied that it was their custom.
> At a feast she gave away quilts, blankets, and moccasins that had taken her the
> entire year to prepare.

An interpreter on the same Reservation gave the following account:

> My step-grandmother must have had many deaths in her family, for I never
> saw her unless she was carrying a babylike form or bundle. In the bundle was
> a dish. When anyone died she was asked if she wanted to do this. If she did
> not she was released. If she said yes, she carried the bundle with her for a
> year. When visiting, she set the bundle down, opened it, took out the dish, and
> ate from it. This was a tin dish. Besides the tin dish the bundle contained
> something that the dead person had liked, such as a pair of moccasins. A year
> after the death, everything that the dead person had owned was given away.
> This was done for deceased near relatives including grandchildren. The pagans
> still do this. [Hilger, 1936 c, p. 40.]

A 16-year-old Mille Lacs girl had seen persons carrying a small bundle during the year of mourning: "My mother did not carry one when
my father died, but she did when my little brother died. There is no
hair of the deceased in the bundle, but only a dish and a spoon. These
are wrapped in some piece of cloth and carried in the arm, not on the
back. At mealtime food is put on the plate."

Formerly for one year following a death all the members of the
deceased person's family were not permitted to participate in seasonal

occupations, such as production of maple sugar, gathering of wild rice or berries or garden vegetables, or hunting or fishing, unless someone fed them a portion of the food being gathered. After having eaten from the hands of another, the mourners gave a feast and were thereby released from the taboo. "When my little girl died, my mother gathered vegetables of every kind from the garden, cooked them in her own home, and brought them to me to eat. After this I could gather my own vegetables. She also picked berries of every kind, green ones of those that hadn't begun to ripen mixing them with ripe ones, and offered them to me to eat also. After this I picked my own berries."

If the taboo on food gathering was violated, all things produced by nature died, or "something happened to them—grasshoppers or worms, or disease took them." An aged Lac Courte Orielle informant was certain that the flagrant violations of this taboo and of the one which forbade menstruating women to participate in the same food-producing activities (pp. 52–53) was the reason, and the only reason, for the lessening within recent years of all growth productive of Indian foods, such as maple trees, berries of all sorts, wild rice, gardens, fish, and other animals. She added:

Whenever a man lost his wife or a woman her husband, in the old day, the person left behind could not gather nor eat anything like venison, fish, sirup, berries of any kind, nor wild rice, until a feast was given at which they were fed. This gave them the privilege of again gathering and eating these things. If they had ignored this custom and fed themselves, they could reasonably have expected that the berries would be eaten by the birds, that the rice would have been shaken off by a storm, and that everything would have gone to nothing.

An interpreter at L'Anse had had the following experience:

One time a woman who was still in mourning period came to visit me. We were in the orchard and she admired the apples. I said she might have the apples. She wanted me to pick them, but I insisted that she would have to do that. After much talking she came the next day and picked the apples. She told me that the tree would die; and it died the next year. The old belief is that anything touched by a mourning person dies. [Hilger, 1936 a, p. 22.]

Pronouncing the name of one's deceased parents and their brothers and sisters, one's own brothers and sisters, and one's children was taboo for all times. "My mother never pronounced my deceased sister's name, but always spoke of her as, 'The one that is no more,' or 'The one that died.'" One constantly heard informants and interpreters speak of their "deceased" relatives.

HEALTH MEASURES

Curative powers and procedures were of two types: those closely bound up with shamanistic powers (mīdē'win) and those primarily secular in nature in which curative measures had intrinsic value. Knowledge of the first type, and some phases of the second, had their origin in prepuberty dreams (pp. 39–49). Those possessing such knowledge and exercising it either had obtained it themselves during their own fasts and dreams or had purchased it from someone who had been so favored. Shamanistic procedures, however, were known to only a few persons. Knowledge of intrinsic value of herbs, bark, roots, tattooing (āgȧ'sōwin), and bloodletting (pā'pāīcŏȧng), on the contrary, was held by many: it was specialized knowledge, to some extent, for persons had knowledge only of certain herbs that cured certain diseases. Some were adept in bloodletting, others in tattooing. Preventive measures were known to all.

SHAMANISTIC POWERS

Shamanistic powers were applied not only when the occasion for the disease was ascribed to evil powers but also when it was considered due to natural causes (pp. 88–90). If the cause was thought to be a natural one, the remedies found in nature were applied; if no cure resulted, a medicine man was summoned. In more recent times, if the patient shows no improvement after both natural and shamanistic treatments have been applied an American licensed physician may be called upon. If foul play is suspected a "tipi shaker" may be hired to discover not only the cause but the type of cure and the possibilities of a recovery (pp. 75–78).

Preparatory to exerting his supernatural powers, a shaman took a sweat bath (mȧdōdō'sōn) in a low, circular, dome-shaped wigwam (mȧdōdō'swȧn). When exercising his power he usually beat a special drum (cīgī'gwān), sang special songs, breathed upon or blew at the affected part of the person and sucked it through several hollow bone tubes made from leg bones of fowl (ōdōkā'nīgān) (leg bones of geese being preferred because of their length). He finally swallowed the bones, and then ejected them (cf. also Densmore, 1910, pp. 119–125).

A drum used for shamanistic cures on the Red Lake Reservation had been made by stretching wet untanned deer hide over both sides of a band of wood 7 inches in diameter and 2 inches in depth. The two pieces of hide were sewed together around the band with sinew and after drying formed taut drumheads. In the interior were two cross sections about one-half inch in thickness of a long bone of a large animal. "Any bone that was about 2 inches in diameter and that had contained marrow could be used." The drum could either be beaten with two small drumsticks or used as a rattle.

A Red Lake informant had seen a medicine man blow on the affected area of a man's body through two hollow leg bones of a fowl.

He blew furiously at it; you can't imagine how hard he blew! Then he swallowed the two bones—swallowed them right down into his body, he didn't keep them in his mouth—took the drum and rattling it repeatedly struck his breast and his back between the shoulders with it, coughed up one of the bones and ejected it into a little dish, and soon he spat out the other. This is the truth. And that fellow treats all diseases that way.

Some 20 years ago I and my mother were caught in a snowstorm, [remarked a Red Lake interpreter]. So we stopped at an Indian home on the road and asked to stay over night. The old man, the owner of the home, was sick in his floor bed but he welcomed us and said he was sorry he couldn't feed our horses. I and my mother attended to our horses, ate our supper, and laid down to sleep. During the night we heard sleigh bells; soon an Indian walked into the house. It was an old lady. She had come a long way. She told the old man that her son hadn't slept for 3 days and 3 nights; that he had been struck by a tree he was felling, and that splinters had entered his ear. The American doctor who lived right near them had been unable to remove them, and would the old man please do something for the boy. The son was brought in. The old man addressed the splinters in a speech ordering them to leave the young man's ear as Jonah had left the belly of the whale. While he beat the drum, he ordered his old woman to bring him a bundle. He carefully unwrapped this and from it took several hollow bones through which he blew into the young man's ear several times. He then asked for a dish, and presented the mother with the splinters. After this the boy fell sound asleep.

An old L'Anse man and his wife related the following:

One day while we were fishing, we stopped at a relative's for a meal. My old woman had suffered from a toothache for some time. The relative who was a medicine man asked her to lie on a bulrush mat on the floor, with the sore side of her face toward the ceiling. (I was sitting there watching him.) He then covered her face with a clean cloth, sat down near her, and began to beat his drum and to sing. Then he swallowed three bones. Soon I heard a noise like a crane, and I looked out across the lake to see the bird. After a little while I heard the same sound, and I was puzzled again; but an old woman who was in the room pointed at the medicine man to let me know that it was he who was making the noise. And then I heard a noise for the third time and here he was, coughing up the other bone. He had asked for a clean saucer containing some water and in it he now had three small worms. [His wife added, "Yes, that's true, and each worm was black at both ends, and about so big"—indicating their size by pressing the tip of her small finger between her two thumbnails.]

The following was related on the Lac Courte Orielle Reservation:

Suppose there is something wrong in the chest or some part of the body. You call in the medicine man. He has bones of a bird, for example, a goose, the largest ones of which are probably 2 inches long. He will have two or three of these bones, cleaned and smoothed. When he is ready to perform on the patient, he puts the bones into a dish of clean water. One by one, he puts them into his mouth and swallows them. He then puts his mouth on the chest, or on the bare skin of the sick part, and one by one he will cough up the bones. He sucks the sick part through the bones, and sometimes worms or whatever causes the sickness, appear. [Hilger, 1936 c, pp. 45–46.]

The same informant had witnessed the "killing" of the cause of a disease:

One time at Long Lake many Indians were gathering rice. They were camping across the bay. They had a drum. We used to go over at night to watch them, and to dance. Old Omazig was their speaker. He was a brave. He made a speech. A girl was sick and was getting worse. This old speaker said, "We are going to kill the cause of the disease which troubles her." He gave no explanation of how he was going to do this. He simply said, "In the morning you will know." Early next morning at sunrise—it was foggy—we heard a big noise across the bay; then a gun shot. We wondered if there was some truth in what the old man had said. Someone said that the people had fashioned bulrushes into the shape of a person. Then they attributed the sickness, as it were, to the statue. The noise we heard was made by the women, who, with hatchets, were attacking the statue. The old speaker had shot at it with the gun but missed it, and everybody laughed about it. The women chopped the statue into pieces. The old fellow predicted the girl would get better, and she did. I was twenty-five years old at that time. Yes, the old fellow missed that statue, and with a shotgun at that! The shot scattered a considerable distance, and yet he missed the figure! The man may have had poor eyesight, or perhaps the fog obscured the target. [Hilger, 1936 c, p. 40.]

HERBS, ROOTS, BARK [25]

The administering of plant life, namely of herbs, roots, and bark, was more widely known and practiced than were tattooing and bloodletting. In order that herbs, roots, and bark be efficacious, the collector offered a small piece of plug tobacco (pákī'djīwin). It was placed in the ground "very near the plant, if an herb was gathered; right near the trunk of a tree, if bark was gathered; and in the hole from which the root was extracted, if a root was gathered." Some Chippewa not only offered tobacco while collecting herbs and roots, but also smoked their pipes; some addressed prayers to the spirits involved in plants they were gathering. "Before old people set out to gather plants they cut plug tobacco into small pieces. They place these as offerings in the ground wherever they dig up a root or gather an herb. Their belief is that the better they pay, the more efficacious the medicine will be. You can't have anything for nothing! In early days, when the old fellows brewed medicines, they sang songs too." A L'Anse man remarked that one day he and an old fellow were coming from Copper Harbor:

On the way we saw some valuable roots. "Let's dig these up," I said, "but let's offer tobacco first." My friend laughed, and wouldn't offer any. Well, I began to dig; I offered tobacco every place I took a root. He, too, dug and found a few at first; but in the second place in which he dug, a frog jumped up; and the next place a lizard. That was enough; he stopped gathering them. But he was served right!

"Indians who know the medicinal value of plant life consider this knowledge personal and will not share it with anyone without good pay," remarked a Lac Courte Orielle interpreter. "They may give decoctions brewed from herbs for little pay, but will not give knowledge of how and where to collect the plants unless they are well

[25] Cf. also pages 10, 15, and 31 of the present study; Densmore (1928, pp. 299–305, 322–368); Smith (1932, pp. 348–392); and Reagan (1921 b, and 1928).

paid." Some knowledge regarding the medicinal value of plant life cannot be bought at any price, and "dies with the one possessing it." (Cf. Preface.) Usually, however, parents or grandparents are willing to transmit knowledge they possess to their children or grandchildren. Many informants remarked that such knowledge had come to them from parents or grandparents. A Red Lake woman bought the prescription for sore eyes, the name of a root, by paying the owner "a blanket, a sap kettle (kettle used in making maple sugar), a pair of fancy pillow cases, and yards of calico." A Lac Courte Orielle informant had paid tobacco, dry goods, quilts, buckskin, mats, and kettles for information regarding medicinal decoctions. "I wouldn't think of asking for such information for nothing," she added.

Medicinal knowledge, when purchased, included the ingredients to be used, the direction for making the decoction, and the manner of administering them; the method of inhaling herbal fumes or of masticating roots or bark; and the songs used in preparation and application, if such there were. If only the decoction was purchased, the price, as noted before, was less; the "recipient probably payed a little tobacco first, and then a piece of cloth."

A La Pointe interpreter contributed the following prescription applicable in cases of tuberculosis, or of any lung trouble:

Cut into pieces and boil in a gallon of water: (a) about 12 inches of the trunk of saplings of each, pine, spruce, and ironwood, that have grown to the size of your wrist; both bark and pulp are used; (b) two pieces of cherry-tree roots (bāwā'imī màmàgà'wàc), about the length of your hand; (c) two hazelnut roots (bàgànī'mic); and (d) 1 tablespoonful of bambilian buds (mānāsō'dī), Keep the decoction in a crock jar and drink a cupful at a time as often as thirst requires, and also before going to bed. When all has been used, reboil the ingredients, but a longer time than before. Reboiling can be done a third time, but after that discard the material. Keep the tea in a cool place. I shall send you any ingredients that you may need and cannot find, for we have all these trees and roots right here on our reservation. This really benefits a person when taken in time; I mean when taken in the first stages of lung trouble.

A Lac Courte Orielle informant after being presented with both tobacco and calico for a dress, took the writer and an interpreter through fields and woods, gathering the material for a prescription used in treating "internal abdominal troubles" (pl. 30, 3). She slashed a piece about 3 inches in length from the trunk of an ironwood tree. "Only the core of this, the yellow part is used," she said, "and this can be gathered at any time of the year. When used alone it is good for pleurisy; it also serves as a physic." Then two chips of the basswood tree, about the size of the palm of her hand, were got from near the root of the tree, only the inner bark being used. Next her hatchet severed two chips off the butternut tree, also the size of the palm of her hand, but both outer and inner bark were collected. She then added a chip of the slippery elm, and remarked, "And now we'll have to find an old stump." In our search for it she ran across the false solomon seal and the "cat's eye," and dug up roots of both of these. From a wild currant bush close by she cut a twig, and then dug up a root of the maidenhair. We finally found a stump and loosened from it the vine she knew would be growing on it. She took the entire vine—root, vine, leaves, and flowers. "When used alone this will bring about menstruation, if it fails to occur at the proper time," she remarked, "my daughter-in-law used it successfully." She searched in vain for the following plants which were essential to the prescription: jábō'cīgăn, wīsōgī', djĭbik', ōkō'dok, ănicĭnă'pīkō djibik', nábánē'ánīkwēyák, mīcīgī' nīmīne'kwāwic, and wábic kă'ki wī'cgăgōk. Had we intended to gather ingredients of the above prescription for curative purposes, we should have had to offer tobacco at each collection. "But," said the informant, "since I did it only to show you which plants to use and how to find them, tobacco was not necessary." A few roots, however, had been gathered by the informant to take home, since her supply of them was nearly exhausted. In these instances she dug little holes with her hands, placed a small piece of plug tobacco in each, covered it with dirt, and spoke to the plant saying: "I'll take just a little for my use, and here is some tobacco for you!" The above ingredients were to be boiled in a gallon of water and could be reboiled twice, each time, however, prolonging the period of boiling.

Information regarding several commonly known remedies were volunteered by informants: Skin eruptions are sponged with a decoction made by boiling strawberry roots and alum. Dried resin, ground to powder, is dusted on skin sores. Chewing the root of sweet flag (wībănk'), gathered late in fall after growth has stopped, cures sore throats. Decoctions of roots of wild celery is thought to cure tuberculosis; the leaves of "zens" stop sweating that occurs with colds; flowers of the boneset, if picked "just before the frost sets in," subdues a fever; sturgeon potatoes (nămă'pin), gathered in the fall when they are filled with strength, cure heart trouble; mixing a root found in swamps (mćkwō' kāwăc) and catnip (nămēwăc') revives fainting persons or quickens weak heart beats.

One informant had medicinal knowledge of herbs "that are useful in case of pleurisy, and can also be used as a cathartic." Another knew that "pine lumps" (pine knots) had medicinal value. Another, born with weak eyes, had sight partially restored as a child by an Indian doctor who used eye drops made "from something that looked like green peas." An interpreter's mother had bought knowledge of medicine for sore eyes which consisted of the inner bark of the root of the wild rose and of an ingredient which she preferred not to tell. Her friend made medicine by boiling the inner bark of the Juneberry tree and a stick of some plant (this was secret knowledge) sliced into four pieces. After boiling, the sticks must be burnt. "One-half a cup of chopped potatoes boiled with pine lumps is good for earache." Earaches are also cured by blowing tobacco smoke directly from the smoker's mouth into the ear. Inhalations were made by placing herbs on some heated object and catching the fumes under a blanket that covered both the patient's head and the heated object.

Several very old informants spoke of the days of smallpox epidemics. The disease being unknown to the Indians, they had no cure for it; remedies that it was hoped might help were applied without success.

We had no cure for white men's sickness like smallpox. I remember an event of the smallpox time [said a Red Lake informant]. Some Canadian Indians who happened to come down our way found all the Indians in one place dead—all but two children. One of these children was Ghost Head. This woman grew up and lived in Red Lake a long time; I knew her well. The Canadians found Ghost Head suckling her mother who had been dead of smallpox 8 to 4 days. Big flies were on her body, but still the child nursed on the woman. They put the children into their canoe, took them home, and cared for them.

TATTOOING (ĀJĀ′SŌWIN)

Tattooing was used as a health restorative in cases of muscular pains, "such as rheumatism, dislocated joints, and backaches." Few persons, however, had knowledge of the procedure and ingredients to be used. Both adults and children were treated. A Red Lake informant had found relief from pains in her knee and elbows after several tattooings. She had tried various medicinal remedies previously without success; she had "even tried the U. S. agency doctor." Marks were in evidence on her legs and wrists. Another informant had been cured of rheumatic knees by being tattooed in May 1932. Both Red Lake and Lac du Flambeau informants had been cured of goiter by being tattooed. "I never heard of any herb used in curing goiters; in fact, I never saw goiters when I was young." A number of informants were convinced that their people had "caught" goiters from the Whites, along with tuberculosis and smallpox.

No pattern was used in tattooing. Tattoo marks were of various sizes: the variety in both size and color reminded one of blueberries.

Tattooing was done on the affected part. The woman cured of goiter had many marks on chest and neck; the one cured of rheumatic knees was spattered with marks in the knee area and just above it. Several women had marks on the side of the face; others said their backs were covered with them.

The implement (djàbōn′īgan) used in tattooing consisted of a stick, usually a twig of a tree or bush, into one end of which three or four needles had been inserted—occasionally the needles were tied around the stick. Tattooers were reluctant to give information on ingredients used. Informants as well as interpreters who had been tattooed thought them to be gunpowder mixed with some pulverized roots. One informant was certain that sarsaparilla roots were used, "the root that's really not a root, but runs along in long strips."

A tattooer's outfit—that of a 60-year-old Red Lake informant—contained a needle applicator and some pulverized substance. Both were securely wrapped in a piece of birchbark and stored in a closed sandwich-spread jar. The applicator had been made by slicing one end of a hazelnut twig and inserting into this three needles in a row. "There should be four needles," remarked the owner, "but I'm using one for buckskin sewing." The needles were held in position by being tightly tied with some white woolen yarn. The medicine consisted of a bit of moldy substance the ingredients of which the interpreter thought it best not to inquire about. The tattooer remarked: "My mother taught me how to tattoo and she learnt it from an old, old woman years ago. Men seldom have this knowledge."

Tattooers had used two procedures. Some dipped the needles into the medicinal substance and then pricked the skin; others applied the medicinal substance with the end of a small stick, and after that pricked the area with needles. A Red Lake tattooer used the latter method: "He dipped a little stick into some black medicine contained in a small birchbark dish, and dotted my arm. After that he took a stick that had a row of three or four needles in one end and pressed the medicine into my arm. It cured the crawling feeling I had had in my arm for a long time." An informant on the same reservation had been tattooed by the first method in 1926: "I had dislocated my knee and was so badly off that my old man had to carry me from place to place. The woman who tattooed me dipped a bunch of sewing needles that had been tied around a stick (about ¼ inch in diameter) into some black medicine and kept pricking my leg. It was very painful; but it cured my leg." Marks were scattered irregularly from ankle to hip, except for two rows, about one-half inch apart, which extended from ankle to upper leg.

On the Lac Courte Orielle Reservation the procedure to be used was described as follows:

If you want to tattoo, in order to cure a sickness, take a small piece of wood, split one end of it and tie a few needles into this end. Mark off the space that is to be tattooed, an area about 1 inch square, dip needles into medicine, and with them prick the marked area. I broke my hip some years ago and used to have great pain driving a lumber wagon. I drove this wagon practically every day, hauling lumber to build a new house. I had a spot tattooed on my hip. I found great relief but after having it done so many times, I no longer found that it helped any. After it was pricked, I was supposed to rest. Once I felt that the whole thing was taking too much of my time, so I took the needles and instead of pricking my hip continuously for a long time, I drove the needles down deeper. But this made my hip very sore. After each pricking, the pricked part oozed blood. It was covered with the down of any bird. The down sticks to the wound until it is healed.

In '81 I saw an old woman on the Reservation who had tattooing in the form of a cross on her forehead. The parts of the cross were all equal. They were made up of four ½-inch squares. The color was a deep blue. The design, so far as I know, didn't mean anything. This woman had merely been treated and cured of some trouble. [Hilger, 1936 c, p. 44.]

BLOODLETTING (PĀ′PĀĪCŌĂNG)

Bloodletting was done to remove "bad blood." It could not cure "aches inside the body; herbs and roots and teas were good for that." Nor could it cure cases in which pus infections were involved; "the medicine man had cures for these" (cf. pp. 88–89). Bloodletting was done at the temples and at the inner arm at the elbow. When applied at the temples it relieved headaches or insanity, "the kind of insanity which does not make people violent and which is caused by evil powers". When applied at the elbow, it relieved strained backs or arms.

Incisions were made with sharp-edged flint stones (bī′wānăk), with pieces of broken porcelain sharpened to an edge, or with points of knives. If the blade of a knife was used it was completely wound about with string, leaving only as much of the point exposed as was needed for the depth of the cut. The gash was made by holding the point over a vein with one hand and tapping the handle end of the knife with the other.

After incisions were made in the temples—at times as many as three were made in each temple—the larger end of a horn "of any critter" (wīkwȧ′cīgăns) was pressed firmly against the temple so as to cover the incisions, and the blood sucked through the small end, this end having been filed or cut off so as to permit the passage of air. If the blood was let at the elbow, no sucking was necessary since a vein was tapped and blood flowed freely. When the required amount of blood had been let—probably a teaspoonful from each temple or a half cupful from the elbow—the blood flow was clogged by the application of chewed tobacco, chewed bark ("he won't tell what bark it is because it is secret knowledge"), a green poultice, or a decoction of gray medicine.

Both temple and elbow bloodletting were being done during the time of ethnological research covered in this work. Several persons so treated were seen with bandages about their heads, or adhesive tape over temples. A L'Anse informant found relief from a prolonged "terrific" headache by being bled by an Odanah woman (La Pointe Reservation) blood-letter. "This woman," she said, "rubbed her fingers over my temples, made three incisions—none of which I felt—

with a knifelike thing made from a chip of a dinner plate and sucked about half a hornful of blood. Then she pasted a green poultice over the incisions. I haven't had a headache since; and that was 11 years ago."

SWEATING

Sweat baths (mȧdōdō'sōn) were resorted to as both curative and preventive measures. Since sweating released impurities, it was often resorted to in cases of pain or stiffness in arms or legs. Sweat lodges, low, circular, dome-shaped wigwams (mȧdōdō'swȧn), were seen on all reservations. One on the Red Lake Reservation, 4 feet high and 4 feet in diameter, had been made by planting eight hazelnut stalks in the ground, about 1½ feet apart. The upper opposite ends were overlapped and tied together with basswood fiber. The entrance was indicated by two twigs, each 18 inches long, that had been planted parallel with two of the hazelnut stalks. To one side in the interior was a pile of eight stones, each approximating the size of a man's fist. A sprinkler of balsam twigs with handle made by tying two places near one end with basswood fiber lay nearby. Indentations in the sand indicated recent sprinkling. Encircling the lodge, close to the framework, was a ring of balsam twigs. A path of an unidentified weed led from the door of the lodge to a place about 2 yards away where charred remains of a fire and a pail half filled with water stood. A similar wigwam on the same reservation was made of branches of the elder tree. Its owner sweated in it for an hour and a half, "never longer," whenever afflicted with rheumatic pain. After covering the framework with blankets, he heated stones, carried them and a pail of water into the wigwam, undressed inside of it. (His clothes were pushed to the outside so as to keep them dry.) He then sprinkled cold water on the pile of heated stones producing as much steam as he desired. Four men on the White Earth Reservation were seen crawling out of a sweat lodge. "All those men worked hard on road building this week, and their muscles ached," said the wife of one.

PREVENTIVE MEASURES

Preventive measures began with a baby's first bath in herb and root decoction: this was to give it a strong constitution (p. 18). As the child grew older, it was allowed to eat all the charcoal it wanted, strips of burnt cedar preferably, in order that its bones might thereby be strengthened and it be given some resistance to sickness. There were no measures taken to establish resistance or immunity to sickness in older children or in mature persons. Some informants thought that eating bear grease in the early days had given their people some resistance by making them physically strong. "We eat it sometimes now

and everybody feels better." It was thought that epidemics "carried
by Whites," such as measles and scarlet fever, could be checked by
making a smudge of cedar in the room in which the disease was found;
or if no one in the family was afflicted, the sickness could be warded
off by filling the air of the entire house with the fumes of a similar
smudge. It was also believed that cedar boughs on doors kept
epidemics from entering.

People were at times warned of impending sickness by the song
of the robin, for "a robin has two ways of singing: if he sings one
way sickness will occur; if he sings the other way, it won't." When
robins announced it, or rumors had it, that an epidemic was spreading, the Indians hunted for skunks to secure the musk. They dropped
this into toilets, woodsheds, and around the outside of the home. Some
people saved musk in bottles for emergencies. "It keeps away smallpox and other sickness, the kinds Whites get mostly. It's just like
your fumigation."

It is possible, too, that the Chippewa were immune to certain ill-
nesses. On Vermilion Lake Reservation no Indian is known to have
been poisoned by ivy although the reservation has a profuse growth
of it. "The only one that is ever poisoned is a Finnish woman who
lives here."

MORAL TRAINING

KINDNESS

Children were taught proper etiquette in an informal way whenever an occasion presented itself. "It was really not manners that
were taught; it was more like kindness." "We were told not to look at
any person a long time; nor to make fun of anyone, but to respect all
people. We were told, too, to say 'goodbye' or to look at people once
more just before they left: that was a sign that they were welcome
to come again. Children were often given tobacco and told to present
it to older persons as a sign of good will and friendship. It was customary for any one arriving in a home to offer a pinch of tobacco to
all adults. The acceptance of it signified peace and friendship among
all present".[26]

Densmore's informants had been taught "that they must not go
peeking in the wigwams after dark and that they must not laugh at
anything unusual nor show disrespect to older people. They were
also taught that they must not go to the neighbors when they were
eating and look wistfully at the food. Little children were taught
not to go between older people and the fire" (Densmore, 1929, p. 58).

---

[26] When Chippewa friends instructed the writer in the etiquette of their people, they
emphasized the importance of tobacco giving and advised that commercial tea be offered
in the event that no tobacco was at hand.

Respect for older people, evidenced in speaking to them in a civil way and in listening to them attentively, was well impressed upon children. "It was one of the main things taught us; we were told no one would respect us if we did not respect older people." "Mother would talk to us children and tell us that if we met a blind man, to lead him; if a hungry man, to feed him; or if we found an old person alone, to help him."

Assisting the aged in a material way, however, does not seem to have been part of the training of the Chippewa children. On all reservations old persons were seen to shift for themselves; their able-bodied sons felt no obligation to assist them. Daughters, more often, seemed to feel a responsibility. Old parents seemed indifferent to their neglect; none offered any complaints against their children. Gilfillan (1901, p. 96) found this condition to exist in his time. He wrote:

> But it seems to be an unwritten law among them that an old man, and especially an old woman, must shift for himself or herself somehow. They have a contempt for the aged and useless, like all heathen. The son never seems to think he is under any obligation to do anything for his aged father or mother. Nor do they make any complaint of him, for they do not seem to expect anything. And one always hears the complaint that food given by the government, or by charitable persons, does not get to the old persons for whom it was intended, but is eaten by the well and strong.

Sharing what is over and above the necessities of life is a virtue of the Chippewa. Children in the early days were taught this by observation and participation: "A mother would put some food into a dish and tell her child to take it to the neighbors, and so teach the child to give and share." "A mother seldom gave anything away herself; she always gave it to one of the children to give, so the child would grow up to give and be willing to give." "Children learnt one of the main customs of the Indians, namely that of feeding each other, from their parents. If a family had much meat because of a successful hunt, everybody was invited to come and get some, and the children saw this."

STEALING

Various informants named families, members of whom they never trusted, because they knew that they had not been taught to respect the property of other people. "They belonged to the lower class and everybody knew they had no training."

In the better families, however, honesty was highly respected and was taught to children. If a very small child brought home an article that did not belong to the family, "the parent took the thing, carried it back, and explained." If the child had nearly reached the age of reason, "he was taken by the hand, marched back with the thing, and made to put it where it belonged. If he was old enough to be reasoned with, I sent him back by himself, after talking to him. I teach my grandchildren the same as I taught my children." "If a child took something from a neighbor, it was told to carry it back. If it refused to do so, the mother marched it back with the article—the child had to carry the article and hand it to the owner."

Older children who were caught stealing were whipped by a parent and made to return the stolen object. "I used to take my son and spank him, and make him take the thing back," said an old man. Another informant gave his grandson "a licking, and made him return the stolen thing."

LYING AND BOASTING

A lying child was told that it was making a wrong start in life, and that it would never be of any account if it continued to lie. Parents scolded lying children, "spanked them with little sticks on their legs," or "hit them in the mouth." Lying children were not liked; "a grudge was held against them and they were ignored to make them feel it for a long time."

A boasting child was usually not listened to. Sometimes boys boasted: "if what they boasted about was true, their elders listened; if not, they ignored them or walked away from them."

TALEBEARING

A talebearing child was not listened to: either it was pushed away or people walked away from it. Some parents punished children that bore tales by slapping the mouth or shoulders. "I wouldn't listen to a child that brought tales; I chased it away and told it, 'I don't want to hear that.' Those who listened to children spoilt them and made tattletales out of them."

QUARRELING

Often when children quarreled with neighbor children, they were not allowed to play with them again. Parents who took sides with their own children against those of neighbors' caused ill feelings to grow up between the families. Usually quarreling was ignored by the parents. "I never defend my children when they complain about other children being mean to them; I say to them, 'Oh, that's all right, so long as you weren't killed'." Densmore (1929, p. 60) writes that stern and oft-repeated advice by grandmothers to mothers was ". . . if your children go among the neighbors and make a quarrel, don't take their part. You must bring them home and make them behave themselves. Do not get into a quarrel with your neighbors because of the quarrels of the children."

When children of the same family quarreled, parents either paid no attention to them or gave them a little switching. Some parents "just wouldn't allow quarreling. If we quarreled early in the morning we were chased away from the house before breakfast and were given nothing to eat until evening; we were not allowed to come home for meals." A 4-year-old boy who had formed a habit of settling a quarrel by biting his opponent had repeatedly been told by his mother that "it was naughty and not to do it. But one day when he was biting a boy, I took a stick, opened his mouth, and told him that I would knock out all his teeth and that then he wouldn't have any when he grew up to be a man. He seemed to realize that he was doing wrong, and never bit anyone again. I had to tell it to him in this way just once. I did not touch his teeth, of course."

Quarreling children, and grown-ups too, might call each other "dog" or "ghost", or "snap eyes" at each other, or say "Gā!", an expression accompanied by a gesture of the hand.

"Dog" (ȧnīmūc′) or "You look like a dog" or "You are like a dog" are the most insulting expressions a Chippewa can use; "they are the worst thing that can be said in the Chippewa language." "When we called each other 'dog' or 'ghost' (cībȧī), we were using the worst names we had; really, they were about the only bad words there were in those old days."

"Snapping eyes" (nīmicgȧ′bin) consists of looking sharply and reproachfully from the corner of one's eyes directly into the eyes of another person and then, while turning the head disdainfully in the opposite direction, walk away from him. This gesture was done rather quickly and no words were spoken. The writer has seen, and repeatedly heard of, children and older girls who wept bitterly because someone had snapped eyes at them. "Indians are very, very sensitive to snapping eyes," said one old informant after she had demonstrated the act. Only after repeated requests did she give a demonstration and then only on condition that the writer understood very well that she "had no thoughts back of the snapping."

"Gā!" was an expression that was uttered in a loud annoyed tone and was accompanied by a gesture of the hand which was formed as though it held an egg (tips of all fingers were brought to tip of thumb), fingers and thumb were released full stretch with a quick movement while the person said "Gā!". A mother was seen using the gesture in order to disperse her annoying children: they stopped play instantly, and quietly and doggedly found their way behind the house. The grandmother seemed amazed at the mother's action and was no longer willing to give information through her as an interpreter. After 15 minutes the children were still huddled against the back wall of the house, out of sight of everybody.

INTOXICANTS, SUICIDE, CANNIBALISM, REVENGE

The Chippewa before the coming of Whites had no intoxicating liquor; its devastating ravages among the tribe today are well known.

Suicide occurs today, but none of the old informants recalled ever having heard of it in the early days. Gilfillan wrote in 1901 that there had been only one case in 25 years, "this being an elderly woman who hung herself at the gate in front of her door, after a family quarrel" (Gilfillan, 1901, p. 60).

Cannibalism was resorted to, but only very rarely. Warren (1885, p. 501) relates that a man, his wife, his two daughters, and a son-in-law had killed and eaten 15 persons, most of whom were their own children and grandchildren. He also quotes from the Minnesota Democrat of July 29, 1851, describing Indians at the point of starvation as eating their own children. Father Belcourt affirmed that the Chippewa of Canada ate the flesh of their vanquished enemies but, aside from this, looked upon cannibalism with horror (Hodge, 1907, pt. 1, p. 278). Several Red Lake informants knew that Sioux had been eaten by the Chippewa—"just a little by each warrior"—after a successful war. Two aged informants on the same reservation had heard of a woman of their band having eaten her own children, but "she had been 'grand-medicined'" (p. 73). On the White Earth Reservation cases were reported to have occurred about 1850 (Watrin, 1930, p. 44).

Revenge for the death of a relative culminating in the murder of the offender was an unwritten law of the Chippewa. "There were no laws among the Indians like among the Whites; but if a man killed another man, the second man's relatives killed the first man; and that was considered all right."

The following account was collected on the Lac Courte Orielle Reservation:

And now I'm going to tell a true event: An old fellow, before the eighties, killed two brothers of a man still living at Reserve (Lac Courte Orielle Reservation) ; after that he moved to Mille Lacs. Some years ago some Mille Lacs Indians, among them this old fellow, came to Reserve to give a dance. On the last day, when recounting experiences which showed bravery, the old man got up and made a speech in which he told of the killing of those two brothers. All the Indians from Reserve were tense, for the brother of those two men was present and they knew what would follow. The brother rose to leave the place, but they held him. In the evening the friends of the old man offered to take the old man back to Mille Lacs some other way than that of going with the crowd. But he said he didn't care: he was going with the crowd. In the morning all danced, and then the band of 50 Indians from Mille Lacs started home. They went in single file except those around the old man who tried to keep him in the center. When they came to the path between Wolf and Whitefish, "Bang!" came a gunshot. That was the end of that old fellow. He was shot at long range. That was the way that ended!

MENTAL TRAINING

COUNTING TIME

Time of day was told rather accurately by the old Chippewa by means of sundials. Sundials are used occasionally today in camping grounds and are made as in the early day: On a clear night a man will stake a stick, about a yard high, and, lying flat on the ground, move about it until it is in line with the North Star. The position of a second stick will be determined by laying a pole to the south of the first and in line with it and the North Star. (An informant on the Lac Courte Orielle Reservation did not stake a second stick but simply draw a straight line north and south through the first stick keeping the North Star as a guide.) In the morning he will draw a line through the base of the south stick and at right angles to the line joining the two sticks. When the shadow of the south stick falls on the westerly line, the first half of the day is beginning; when it falls in line with the north stick, it is midday; when on the easterly line, the last half of the day has ended. The remaining parts of the day are only approximately read.

An old Red Lake Indian staked two sticks as described above. In the morning, a third one was planted to the south and in line with the first two. A semicircle was then drawn through the third stick, convex to the southward. When the shadow of the third stick fell west and tangent to the circle, it was approximately 6 o'clock in the morning; when it fell in line with the two sticks to the north, it was noonday; when, to the east and tangent to the circle, it was approximately 6 o'clock in the evening (Hilger, 1937 f, p. 179).

Days were counted by nights; nights were not named. Neither had informants heard names assigned to days of the week other than the ones now used. Sunday is called ánā'mīē gīcīgod' (prayer day); Monday, ĭckwá'ánámĭē gīcīgod' (day after prayer day); Tuesday, nīcō'gīcīgod' (second day); Wednesday, ábátō'seg gīcīgod' (middle day); Thursday, nīō'gīcīgod' (fourth day); Friday, nánō'gīcīgod' (fifth day); Saturday, Mārī'gīcīgod' (Mary's day).

When time counts needed to be kept, either nights or moons, as they passed, were marked on a stick or on the bark or the poles of the wigwam. Moons began with new moon. New moon was called ōc'gēgágin gīsīs (moon hangs new); first quarter, pákwē'wĭ gīsīs (moon has piece bitten off); full moon, wāwĭás'si gīsīs (moon is round); and last quarter, ĭckwāyá'sĭ gīsīs (moon ceases to burn). The following moons correspond to our months. (Informants were not able to account for an additional moon in the 12 calendar months.)

January	kit'cī măn'itō gīsĭs	Big spirits moon
February	nămībī'nī gīsĭs	Suckers-begin-to-run moon
March	ōnăb'ănĭ gīsĭs	Crusted-snow-supporting-man moon
April	iskīgăm'issīgē gīsĭs	Boiling-down-maple-sap moon
	bībōkwădájăm'ik gīsĭs	Putting-away-snowshoes moon
May	wábīgon'ī gīsĭs	Flowering moon
June	ōdēn'īminnī gīsĭs	Strawberry moon
July	ābītănī'bin gīsĭs	Midsummer moon
	mīnī' gīsĭs	Blueberry moon
August	mīnī'ka gīsĭs	Plenty-of-blueberries moon
	mánōm'ini gīsĭs	Wild-rice-gathering moon
September	wátăbā'bī gīsĭs	Turning-of-leaves moon
October	bīnă'kwā gīsĭs	Leaves-falling moon
November	gáckăd'īnō gīsĭs	Lake-freezing moon
December	măn'itō gīsĭs sōns	Little spirits moon [27]

Seasons are called sīk'wăn (spring), nī'bin (summer), tákwā'gīk (fall), bī'băn (winter). These words do not lend themselves to translation.

Dates were not recorded. Events were remembered by being associated with significant happenings or with a phenomenon of nature that occurred at the time of the event. "I shall be married 50 years next rice-gathering time." "My father used to say that since the last Sioux fight he had seen a certain set of stars appear 5 different times." "When the Chippewa and the Sioux fought their last war, that was the time I was born."

The age of individuals was not recorded. Events in the lives of informants were placed in a developmental period: before I could walk; when I was so high; before I had sense; when I was already an old woman; after I was a grandmother the first time. "That happened when the blueberries were ripe and I was so high." "My mother died before I could walk." "We admitted two children, just old enough to remember, into the Mīdē'wiwin this spring." "No one blamed a child that took a neighbor's moccasins unless it was old enough to have sense." "I was laughed at for playing with dolls when I was as big as that girl (11-year-old girl), for I was already an 'old woman.'"

LINEAR MEASUREMENTS AND COUNTING NUMBERS

Measurements were based on the palm of the hand (nāgá'kīmi); the width of four fingers (nīōn'inj); the distance from tip of thumb to its first joint (ōgīcīninj'); a hand stretch, one consisting of distance from either tip of long finger to tip of thumb, or from tip of small finger to tip of thumb (ningōtwá'cīninj); distance covered by a fist with out-

---

[27] Cf. also Cope, 1919, pp. 165-166, for Chippewa names for moons as found in other sources.

stretched thumb (àbītō'sid) ; distance from tip of long finger to elbow (īkōdō'swânk) ; and on an arm stretch, either on one arm from end of fingers to face (ābitā'wīnik) or on both outstretched arms from end of fingers to end of fingers (nīgōtō'wīnik or nīcā'bīgōns).

A navel-cord container was made of two pieces of buckskin "as large as the palm of my hand." Arrowheads were measured in length and in width by a certain number of thumbs—from tip of nail to first joint. In making buckskin jackets women used "big hand stretches," stretches from tip of thumb to tip of middle finger. (In demonstrating the informant moved the tip of the middle finger to the position of the tip of the thumb, the hand thus gliding along the length of the skin in the direction of the thumb.) The length of a baby's birch-bark bathtub extended from the tip of the long finger to the elbow; in width it covered two stretches of the hand. (In demonstrating, the thumb of the informant glided to the position of the tip of the little finger.) An informant measured the length of an arrow shaft by closing both of his hands with thumbs extended around the left end of the shaft, outstretched thumbs resting on shaft and nails touching. He released the left hand and placed it snugly against and to the right of the right hand. This gesture was repeated until he had measured the stick. Birchbark dishes used in collecting maple sap varied in length; the largest ones measured from tip of long finger to elbow.

An informant measured the width of a bulrush mat with seven hand stretches (from tip of thumb to tip of long finger), by gliding tip of long finger into position of tip of thumb. The length of a mat was a double arm stretch and a half (one-half was distance from tip of hand to shoulder). When a mat was completed, it was stretched, the give of the weave lengthening it to two double-arm stretches. "I often saw my mother use this measurement," the 53-year-old informant remarked.

The pattern for moccasins is made by tracing the foot of the person for whom they are intended, adult, child, or baby, on a piece of paper on which he stands. Formerly a thin layer of birchbark and charcoal were used in the tracing. The foot may also be traced while the paper is held against it. The tongue for the moccasins of adults is of standard size, a pattern being kept on hand; the size for a child's or baby's is guessed. The length of moccasins "that are sold to stores today" are measured by placing the palm of the hand on a piece of buckskin and bringing it over the tip of the fingers to the joint of long finger and palm; the complete width—sole and top—is a single hand stretch; the tongue is standard size.

A Red Lake informant attached floats to her nets a double arm stretch apart, "both arms must be outstretched at full length in line with my ears; not by holding hands backward." "I often saw my grandmother measure something between the hands of her two out-stretched arms. This is called nīca'bīgŏns. Today, women consider this equivalent to 2 yards."

Chippewa count numerals in the following manner: One, two, three, four, five, six, seven, eight, nine, ten; ten one, ten two, ten three . . . ten nine; two tens, two tens one, two tens two . . . two tens nine; three tens, three tens one, three tens two . . . three tens nine; etc.

DIRECTIONS

Chippewa who were acquainted with the locality of their habitat and with the country surrounding it relied on the position of the sun or of the North Star to find directions; when not well acquainted with a locality, they marked the trail in order to make return possible. "When men went hunting in those early days, they didn't need to mark the way; they always found home without difficulty. However, if some families were moving and expected others to follow them at a later time, the first ones chipped bark off trunks of trees or broke branches along the way. If the direction changed en route, the tree was chipped on two sides, one chip in line with the direction from which the family came and the other in line with the direction to which they had turned. If the distance to be traveled was long, and no chances were to be taken of having the second detachment lose its way, a small piece of birchbark was fastened to a tree at turns in the trail: a +, "a star," engraved on the birchbark indicated a turn toward the rising sun; a −, one turning toward the setting sun. This was done in addition to chipping the tree.

A woman going only a short distance from home—she might be gathering berries—broke little twigs, one at a time along the way and several at a turn in the direction in which she turned. Today, when ever it is difficult to find brush, because of clearings in many localities, sticks are driven into the ground and rags tied to the upper ends.

Some informants had not heard that the Chippewa used smoke signaling; others said it was used whenever fear arose that someone had lost the trail. In such cases a fire was made on an elevated area and covered with a buckskin, thus smothering the flames and at the same time preventing any smoke from rising. When all was ready for signaling, the buckskin was lifted and all smoke allowed to ascend. Immediately afterward, grass was thrown on the fire to smother it and all was again covered with the skin. When the first signal had well dispersed, a second was sent up. This was repeated as many times as it had been agreed upon before families separated, or as many times as it was customary to signal.

INTERPRETATION OF NATURAL PHENOMENA [28]

Northern lights were ascribed to the thunderbird, to electric storms raging in the far north, to reflection of the sun on snow, ice, or water, to currents of wind in high elevations, or to spirits or ghosts dancing far to the north. "The people said last night when the northern lights played (Vermilion Reservation, August 19, 1939) that the souls of the old people who lived long ago as well as those who died recently were dancing." "The ghosts of the departed Chippewa, other Indians, and Whites have a dance." All informants were agreed that northern lights predicted rain or snow, strong winds or storms. "Two or three days after northern lights appear bad weather will invariably follow."

Most informants had not heard any explanation given for the origin of the rainbow. A very old Lac du Flambeau woman had heard old Indians say when she was a child that after a rain Mōdjīgēkwe' extended her arms over the sky, joining her fingers; the colors in the rainbow were those of the sleeves of her dress. La Pointe and L'Anse informants had not heard this explanation, and they doubted it because buckskin clothes and not rainbow-colored ones were worn formerly. A rainbow predicted fair weather when it appeared in the east; rain, when in the west.

Sundogs predicted snow. A large circle about the moon gave warning of warm weather; a small one, of a storm, "and that is true, for it never fails to storm when a small circle is seen." Thunder and lightning did not predict weather; both were caused by the thunderbird, Anīmī'kī. The movements of his wings and tail caused the thunder; the opening and closing of his eyes to see where he was going, the lightning. Weather, too, could be predicted "by the way the stars and clouds hung. An old woman here can do that, she can tell for instance whether or not we'll have a good sugar-making season."

The behavior of animals, too, predicted weather: when tree toads sang, rain or storm was in the offing; rain could be expected when birds ended their songs abruptly; whistling lizards, small ones that live in rotten wood and whistle like persons, predicted rain; when large animals "tracked around in the woods rather aimlessly, going round and round, a change of weather could be expected. The ordinary way for animals to act is to go around quietly and to act as though they knew what they are about."

Human beings, too, brought about change in weather; killing frogs brought rain; throwing rabbitskins on fire brought north winds or caused a "big storm." Swinging one's hands back and forth in the water while going places in a boat also caused storms.

---

[28] Cf. also Hilger, 1937 a, pp. 178–179.

I was often corrected by my grandfather when swinging my hand back and forth in the water while traveling by boat. I was told it would cause a storm. However, I might play in the water after the boat landed.

Throwing dogs or cats into the lake will cause a storm almost at once. The spirit of the water, it seems, doesn't like nasty things in the water so it produces a wind that will take the things to shore. Winds thus produced may blow in any direction. As soon as the cats or dogs are thrown on shore, the wind ceases. Pappin often saw this take place. One day he and one of my uncles wanted to fish off Keweenaw Point. They threw a cat into the bay and had a favorable wind for 3 days.

Not long ago, Pappin was out in a boat with two men. They intended to fish. He noticed a bag near one man and said to him, "What have you in there?" He said, "A cat that I am going to drown." Don't put it in the bay or you'll have a wind." They were conversing in the boat, when suddenly a storm arose. Pappin turned to the man and said, "What did you do with the cat?" "I threw it into the bay." "Well! there is your storm." [Hilger, 1936 a, p. 20.]

The Chippewa did not cause winds by plucking feathers off a bird's back, "but any man who wanted to do so could change the wind by shooting an arrow in the direction in which he wished it to blow. My uncle often did that."

No significance was attached to an eclipse of the moon. Several explanations, however, were given for an eclipse of the sun: Spirits were thought to be hiding the sun and hence arrows were shot toward it until the eclipse passed, the belief being that the spirits were killed; some believed that the sun was dying or dead, and shot arrows to revive it; others thought it a bad omen. "I have seen Indians shoot at an eclipse of the sun with guns in order to kill the bad luck. The Indians were much frightened by an eclipse."

Both sun and moon "were like persons. The moon at one time had been a man who, while on his way to fetch water, was taken up into the air. That is why in a full moon one can see a man with a pail."

A comet forbode evil. "While we were living at Copper Harbor," said a L'Anse informant, "my mother called us outdoors one night and said, 'Look!' The sky was red and then it became white. The stones were red from the reflection. It was night but it seemed like daylight. This thing had a long tail which was lighted. My mother said some catastrophe was going to happen, and soon the war between the North and the South broke out. My father went away and was gone for 3 years." [Hilger, 1937 f, p. 178.]

LANGUAGE [29]

Children were taught certain words of their native language by imitation. Names of objects might be taught by holding the object before the child and pronouncing the name until the child was able

[29] For pictography, see Hoffman (1888, pp. 209–229) and Reagan (1927, pp. 80–83); for pictography and sign language, see Tomkins (1926, pp. 74–90).

to repeat it correctly. Often a child was rewarded by being given the object after pronouncing its name. Most of the child's vocabulary was learned by hearing elders speak. The various bands spoke dialects of the Chippewa language, "but all could make out what other bands were saying."

The sign language was not taught to children; it was not part of the Chippewa culture. Only a few old persons were able to communicate in it. "Some of us had to know it so that we could talk to the Sioux and some other prairie tribes," said a Red Lake informant.

The Chippewa had no written language (Baraga, 1878; Jones, W., 1919). A form of pictography, consisting of symbolisms that represented numbers, directions, days, hills, lakes, sky, and earth, and of crude delineations that represented men, birds, animals, and material objects was known to a few persons in every band.[30] Those who were well versed in it could combine these delineations and symbols into ideographs that represented progressive action. Such ideographs, if used in messages, records of time, directions, or maps designed for travel, could be interpreted by many, but only members of the Mīdē′wiwin could read the ones related to their lodge (cf. also Densmore, 1929, pp. 176–183). "My father had birchbark with writing on it. It was too sacred for me to look at; young people were not allowed to look at it." "Once before they had a medicine dance, they sang initiation songs four successive nights. I saw my grandfather go to his bundle and take out a roll of birchbark. He opened the roll and looked at it. There was no writing on it; there were only birds and animals marked on it. He looked it over carefully and selected some songs and hymns. I looked at it too and asked how he could read it. He said, 'I know what it means. I can read it'" (Hilger, 1936 c, p. 45).

Picture writing was done with a bone on the inner surface of birchbark, or occasionally on slabs of cedar or ash. In order to give the pictures some relief, charcoal or colored soil was rubbed into the markings.

If a Red Lake band was in danger or needed help and no one in the group had the ability to write a message, several scouts were sent to a neighboring tribe with a belt to ask for help. This belt was undeniable evidence that the group was in trouble and that the scouts were delivering a truthful message. The belt was about 3 feet in length, broad in the middle and tapering toward the ends. On both sides eagle bills were attached in a scattered manner. "When these were removed the belt was like a carrying strap that women used in packing

---

[30] Mnemonic records were exhibited in Case 6, Hall 4 of the Field Museum, Chicago, July 25, 1935. A descriptive label read: "The Ojibwa had developed a system of mnemonic records which more nearly approached writing than any other form found north of Mexico. The records consisted of more or less conventionalized figures incised on birchbark. Each figure represented an idea or event but the figures were not sufficiently conventionalized to be classed as true ideographs."

wood or anything else on their backs [p. 141].   I never saw such a belt but my father told me about it," said an old Red Lake informant.

DIVERSIONS

Chippewa children were given much freedom and therefore spent much time in play.   Their developmental age, it appears, was not unlike that of other children.   While small they played with toys made by their elders; when a little older, boys and girls played together in games and in imitation of elders; when still older, sexes excluded each other and played apart and tolerated no interference from each other; in adulthood, some games were played by each sex exclusively, some by both sexes but apart, and others by both sexes together.

Formerly the child had little choice in companionship, since the only children within its environment were those of its own family or of the few families that lived in its group.   Groups of families were of necessity small since all had to live upon nature in the locality. They usually moved en masse in following the seasonal occupation of maple-sugar making, berry picking, wild-rice gathering, fishing, and hunting.

Both boys and girls in late preadolescent years had a chum; many informants spoke of these with affection, having been lifelong friends. "Chums were like brothers or sisters to each other, and no matter what happened after we were married, we could always count on a chum if we needed help."   Old men informants did not think that gang life, such as is found among American boys, existed among the Chippewa boys.   Boys of various groups banded together to fight the boys of another group, but this seems to have been the extent of their planned activities.

Groups of families of close social affinity exist on reservations today.   Small children of such groups play together.   Parents seem free of worry when their older children seek companionship only within the group.   In some instances the families of a group are consanguineous; in others the affinity is dō'dámic; in still others it is thought that the common possession of drums in early days is responsible for their grouping.

Diversions within and between groups consisted of story telling; of smoking, chewing, and snuffing while visiting; of playing games and gambling; and of dancing.   The children, if not actual participants in these activities, could always be nonparticipating observers.

CHILDREN'S PLAY

The earliest toys of a Chippewa child were those hung on the bow of its cradleboard.   Among these were usually the bag with his navel cord and strings of claws of animals or of skeletal heads of small fowl (p. 23). Small girls played with dolls; boys, with bows and arrows. They mimicked their elders in the various occupations of housekeeping, caring for dolls (pl. 5, *3*), hunting and fishing, and dancing. During this study children on several reservations were seen imitating their elders. On the White Earth Reservation, either commercial dolls or ones improvised from old rags (hose stuffed with rags to toe and then wrapped snugly into a piece of cloth "so that it looked just like my little sister when mama gets her ready for sleep") were put to sleep under soothing one-syllable lullabies in hammocks stretched between twigs of berry bushes or poles of a swing. One-room "houses" with walls of 1-inch-deep ridges of soil were marked off on well-scraped ground in the yard. These houses were equipped with household furniture, such as is found in their own meagerly furnished homes, made of most perfectly modeled clay forms—the gumbo soil in the area (western section) being well adapted to modeling. Although models were only 2 or 3 inches in length, tables had grooved legs and rounded corners; chairs had curved or straight backs; rockers had runners; and sideboards, designs on doors! Several tables had plates and cups with handles. None of the furnishings were considered precious enough to be saved for the next day's house playing; new ones were made three successive days. In the yards of these "houses" tripods were erected and cooking was played at.

A question as to the differences in steps and rhythm of the squaw dance and the rabbit dance was answered by several third-, fourth-, and fifth-grade girls on the White Earth Reservation by fetching an old rusty metal pail and some pieces of kindling—these serving as drum and drumsticks—and demonstrating both dances (1938). (Pl. 10, *1, 3*.)

GAMES AND GAMBLING

Densmore classifies the games among the Chippewa as games of chance, such as the moccasin, hand, plate, snake, and stick games; and games of dexterity, including the bone, bunch of grass, awl, woman's, and lacrosse games. Children's games are listed by her as the coasting erect game, snow snake, deer sticks, marbles, spinning stone, woman's game, bunch of grass game, playing camp, hide-and-seek or butterfly game, blindfold game, windego game or cannibal game.[31]

The only game which came under the writer's observation was the moccasin game (mǎ′kisin ǎtǎ′dīwin—shoe gambling) which was being

[31] Cf. Densmore (1929, pp. 67–70, 114–119). For quotations from Densmore's study, see Brown (1930, pp. 185–186). For games played by children and adults, see also Copway (1851, pp. 49–60) ; Hoffman (1890, pp. 133–135) ; Reagan (1919, pp. 264–278) ; and Culin (1907, scattered between pp. 61–791).

played by men on the Red Lake Reservation and by boys on the Vermilion Lake. On the Red Lake Reservation (1939), six men (women never participated in it) were seated on the ground, three in each of two opposing rows. "Moccasins" consisted of four oval-shaped pieces of blue serge about the size of a man's hand, lined with brown cloth, and hand-sewed about the edges. The serge was the upper side. One of three drums used in this game was made by stretching scraped but untanned deer hide over a band of basswood, and fastening it there by passing a strip of hide back and forth on the opposite side through holes made near the edge of the hide. When completed this side gave the appearance of the spokes of a wheel. The drummer held the drum by clenching the spokes with his left hand. With his right, he beat the drum, all drummers singing to the rhythm of the beats.[32] One drummer had to be a participator in the game. Other implements necessary for the game were four ball bearings (mȧ'kisin ȧtȧgīȧ'win—bullets used in shoe gambling), one of which was marked with two crosses carved on opposite sides, all parts equal; a switch of the hazelnut bush used in designating the moccasin under which the marked ball bearing was hid; 20 knitting-needlelike sticks of wood (bēmēȧg'ȧnōn) used in paying the penalty for a wrong choice (these were all passed to the opposing side when a "deal" had ended); and 10 small slabs of cedar wood, pointed at one end so that they could be easily planted in the ground. The small slabs were counters and each represented 20 of the small knitting-needlelike sticks, their total making up the final score and showing the winning side.

The game was played in the following manner: One of the three persons on a side, each taking his turn, hid the ball bearings, one under each moccasin. The hider did this with many amusing gestures of arms following the rhythm of the drums and the songs. Drumbeats, songs, and gestures were intended to confuse the opposing person whose turn it was to find the marked ball bearing. When all were hidden, the hider clapped his hands. The opponent whipped the ground slightly with his stick for a time in thoughtful search, and finally slapped the moccasin that he suspected was hiding the ball bearing. Before doing so, however, he was permitted to uncover two of the moccasins, if he so wished. His choice was always undeniably indicated by the decided manner in which he slapped the moccasin. A wrong choice was penalized, a knitting-needlelike stick being passed to the opposing side. A loss of 20 of these gave the opponents one of the cedar-wood slabs.

---

[32] See also Densmore (1910, pp. 156–161, 186–191; 1913, pp. 240–242, 282–284, 299) for moccasin game.

Old clothing—a pair of trousers and faded shirt topping the pile—was staked by the men who were gambling. Twenty-four persons of all ages and both sexes, including children, were nonparticipants. The men, all of whom were WPA employees who had worked the allotted hours for the week, had played for 3 days. "Long ago valuable things were staked," remarked an observer. "But that's not done any more; men today play for amusement rather than for stakes." Copway wrote of the moccasin game in 1851: "So deeply interesting does this play sometimes become, that an Indian will stake first his gun, next his steel traps, then his implements of war, then his clothing, and lastly his tobacco and pipe, leaving him, as we say, 'Nah-bah-wan-yah-ze-yaid,' a piece of cloth with a string around his waist" (Copway, 1851, p. 54).

On the Vermilion Reservation, August 1939, a Chippewa, over 80 years of age, was teaching the moccasin game to four boys, aged 7 to 11 (pl. 10, 4). He used ball bearings like the ones described above whenever he played the game, but "these kids do just as well using three white marbles and that yellow one," he remarked. The moccasins and counters, however, were the ones used by him whenever he played the game with adults. The moccasins—oval-shaped and of black material with edges sewed by hand—were 8 inches long and 6 inches wide; the knitting-needlelike counters, 10 inches long. The large counters, each worth 20 of the above-mentioned, were of birch wood, 7½ inches long and 1½ inches at greatest width. Ten of these were used in counting; the eleventh one, easily differentiated because of one scallopped end, was shifted back and forth by the old man, thus indicating the side that was hiding the marbles. The willow stick used in slapping the moccasin was a yard long. One of the boys beat the drum while he and the old man sang to the rhythm. "The drum may be of any size," the old man said. His, covered on both sides with undecorated and untanned deer hide, was 17½ inches in diameter, and 2 inches in width. A strip of deer hide with four 2-inch sticks tied to it at intervals, extended across the diameter on one side. The drummer held the drum by slipping his hand between the drumhead and the strip. All-day suckers which the writer had distributed among the children in the group formed the stake. In early days the old man had staked, won, and lost blankets, canoes, tanned hides, and "other valuable things."

Some informants had participated in the lacrosse game when young. "It was no gambling game, but the winner got a prize. I once took off my waist and gave it as a prize," remarked a Lac Courte Orielle informant.

DANCES

One of the most enjoyable diversions of the early Chippewa was the social dance, for dances gave opportunities for friendly gatherings and fun. Catlin wrote in 1832–1839 that the Ojibway had entertained his party with picturesque dances. He wrote: "They gave us the *beggar's dance*—the *buffalo-dance*—the *bear-dance*—the *eagle-dance*— and *dance of the braves*. This last is particularly beautiful, and exciting to the feelings in the highest degree" (Catlin, 1926, vol. 2, p. 154). Densmore (1929, p. 107) lists the begging dance and the woman's dance as social dances.[33]

All informants had participated in the squaw dance, a dance still prevalent on all reservations, most especially at the time of the commercial pow-wow—an Indian dance held for tourists (pl. 11). A Lac Courte Orielle informant gave the following account of a squaw dance:

When I attended squaw dances as a young man, it was done like this: Women chose their partners for each occasion. If the man chosen by a woman for the first dance gave the woman a whip, he signified thereby that he would present her with a pony later. She, in turn, might then give him a beaded-bag outfit. In the dance the woman follows the man. In old days these dances sometimes lasted 10 to 14 days but were not given very often; today they are given every Saturday night.

The feather dance is still held on the Lac Courte Orielle and the Vermilion Reservations. Although it was formerly considered a social gathering, the Vermilion Indians in recent years have attached to it a ceremonial which the interpreter was certain was an intrusion. "An old man here leads this dance every spring and fall in the dance hall," she remarked (cf. pl. 12 for similar dance hall). "He offers food in memory of certain Indians—it is as though the spirit of the food went to these dead Indians—and after that the people eat the food. My mother said it wasn't conducted that way years ago."

The forty-nine dance, a new dance only 5 or 6 years old, was much in vogue on the Lac Courte Orielle and the La Pointe Reservations in the summer of 1935. "It's all the rage here now," said a Lac Courte Orielle informant. "It is not so much an Indian dance as it is a waltz. It originated after the World War: 50 men went across but only 49 returned. These 49 originated the song and the rythm for the dance." The La Pointe Chippewa who had held the dance for 3 years previous to 1935 gave the same explanation for its origin. Some informants believed the 49 men to have been Chippewa. Others thought they were Winnebagos, and that these had introduced it among their own people. Still others had heard that it had originated with the Dakota and had been introduced by them.

"Other dances that were not known among the Chippewa years ago but are found among them today are the fish dance, the snake dance, the deer dance, the horse dance, and the corn dance," said a Lac

---

[33] Cf. Culkin (1915, pp. 83–93) and Reagan (1934, pp. 302–306) for social-ceremonial dances.

Courte Orielle woman. "It is possible that the Winnebagos introduced these. They are all social dances." On the White Earth Reservation, children imitated their elders in the squaw dance, the rabbit
dance, and the side dance (pl. 10, *1*, *2*, *3*).

VISITING

One of the most prevalent diversions of the Chippewa consisted of
visiting. Time was spent in conversation, or in silently sitting in each
other's presence. In the summer, visiting was done out-of-doors under
sun shelters; in the winter, in the wigwam around the fireplace.
Children, when not romping around and playing, sat by and listened
in. Topics of conversation were often mere gossip, but many times,
especially in the winter, historic events such as wars, traveling, and
visits of other tribes, were recounted. Many times, too, traditional
legends—some with lessons for the young, some for mere entertainment—were related, especially by those well versed in them. Densmore's informants said that one old woman "used to act out her stories,
running around the fire and acting while she talked." [34] Stories of
Windē'gō and Bā'kȧk were also told. Windē'gō is variously described as a "giant, an overgrown person who eats human beings;" or
as "a giant who ate and drank a lot of grease, and then sat down and
became tall and bloated;" or as "a giant Indian who eats other people,
who may eat a whole person at one meal and then not have enough."
An old Lac Courte Orielle man told this story: "An old man once told
me that while a man was trapping he stooped over to look at his trap.
Just then someone put a shawl over his head. The man said to this
being, 'What are you doing?' The being answered, 'Oh, nothing!'
But he took the man into a boat into which he had already taken his
two children, and this being ate all three. And that was Windē'gō!"

Bā'kȧk is a skeletal being who is always going about harming other people
[said a Red Lake informant]. At the first thunderclap he comes from the east,
and stays around until deer hunting time in the fall, when he goes west; sometimes too in winter he returns from the west and goes east. He does his
mischief on his way westward, never on the way back. · Sometimes he is seen
walking in the clouds. My husband tells me that when the Indians are out
hunting and have no tent, they must hang their clothes above their heads in
order to be protected against this skeleton. Once while camping, a man, his
cousin, and his brother slept near the side of the fire. The cousin woke up,
heard something like a little squeak, and saw something fall; and that was
the skeleton. The brother, too, heard it and was frightened. The skeleton,
using something he had in his hand, cut the man open down the front, took
the tissue called "weese" (omentum)—it is right over the abdomen—put it on
the fire, and finally ate it. His brother saw all this. The skeleton put the

---

[34] Densmore (1929, p. 29). For traditional legends, see Chamberlain (1889); Blackwood
(1929); Jones, William (1919); Laidlaw (1915–22.)

man's skin together again, covered him up so all looked the same as before, and started on his way. The brother went over to the man, woke him, and said, 'Are you alive?' The man didn't know anything had happened; so his brother told him. Soon the man began to fail and before long died. This really happened.

Good humor, telling jokes, and smoking added their share of entertainment. Men, women, and children smoked, Gilfillan (1901, p. 97) noted: "All the children think they must have tobacco the same as their elders." Pipes were often passed from one person to another, each person taking a few puffs. When empty, they were refilled and passed again. On the Lac du Flambeau Reservation an old couple who had joined our group of informants passed a pipe between them, the woman refilling and lighting it as many times as her husband. Many Chippewa today smoke kinnikinnick, chew plug tobacco, and use snuff.

Visiting was often done in silence, persons merely sitting or reclining in each other's presence. Old Indians on several reservations complained that they had been indirectly told by white people that they were not wanted on their porches or on their lawns. They were asked: "Do you want anything?" "So now I don't go visiting there any more, for I'm not wanted. I used to enjoy visiting on the porch, just sitting and smoking, thinking of so-and-so when he used to live there." Children on the Lac du Flambeau and the Lac Courte Orielle Reservations repeatedly dropped in to see the writer, squatted at once in a huddle on the floor near the wall, stayed awhile without uttering a word, and when bidding goodbye quite agreed that they had had a pleasant visit. On the White Earth Reservation girls entered the writer's room after a gentle rap, quietly announcing that they had come for a visit. Clearing rockers and chairs of paper and books, they sat for an hour in perfect silence, observing the writer and studying all that was to be seen in the room, and finally left thanking her for the "nice visit" they had had.

VOCATIONAL TRAINING AND DOMESTIC ECONOMY

CANOE MAKING [35]

Birchbark canoes were used by the Chippewa in summer traveling on lakes and rivers; for movement of household goods and families; for fishing, hunting, berrying, and rice gathering. Families usually owned several of various sizes, smaller ones for berrying and rice gathering, and larger ones for transportation. Both men and women rowed: the man paddled sitting in the prow, the woman in the stern. The weight of a canoe ranged from 65 to 125 pounds. "My father

[35] Cf. also Densmore (1929, pp. 150–152) ; Warren (1885, pp. 98, 105, 473).

helped to make one of the largest canoes our band had; it seated 30 warriors and it took 2 men to portage it," said a Vermilion Lake canoe maker. When portaging either the man or the woman carried the canoe by balancing it on head and shoulders (cf. pl. 17, 2). The delicacy of balancing often depended on the manner in which the paddles were fastened inside the canoe. Catlin says of the canoe:

> The bark canoe of the Chippeways is, perhaps, the most beautiful and light model of all the water crafts that ever were invented. They are generally made complete with the rind of one birch tree, and so ingeniously shaped and sewed together, with roots of the tamarack, which they call *wat-tap*, that they are water-tight, and ride upon the water, as light as a cork. They gracefully lean and dodge about, under the skillful balance of an Indian, or the ugliest squaw; but like everything wild, are timid and treacherous under the guidance of a white man; and, if he be not an experienced equilibrist, he is sure to get two or three times soused in his first endeavors at familiar acquaintance with them. [Catlin, 1926, vol. 2, pp. 157–158.]

Although both men and women made canoes, canoe making was usually considered to be a man's occupation. Boys past puberty were expected to learn to construct them. Today the art is nearly lost. Although birchbark canoes were seen on nearly all reservations, the making of them was known to only a few old men. "The Indian arts are dying out. Here on the Lac Courte Orielle Reservation there are only two men left that can make a birchbark canoe. It is difficult, too, to have snowshoes made these days," said an informant. No dugouts— boats made by carving out cedar tree trunks and then covering them with hides, "the kind they used years ago"—were seen on any reservation. Several old men remembered well how to make them but had neither strength nor material to do so. "Anyway the cedar trees around here are too young; you need a pretty good sized one to make a dugout," remarked a Red Lake man.

A canoe exhibited at the Mille Lacs Indian Trading Post on Mille Lacs Reservation was made by a fullblood Chippewa, her son, and three other women (pls. 13–17). "It really takes four women, and two men to do all the work in making a canoe." The men did the work requiring the use of tools, such as shaping the wood for ribs, floor, bow, and stern. The women prepared the bark and the pitch, and did the sewing. All material used in making the canoe came from trees: the bark was of the birch; the gunwales, ribs, and flooring, of green cedar saplings; thread, of the split roots of spruce; and pitch, of spruce resin, "boiled until it pulls like taffy, after which it is fried in grease mixed with powdered charcoal made of cedar." All measurements were distances between body parts. The depth at middle distance between bow and stern was the distance from elbow to tip of thumb; the distance between ribs was one hand stretched from tip of little finger to tip of thumb.

A 75-year-old Vermilion informant completed a canoe on August 18, 1939, which he intended to use for wild-rice gathering within a week, "just as soon as the licenses for wild-rice gathering have been approved." The floor of the canoe measured 14 feet 2 inches in length; the distance between stern and prow at the opening, 12 feet 2 inches. Its width across the middle at the opening was 3 feet 2 inches; its depth, 1 foot 6 inches. All material used had been gathered from trees: the framework and all wood was of cedar; the outer cover, of birchbark; the pitch, of spruce; the fibers used in keeping framework and parts together, of spruce roots. It had taken a week to gather the material and to make the canoe. The framework consisted of 43 ribs of 2-inch width and ¾-inch thickness. Underneath these and running lengthwise, about 1 foot apart, were slats of the same width but less in thickness, some being a continuous piece and the full length of the boat. The ends of the ribs and of the slats were fastened to a strip of cedar wood which formed the rim about the opening of the canoe. The rim was held apart and in position by four 8-inch boards which extended across the opening and were fastened to the rim. All parts of the entire framework were held in position by stitches of spruce roots, a metal awl having been used in making holes for the sewing. Formerly, sharpened and pointed moose bone, "or any hard and tough bone of any large animal," was used. The exterior of the entire framework had been covered with birchbark, with inner side of bark toward outside. Cracks or weak parts in the bark were well soldered on both sides with spruce resin. For the first application pure resin was used since it was soft enough when heated to be pressed well into all small breaks in the bark. A second application, placed only on the very weak parts, was made of resin mixed with charcoal—charcoal making the resin less brittle than the pure. The pure resin appeared brown; the charcoal mixture black.

Both paddles were also of birch wood; one was 61 inches in length, the other 64. The greatest width of the ladle ends was 8 inches; the narrowest, the handle end, 7½.

An informant stated:

As a young lad I had often watched my father make canoes and in that way learnt how to do the fine details. My father was considered an expert canoe maker: he had learnt it from his father who also had a reputation for canoe making. I made my first one when I was 14 years old; an old woman directed me and showed me exactly how to put the parts together. It was the same size as this one; 14 feet 2 inches long, 38 inches wide, and about 18 inches deep. No one today wants to help me, nor learn. These boys you see around here watch 10 minutes and then run away.

SNOWSHOES AND TOBOGGANS

Snowshoes, well adapted for winter travel, were worn by both men and women. Men's snowshoes (ā′gēmȧk) often had pointed, upturned toes; women's (īkwē'ōdȧgēmȧk), round toes. The framework of a pair of men's snowshoes on the Red Lake Reservation (1932) was made of elder wood. One-half of the woven network, the center section, was made of cowhide; the sections to the front and back of this, of deerhide. When in use the foot was inserted into a strap of rags fastened in the middle front section of the cowhide weave. "When using these snowshoes, moccasins must be worn; shoes would get caught in the network;" said the owner. "Without snowshoes I'd never venture out to trap and hunt in the winter."

A pair of men's snowshoes on the Lac Courte Orielle Reservation measured 46 inches in length and 14½ inches in greatest width (pl. 18). The middle weaving (14½ inches in length) was of horsehide; that to the front (9 inches in length) and to the back (14 inches in length), of deerhide. The weaving of the middle section was held in place by being tied over two bars, one toward toe end and the other toward heel end; the bars also served to hold the framework in position. The strands used in weaving the back and front sections were passed through holes in the same bars. The wife of the owner had hung the snowshoes on a limb of a tree about a rod from the home shortly after her husband's death. "I couldn't bear to see them anymore; they made me very lonesome," she said.

In the spring of 1935 an aged woman on the same reservation had made a pair of snowshoes for her son-in-law for fall hunting. The larger weave was of horsehide; the smaller, of deerhide. "When Indians find a dead horse, they usually remove its hide and use it in making snowshoes," she remarked.

Toboggans (nābāgīdōb'ānȧk, literally flat wagon on ice or snow) were used by trappers and hunters in hauling game and furs. Several informants had seen some but were unable to give details in the making of them. (Cf. also Densmore, 1929, p. 136.) An interpreter remembered one that her grandmother used when she first came from Canada: it had been whittled out of a basswood tree, with a crooked knife.

BOWS AND ARROWS

Material used by informants in making bows and arrow shafts was sinew of nettle twine, fish glue, and wood. Sinew was removed from the spine of the horse, cow, deer, or moose and placed on a flat surface, preferably a piece of timber, and allowed to dry. It was later smoked in order to make it mothproof and flyproof. Dried sinew could be severed into strands fine enough to be used in making beadwork; several strands together were used in sewing buckskin shirts, leggings, and moccasins. Nine were used in making strings for bows and for tying arrowheads to shafts. Sinew was being used by many women on the reservations and was often seen hanging from rafters in homes.

Cords for bow strings were made by drawing either strands of sinew or the inner bark of the nettle (bīgeg'āwắc) through the mouth to moisten them and then rolling them over the calf of the right leg with the palm of the right hand (pl. 19). The procedure was the same as that used in making cords for fish nets (p. 125).

Bows varying in length from 4 feet to "as long as I am tall" (nearly 6 feet) were made of any wood that was strong and pliable, preferably young oak or young ironwood. After the wood was planed with a stone scraper, it was smoothed with sandpaper. Sandpaper was made by pouring sturgeon glue over tanned moose hide and over this, soon after drying set in, very fine sand. After lying in the sun for several hours, preferably a half day, it was ready for use.

Arrow shafts were usually made of ironwood and were smoothed in the same manner as bows. They varied in length, the standard length being 2½ feet. At one end arrows were fastened into grooves with sinew. In order to produce better flying power, the opposite end was tipped off with closely trimmed feathers split in half. The feathers were dipped in glue, inserted into a slit at this end of the shaft, and securely tied with several strands of sinew. Slight engravings were made in shafts and overlaid with color. This enabled the owner to identify his own. Bows, too, were frequently painted or engraved.

Arrowheads varied in sizes and in materials. Some were of flint; some of copper; others of rib bone of moose, deer, buffalo, or any large animal. "Not every man could make arrows; only certain ones in the tribe could do that." Informants knew of no one living that was able to make flint or bone arrowheads. Informants believed that at one time their people knew how to temper copper. Several old men agreed that a copper arrowhead 4 inches in length and one at greatest width found in the vicinity of New Post (Lac Courte Orielle Reservation) had been used on a spear shaft; its weight was too heavy for an arrow shaft. Arrowheads of iron were introduced by white traders.

Blunt arrows were used in hunting birds and small game, the bluntness preventing the tearing of the flesh. Grooves were made on either one or both sides of an arrowhead which was intended for poisoning; grooves were packed with poisonous herbs. Another way of poisoning an arrow was to dip both it and part of the shaft into a mixture of water and rattlesnake poison. In either case the victim of the arrow could not survive.

HUNTING [36]

The chase provided the Chippewa with both food and clothing and was, therefore, a chief occupation throughout the year. It was especially so in the winter when furs were heavier and animals were not

---

[36] Cf. also Densmore (1929, pp. 109–111) and Hilger (1936 b, pp. 3, 17–19).

bearing young.   Families set out for their hunting grounds soon after the cold weather began, about the beginning of November, and returned to the winter camp only after the severe weather set in.   They hunted moose, elk, and deer; bear, wolf, and fox; beaver, otter, and muskrat; mink, martin, fisher, and rabbit; partridge, ducks, and other fowl; and buffalo, if they resided near the prairie lands.

Since hunting was a man's duty, boys were taught the use of bow and arrow at an early age.   A boy's first success in killing any animal used as food was celebrated with a feast: all the village was invited and the meat of the animal served as part of the main dish.   "When my brother caught his first deer, and later his bear, my mother prepared the animal—head, hoofs and insides—and invited all the old people," said a Red Lake woman.   The same celebration took place when a boy caught his first fish.   On the Lac Courte Orielle, the Vermilion, the Nett Lake, and the Mille Lacs Reservations, these customs still prevail. "The first bird I shot was a wild goose," said a Lac Courte Orielle informant.   "I shot it with a bow and arrow directly through the head. It flopped and flopped and flopped, but finally I caught it.   I was about 6 years old then, but since my father was a white man—he didn't believe in Indian ways—no feast was given for me, like that given for other boys, even for boys here at New Post today."   A 38-year-old Vermilion mother gave a feast (1932) when her son caught his first fish.   She invited mostly old people and served the fish as part of the main dish.   An old man made a speech so the boy would continue being successful as he grew older.

The charm most effective in hunting on the Lac Courte Orielle Reservation (1935) was the foetal inclusion found between the skin and visceral lining of an animal—those for rabbit (bītȧwī′ wabōs′) and deer (bītȧwī′ wāwec′kisi) predominating.   At times, as many as three inclusions were found in the same animal.   "Once a man trapped a male rabbit and brought it to me to skin," said an informant.   "Just as I was removing the skin a bag about 2 inches long fell out.   In it were two small rabbits.   I thought it was some kind of 'medicine' (magical power).   I kept one and the other I gave to the man.   I kept it for good luck, but I don't remember that I ever used it."   An old man sitting by remarked: "I carry a little rabbit around with me; I have never found a little deer."

"I heard recently," said another hunter, "that foetal inclusions can be used as lures when hunting, if hunters carry them upon their person.   One fellow here recently let someone carry his—a little deer, completely grown except that it had three heads.   It was found in a male deer.   The fellow who lent it said, 'You will get deer!' and he did; he got eight deer!   Lately a man who found a little rabbit under a male rabbit skin threw it away not knowing its value.   He got a sound scolding from an old Indian for not saving it; the old man himself carried a bear. Deer brings deer; rabbit, rabbits; bear, bears!"

The Vermilion Chippewa had not heard of the charm of the foetal inclusion but believed firmly that finding a fetus—a normal fetus—in a rabbit shot in the fall meant good luck for the entire hunting season. L'Anse Indians believed good luck in hunting would be theirs if they hung skulls of beaver on rafters. A trout skull was hung up by the jaw "inside or outside of the house for good luck in anything." Skulls of various animals were often seen hung from rafters. A Red Lake hunter after smoking a weed found "somewhere out there in the woods, in a clean place," invariably had good success; he smoked only if his first attempt at hunting failed.

Meeting an owl in the woods, said a L'Anse informant, is a bad omen: "I was out hunting a few years ago with a man from Flambeau (Lac du Flambeau Reservation) who insisted on shooting an owl which happened to be sitting on a branch along our way; not killing it, he said, would bring bad luck. Old Indians who meet a fox when out hunting will at once return home; hunting after that would be useless." Another L'Anse informant related his bad luck: "About 20 years ago when I was working across the bay, there were many deer in that area. An old medicine man lived over there. We had no meat, and although I hunted every day and even at night, I never saw a deer. I would see tracks, but never a deer. Somebody told me that that medicine man was using 'bad medicine' on me. I had noticed that every time I'd go into the woods, an owl came from somewhere, swooped ahead of me and sat on a limb. As soon as I caught up to it, it would swoop in front of me again, and sit on a limb. Retracing my steps, the owl repeated its conduct, always keeping to my right. So one day I took a buckshot gun with me. The owl repeated its maneuvers, always keeping to the right of me. If I get a chance I'll shoot you, I thought. I shot, hit the owl and saw it slip down. I ran up to it and stepped on it. A noise like a human cry came from it three times; it looked at me with its two eyes wide open and died. I stooped to pick it up: there was nothing there except the hide and feathers. I took these home and burnt them. After that I never failed to get deer. Two or three days after I shot the owl, the medicine man took sick. He asked to see me, but I wouldn't go. Four days after that he died. That medicine man had taken the shape of an owl and injured my hunting."

Chippewa hunted game for sustenance all through the year, never, however, was any animal killed wantonly. Although no particular family laid claim to any area as its exclusive hunting ground, groups of families that had for years migrated together for the purpose of hunting returned seasonally to the same area. All respected each other's prerogatives. Informants had never heard of difficulties arising from overlapping of hunting grounds; they did know of serious quarrels that had arisen because persons lifted game caught in traps not their own. "This didn't happen often; but it happened!"

The best season for deer hunting was "when the leaves began to fall: the deer were fattest then and best tasting, as well." Doe were not shot while carrying or nursing young.

As noted before, some hunters used charms for good luck in hunting; those who possessed tutelary power related to hunting exercised these (pp. 45, 47). Still others prepared themselves for the chase by giving serious thought to what they were about to do. "The first time that I went hunting my father called me: 'Witigoc, [informant's Indian name], you are now ready to go hunting. (I was told this a few days before we left home.) Don't say anything disrespectful about the deer. Don't boast, saying, I am going to kill a deer, or I am going to shoot two deer. Don't talk that way. God made the deer so he can hear you say that. Simply be quiet and don't talk; and then you will get deer.' The same respect is shown to moose."

Impounding, one of several methods employed in hunting deer, was done by cutting a lane through the woods. The deer was driven down the path and impounded at the end in a space fenced off by saplings. As many as were needed were shot with arrows.

Deer were also caught by means of snares made of a three-strand braid of rawhide, each strand being about one-fourth inch wide. A snare consisted of a noose hung at an angle of 45° and attached to the heavy branches of a tree overhanging the path which the deer were accustomed to take.

At night deer were caught by means of torches. Torches were seldom used in open spaces, and never in the woods; they were of greatest service when hunting from a canoe. When making torches a Lac Courte Orielle informant gathered resin which had collected at a gash which he had slashed in the trunk of a Norway or a white pine several days previously. He heated the resin, saturated rags with it, and while they were still hot wound them around the end of a stick. In earlier days he had used birchbark in place of rags. A White Earth hunter lined a birchbark cornucopia with moss to prevent its burning and then filled it with small strips of birchbark dipped in liquid resin. A La Pointe hunter split one end of a green sapling, 2 feet in length and an inch in diameter, into small splinters and filled the space between the splinters with spruce pitch. This torch threw light at a distance of 200 feet. When hunting deer the torch was fastened to the prow of the canoe, occupants of the canoe hiding behind a piece of bark that was either fastened behind the torch or held there. Today lanterns commonly replace torches. A Lac Courte Orielle hunter (1935) rested his lantern on a 6- by 18-

inch board which he had nailed to the prow of his boat. A board 8 inches square nailed at right angles to the end of the board nearest him served as a shield.

When rustling of the twigs or breaking of dry sticks indicated the advance of a deer, the torch or lantern was lit and light played about in the area. If a deer was in the vicinity, he could easily be seen for "his two eyes appeared like two shining lights. Deer will come toward a light; they are enticed by it." Flashlights have replaced lanterns and torches, especially among the younger hunters today. In order to leave his hands free to use his gun, the hunter fastens the light to the crown of his hat and lights it only if a deer is thought near.

Deer are easily caught at artificial salt licks deposited by hunters in the deer's watering places. La Pointe Indians (1935) watched at night in one such area on lumber laid in the crotch of a tree and in another from a platform constructed of saplings. When a noise was heard flashlights were played upon the space, the deer being easily discerned because of the glare of their eyes.

"Yesterday while rowing around the end of Big Couderay, my husband noticed a deer," said a Lac Courte Orielle woman. "He put salt on the old salt lick and toward nightfall returned, quietly lying in his boat awaiting the deer. Soon he heard a noise, turned on his flashlight—he keeps it securely fastened to the crown of his hat with lens facing directly to the front—saw the deer's eyes like two bright lights, leveled his gun, and shot it."

The "deer call," a sound resembling the call of a fawn that attracts doe, was made either by blowing through one's folded hands, through a roll of birchbark, or through a wooden implement. The father of a Red Lake informant, when out hunting, heard the call of a doe, he thought; brush moved and thinking it was a fawn he fired his gun only to find he had shot his friend. "My father grieved over this all summer. Relatives did not resent it for my father had shown them repeated kindnesses when he stayed at their home."

Bears were caught in deadfalls in the early day. Informants either had seen deadfalls when young or had helped to build them. They were of wood and so constructed that the weight of the bear, as he stepped forward to eat the bait, released a heavy suspended log which fell upon him, pinning him down. Meat of any kind, including that handled by human hands, as well as decayed meat served as bait. "A bear is not particular. I recently saw one eating the decayed carcass of a deer." Maple sugar and fish were also used as bait.

After guns were introduced deadfalls were no longer used. The grandfather of a Red Lake interpreter owned one of the first guns in the area, "an old flint, a muzzle loader, which took three-quarters of an hour to load. Any man who owned any kind of a gun in those days was considered rich. One time, grandfather happened to come upon a tree under which a bear was sitting. He shot at the bear but missed him—just touched his ears. His dogs saved him; for during the time he loaded his gun, they barked at the bear and kept him at bay."

A Lac Courte Orielle informant had heard an old hunter tell how he discovered the winter habitat of bears:

Shabagizig tells about this. In old days in the spring of the year—take a warm day in spring—some fellow would wear snowshoes and go in the direction of a bear lair. He'd beat the snow down with his snowshoes, the snow after freezing making a trail. After dark, this person would get ready, put on his coat, take his hatchet and strike out on the trail. He might go several miles perhaps. It is night. Here is how he told it. This fellow would go along and stand and listen, and stand and listen, and stand and listen. Pretty soon he would hear something. He would hear bear yaps. Sometimes they came from the ground; sometimes, from hollow trees. When he would hear the sound, he would take his hatchet, cut a stick, and place it in the snow so that it would point in the direction from which the yaps had come. The next day he and some others would go out and find the bears there. [Hilger, 1936 c, p. 49.]

A successful bear hunter usually gave a feast at which bear meat was served. While guests (1935) on the Lac Courte Orielle Reservation were sitting around waiting for such a dinner, the host passed tobacco. "Some smoked it; some put it in the stove; I put mine in the corner of my handkerchief and took it home. The man did this just to follow the old custom. Bears are killed in fall and spring, not in summer because then they are carrying their young; in winter, bears live in hollow trees."

Wolves were caught in traps [37] or snares, but with great difficulty. A less laborious way was to fasten a hooked stick to a tree with lower end, the hooked end, 5 feet from the ground and at such an angle that this end was 2 feet from the trunk of the tree. The wolf in jumping for the meat which had been fastened to the hook was caught on the hook, "just like a fish."

Foxes were caught in snares, being enticed into them by the odor of skunk. Skunk musk was scattered in the path on the side of the snare opposite the one from which the fox was expected to come.

Rabbits, too, were caught in snares. Both fox and rabbit snares were like the nooses used in catching deer (p. 122) except that the rawhide strands were less heavy.

Beavers were speared close to the water with spearheads of copper. In order to shield his eyes from the reflected light a hunter covered his head with buckskin or blanket.

Weasels, hunted only in winter when their fur was white, were caught while eating a piece of meat or lard in which a piece of iron

---

[37] For a good account of traps see Lips (1937, pp. 354–360).

had been frozen, the tongue by adhering to the iron caused death. Martins and fishers were caught in traps baited with rabbit meat. All human and other scent had been removed from traps by boiling.

All birds, except the humming bird, were edible and were killed with blunt arrows.

FISHING

Both fresh and smoked fish constituted an important article of food among the early Chippewa. Fishing for immediate use was done at any time during the year. In fall it became a seasonal occupation; groups of families moved to fish for winter storage. "Although no one laid claim to any part of the shore nor to any part of the lake, for persons could fish anywhere, all settled down where they had always settled when fishing. All respected these same rights of others." L'Anse Indians have a tradition that Lake Superior and the large lakes are theirs for fishing but that inland lakes should be left unmolested. "I often heard my father say the old Indians believed the inland lakes and the woods belonged to the animals. They would never bathe in inland lakes. When passing through the woods the father would lead, the children follow him and the mother bring up the rear. They would stay in one line making only a single path and, as it were, tell the animals and the earth that they were using this bit of the land merely to go to another place. Children were told not to run along the sides of the path but to stay in line. People used big lakes, such as Keweenaw Bay and Lake Superior, as though they were their own" (Hilger, 1936 b, p. 2).

Fishing, formerly, was done largely by means of nets, although fishhooks, spearheads, and traps were also used. Women generally used nets, thus securing the best results in numbers and variety.

A Red Lake informant, a professional net maker, in making nets used cord made from the inner bark of the basswood. (Some women used nettles.) The bark, torn into fine strands, was boiled for about one-half hour, and while still soft rolled over the bare side of the right leg with the palm of the right hand (pl. 19, 1). If fibers become dry, they are drawn through the mouth to be moistened with saliva (pl. 19, 2.). No knots were made in joining strands but the ends of two strands were worked between molars and deftly rolled into each other with fingers. Men who assisted rolled cord above the knee.

One old Red Lake informant's great-grandmother made cords for fish nets by boiling nettles, drying them, separating them into fibers, dampening them by drawing them through the mouth, and then rolling them on her leg. "This made fine cord for nets. She used to have balls of it ready for use. That was long, long ago." While rolling basswood fiber women squatted on the ground.[38]

---

[38] For vegetable fibers, see also Huron Smith (1932, pp. 411–423).

The professional Red Lake net maker, referred to above, made nets as recently as 1930, using quilling twine "bought at the store." One of her two shuttles (nābēkwē'ȧgōns) was made of basswood; the other, of a cigar-box cover (pl. 20, 2). The former was 7 inches in length and 1¼ inches in width; the carrier of the thread was 2⅝ inches in height, the space for the release of the thread, 3½ inches. The mesh of the net as demonstrated was 2 by 2 inches. "This would catch pike, perch, and suckers," she remarked. Meshes were measured in the making by pieces of wood (bīmēgī'mīgōn) of various sizes, the size to be used depending upon the kind of fish to be caught in the net. A 2- by 2⅝-inch measure was used if pike, perch, and suckers were to be caught; if "two-lippers," a 3- by 2½-inch; if whitefish, a 2¾- by 3⅛-inch. If the work was well done, our informant noted, the knots of the mesh were immovable. In preparing to set a net as her mother had taught her—the net incidentally had been made by her mother— she held the end of a basswood fiber between her teeth and a stone in her left hand while with her right hand she wound the fiber twice tightly around the stone. She then tied a knot leaving the mouth end long enough so that the stone by means of it could be tied to the edge of the net. Fifteen stones, each about the size of a walnut, were thus prepared and tied to the net, serving as sinkers. On the opposite edge of the net and directly in line with the stones, she attached 15 floaters made of cedar wood. These varied in length from 27 to 29 inches, and weighed approximately 2 ounces each. A second set of floaters, also made of cedar wood, were 5 inches long by 2 inches in diameter, the weight of each again being approximately 2 ounces. A nicety of balance had to be estimated between floaters and sinkers. Notchings, an inch from the narrow end of the floater, permitted fastening to net. When the net was set, the floaters stood erect in the water with only the tips showing. The floaters are made and then the size of the stones chosen, "very large ones would drag the net to the bottom of the lake."

Today Chippewa use factory-made nets. Families on the Red Lake (1932 and 1939) and the L'Anse Reservations (1935) who were fishing for commercial purposes owned from five to seven nets each. Sinkers consisted of flat or rounded pieces of lead; floaters, of elongated cylindrical pieces of wood attached to the net by having the cord, forming the edge of the net, passed through the center. One such net, 300 feet long and 3 feet wide (Red Lake Reservation), had 38 sinkers and as many floaters. Its mesh measured 1⅞ inches square. "One-and-three-fourths-inch squares would have caught many more fish, but this is Government ruling." The owner had paid $15.20 for it. The same informant owned a net measuring 300 feet in length and 8 feet in width.

On Keweenaw Bay (L'Anse, 1935) two young men each owned a net 200 feet long and 3 feet wide; each had 40 floaters and as many sinkers. "We set these nets at seven this evening and expect to raise them at four in the morning the day after tomorrow." They were catching lake trout, large-mouth black bass, and ciscos for commercial purposes.

Nets were thoroughly dried after each usage by being wound on reels, hung on poles arranged lengthwise or in squares, or slid over poles nailed in the form of a plus sign on top of a center pole (pls. 20, *1*; 21, *2*). Poles were peeled of bark and sandpapered so as not to tear nets.

Fishhooks, in old days, were made of bone or wood. Two old L'Anse fishermen heard of a hook 2 inches long made of bone. Both ends had been sharpened and the middle slightly grooved by means of stones, the sliced end of a stick being securely tied into the groove with basswood fiber. When fishing the pointed ends were tipped off with bait— anything edible serving as bait. With a quick and skillful movement a nibbling fish was hooked in the jaw. A Lac Courte Orielle fisherman when a boy made a wooden fishhook by removing bark of a 16- to 20-foot maple sapling, about 2 inches in diameter. After hardening one end of it over the heat of a fire he notched this end in two places opposite each other, thus forming two hooks. Fish were grabbed with either hook while the fisherman stood on the shore. Some informants had heard old people tell of spearing fish with copper arrows, "such arrows as were found when digging the canal between Hancock and Houghton, Mich."

At night fish were enticed by torchlight. One old informant when young had made such a torch by burning roots of Norway pine in a basketlike holder made of old wire which he attached to an iron rod extending from the prow of his canoe. Roots dug about noon and dried in the sun burnt brightly by evening. More recently he had used rags saturated in kerosene in place of pine roots; his neighbors were using discarded automobile tires. Fish, attracted by the light, were both hooked and speared. Fish, whether hooked, speared, or netted, were often killed upon landing by being clubbed. Clubs were made of knots of trees: the knot formed the club and an attached portion of the trunk of the tree, the handle.

In winter fishing was often done through a hole in the ice made with a chisel. In making a chisel a bent piece of iron, sharpened at one end, was inserted into a stout piece of wood and securely fastened there by means of strips of buckskin.

A group of four families, probably not unlike those of early days, had settled on the Narrows of Red Lake for the fishing season of 1932. Women of two of the families were daughters of a third; the fourth family were friends—a young couple with a baby. The old couple occupied a canvas-covered tipi of 12 poles, plus 2 used in controlling wind flaps that regulated the draft.   One daughter and her family lived in a wigwam, a framework of saplings covered with canvas; the remaining two families lived together in a commercial canvas tent. Floors of all places were covered with bedding; corners were filled with wooden boxes and pasteboard cartons used in transporting belongings.   Dishes and cooking utensils were seen on the outside of each home, indicating eating apart.   Toward the center of the grouping, under a long rack, fire was smouldering in two places, charcoal being in evidence in a third.   (See outdoor fireplaces, pls. 30, *1, 2;* 31, *2, 3.*) The rack consisted of several stout 12-foot ironwood saplings, the ends of which either rested in crotches of two poles found at each end of the fireplace or were fastened to the poles with basswood fiber. The two end poles were firmly planted in the ground in the position of an X. All were held in position by being firmly tied together with basswood fiber.   Pails and kettles used for cooking purposes were hanging from crotched sticks attached to the horizontal poles.   Astride the poles with bellies up hung skinned fish, slit down the back, backbone and entrails removed.   These were being dried and cured in the smoke of the smouldering fires.   "It will take about 2 days to smoke these fish; after that we can pack them to take home.   These belong to me," remarked the old woman, "but there's room on the rack for everybody. We all cook here, too."   A short distance away in a small excavation on the side of an embankment, two large whitefish were broiling over a slow fire.   One end of a stick had been thrust under the lower jaw of the fish; the other was planted in the ground in a slanting position. Neither heads, scales, nor entrails had been removed.   "We'll have these for supper in a little while," said one of the men as he poked the fire.   Several large rolls of birchbark, many pieces sewed together since they were intended for a wigwam covering, were used in protecting belongings left outside against rain.   They were not needed for the wigwam since the friend had brought a canvas cover.   Seven partially tanned hides, both deer and moose, lay in a pile nearby; one was tautly stretched on a framework of saplings and exposed to the sun on the shore.   On the shore, also, nets were drying, having been hung from pole to pole, thus giving the appearance of a high fence.   It was about 3 o'clock in the afternoon.   Two men were mending a boat; others were lounging in the shade of trees.   The old woman, using a bone awl as needle and sinew as thread, was sewing herself a pair of buckskin moccasins.   "Since they are for myself, I am not decorating them with beads," she remarked.   Her work kit, a piece of buckskin, contained also a bone flesher made of moose tibia.   "It's a very old one, but the best thing I own."   One of the younger women was sitting against a tree nearby swinging the hammock in which her baby was asleep. (See pl. 3 for hammocks.) A cradleboard rested against a tree. The other two women were soon to return with groceries. At about 5 o'clock, after a lunch, all were going out to set nets. In the early days, the time for setting nets was sundown. A notice posted in various places along the shores of Red Lake by the manager of the Red Lake Fishers' Association (a cooperative enterprise owned and controlled by the Red Lake Chippewa) advised all persons fishing for the Association to set nets at 5 o'clock in the evening and to take them in between 4 and 5 o'clock in the morning, "since this gave everybody ample time to pick blueberries and to attend to gardens." It took two persons to set a net but only one to draw it up.

During fishing season on the Red Lake Reservation (1932) men drew up the nets between 4 and 5 o'clock in the morning (pl. 21, *1*). Women came later bringing the men's breakfast. All nets were brought ashore, women busying themselves sorting fish and removing entrails; men assisted as soon as they had eaten breakfast. Specified sizes of pike, pickerel, perch, and whitefish were marketable; odd sizes were either kept for family consumption or given to old people or to those who were unable to fish. Crappies, suckers, and rock bass were discarded. Of the fish found in one woman's net one morning in 1932, 41 were marketable. Her earnings during the season varied from 5 to 10 dollars a day. (By order of the manager of the Red Lake Fishers' Association the season had opened on July 7 and was to close on August 17.) After the marketable fish had been packed in boxes of ice furnished by the Red Lake Fishers' Association, men rowed out into the lake and discarded all offal. The women in the meantime hung up the nets to dry and all went home; the time was between 9 and 10 o'clock in the morning.

Fishing was done on a similar commercial basis on the L'Anse Reservation in 1935. The fish, however, were collected by "fish trains"—freight trains that furnished ice and boxes, and collected fish early each morning, transporting them to Chicago.

CLOTHING

In the early days adults wore clothing made of finely tanned hides of deer, moose, bear, and elk; and of dressed skins of rabbit, beaver, and other small fur-bearing animals. Children's clothing was made of delicately tanned fawn hides and of skins of beaver, squirrel, and rabbits, whenever these were available.

Tanning hides and dressing skins were a woman's work, but girls, no older than 13 years, assisted. "After a girl had spent her days in her little hut, she was thought old enough to learn everything a woman was expected to know" (p. 52).

Although tanned hides and skins no longer form the clothing of Chippewa, articles of wearing apparel made of them, such as moccasins, jackets, and gloves, were being worn by men, women, and children on every reservation. Tanned deer or moose hide were also being used in making tobacco pouches, money bags, and tool kits; headbands, bracelets, and ceremonial dance outfits, many of these being beaded; straps on cradleboards, wood carriers, and working tools; and network for snowshoes.

Chippewa women on all reservations were tanning hides by old methods. A Lac Courte Orielle informant who had learned tanning from her mother removed all flesh (gīdjēbī′nȧg) when the hide was still fresh, washed the bloodstains from it, and then soaked it in a pail of clear water for 3 days. After wringing it out tightly by hand, she fastened it to a large branch of a tree with a rope passed through the hole left by the removal of the head. She then held the hide tautly near the tail end with her left hand, while with the right she scraped off the hair with a butcher knife, moving across the hide, first to her right and then to her left; strokes were away from her body. This process is called cīgōwē′cīgē. She next soaked the hide over night in a pail of water in which deer brain had been boiled. This process is called nīgōgȧn′gīna. The brain of any animal might have been used; and in the event no brain had been available, a raw egg well beaten and mixed with a pail of lukewarm water would have served the purpose. On the following morning she wrung out the hide by holding the head end in her right hand and tightly winding the hide about the same hand, wrist, and arm (pl. 22, *1*).

She next unfolded the hide and hung it, head and tail ends meeting over the top pole of a rectangular framework which she had erected the previous day for the purpose of stretching the hide. She then rolled the hide from both sides toward head-to-tail line, placed it around a tree (protecting it from the rough bark by a towel which she had fastened snugly about the tree), carefully unrolled the ends, placed one over the other about a hand's length, rolled them together so that they were tightly fastened into each other, placed a stout, smooth round stick into the overlapped ends, and then twisted the hide tightly against the tree, first to right and then to left. Wringing out the hide in this way is called sīnȧkwē′gȧs (pl. 22, *2*.)

The hide was next unrolled and placed on a "horse," a contrivance (ȧpȧkwī′gōn), made by resting one end of a very smooth 6-foot log on the vertex of two raised boards while the other end rested on the ground. It is essential that the log be very smooth, so as not to tear the hide. The informant now standing close to the raised end of the "horse" scraped both sides of the hide, stroking away from the body; this removed any hair, flesh, or moisture that had escaped previous treatment. This procedure she called dīcȧkwȧ'gōn (pl. 22, *3*). The scraper (gīgōkwȧ'cīgōn) made by her husband, was a 5-inch butcher-knife blade inserted lengthwise into a 19-inch piece of oak; the 7-inch extension of wood on either side of the blade formed handles. (On the Red Lake Reservation a 9-inch blade had been inserted in a 21-inch ironwood sapling, handles extending 6 inches on either side.)

After the scraping the informant stretched the hide in all directions (pl. 22, *4*). Holes about 3 inches apart were next pierced along the entire edge of the hide. A stout rope made by braiding three strands of twine was passed successively through these holes and over the top rod of the stretcher. This process continued clockwise until the hide was fastened to all four poles of the framework and tautly stretched there (pl. 23, *1*). Basswood fiber, when available, was preferred to rope.

The stretcher (sȧkȧnȧ'tīgōn) had been made by nailing two horizontal rods about 9 inches from ends of two vertical ones. The framework thus formed was 72 by 55 inches and stood 10 inches above the ground.

The hide after having been tautly stretched was scraped with a chisel-like iron implement (nēcīgȧ'gōn) 11 inches in length with one edge flattened and bent at nearly right angles to handle. The scraper thus formed was 2½ inches in width and 1½ inches deep (pl. 23, *2*). In scraping, the left hand guided the implement while the right hand exerted pressure (pl. 23, *2*). The entire surface was scraped in all directions, with strokes toward worker. This process is called cicȧkwē'ȧgē. Since the hide stretched under this treatment, the rope was adjusted from time to time to keep it taut. Of the entire tanning process this was the most laborious, the entire weight of the body having to be placed on the implement and treatment continued until the hide was dry. Humid days required less energetic work than dry ones did. In this instance—a damp day—scraping took a little longer than 3 hours. The smoothness and softness of the hide depended upon the dexterity with which the scraping was done.

After the hide was dry the informant removed it from the stretcher, laid it on the ground folding it on head-to-tail line, turned both edges over together, and beginning with head end fastened them together by means of clothespins. This made a nearly airtight compartment (pl. 23, *3*).[39] In former days edges were sewed together tightly with basswood fiber. The head end of the hide was next fastened to the branch of a tree; the tail end placed so it encircled the rim of a pail of smudge. This process was called sōwā'sīgōn. Two granddaughters, aged 8 and 11 years, who had assisted the worker by handing her

---

[39] Cf. also Densmore (1919, vol. 70, p. 117) for photographs of a Chippewa woman adjusting a deer hide in the process of smoking.

implements and cord, had prepared the smudge by placing bits of birchbark on burning embers fetched from the kitchen stove and packing the remainder of the pail with white-pine and Norway cones. Punk was sometimes used in place of cones since it was less inflammable. Jack pine cones were not used; they give an unsatisfactory color.

The worker swung the pail back and forth several times to enhance the smudge and then placed it under the hide, holding it there carefully so as to permit the hide to fill with smoke. The informant kept a watchful eye on the fire lest flames shoot up and scorch the hide. Occasionally she peeked into the hide to ascertain the color. When it was sufficiently tanned, she loosened the clothespins, turned and folded the edges and again pinned them. She then tanned the reverse side. Smoking not only gave color to hides but preserved them from moths. Smoking the hide thus is called sōwȧgīgē′ȧkwȧns.

If the hides are not sufficiently softened with one scraping, or if they are scorched in the smoking, the entire procedure—soaking in brain or egg solution, wringing out, stretching, scraping and smoking—is repeated. "When I was about 5 years old," the informant related, "I was playing around where my mother and her cousin were tanning hides. Two hides had been sewed up, hung up on poles, and were being smoked. First one shot up into the air and then the other. Both had caught fire while the women were chatting. The whole process of tanning, from soaking to smoking, had to be repeated. But when they were finished, they were like silk." Moose hides were tanned in the same manner as deer hides. Bear hides were treated only on the fleshy side. They were used for bed coverings, mattresses, and floor mats.

On the La Pointe Reservation, an informant preferred pine punk or crushed cedar bark to cones in making smudge since these are less inflammable. She also added a tablespoonful of soda to the brain solution when soaking the hide. A Red Lake informant had to supply deer brain to the woman whom she hired to tan hides. "She says she cannot tan them unless she uses brains. I must give her a head with every hide." At Red Lake, too, hides were exposed over smudges made in holes in the ground.

A Red Lake informant used a flesher made of 6 inches of moose tibia. When in use she held the knee-joint end in her right hand while with the other end, chiseled to a slanting edge and serrated, she removed the flesh with abrupt strokes. When gripped for use the palm of the hand faced the hide, and the small finger, the serrated part of the flesher. Strokes were away from the body. The implement was loosely fastened to her wrist with a band of tanned hide.

Often articles of clothing made of tanned hide were decorated with porcupine quills or beads.[40] Informants knew of only one Chippewa who was using porcupine quills at the present time. Women were seen on all reservations using beads of various colors in decorating moccasins. On all reservations, too, some individuals owned beaded buckskin suits or dresses which were worn at the annual pow-wows (pl. 11). Designs consisted of conventionalized flowers, leaves, or fruit.

On the L'Anse Reservation rabbitskins were treated by having the flesh side thoroughly soaked with wet salt, soda, and soap. Later they were gently rubbed and scraped. Great care had to be exercised since the hides were very tender. The hair was not removed.

Bed coverings and blankets worn by adults were made of rabbitskins. L'Anse informants either sewed the skins together edge to edge (furry side was then used nearest the body), or sewed together braids made of four 3-inch strands of skin extending the full length of the robe. A braided robe on the L'Anse Reservation was nearly 2 inches in thickness and in size that of an ordinary comforter for a double bed. Vermilion Chippewa neither tanned nor salted rabbitskins but merely dried them in the sun. Robes were made by looping and knotting strands of skin (cf. pp. 26–27).

Head, neck, feet, and ankles of both adults and children were often kept warm by being wrapped in rabbitskins with the fur nearest the body.

BIRCHBARK CONTAINERS AND BULRUSH MATS

Chippewa women, when gathering birchbark, tramp through the woods all day, walking miles in search of a suitable bark. Birchbark is gathered from the time the leaves of the birch have completely unfolded to the end of July, the bark being most easily removed during this time. A Lac Courte Orielle informant clutched her pocket knife in her right hand with blade extending beyond her little finger and carefully cut the outer bark (only the outer bark is removed) from a place as high as she could reach, down to the root. In removing the bark she moved clockwise around the tree, loosening it carefully with both hands so as not to break it. Removing bark from growing birch does not injure the tree. "When large pieces of bark are needed, such as are used in making canoes, trees are felled and stripped. Large birch trees are very scarce today," she noted.

The bark is either rolled or folded at the place of gathering, tied with basswood fiber, packed on the back of the gatherer, and brought

[40] Cf. Densmore (1929, pp. 35, 161, 172, 191–192; 1928, pp. 390–397) and Lyford (1943) for patterns used in beadwork. For plates showing patterns made by biting birchbark, see Densmore (1928, pls. 59–63).

home for storage.[41] Somewhere either inside or outside of homes in which aged women lived, rolls or folded packets of birchbark were seen.

Chippewa women make both leakable and nonleakable birchbark receptacles (pl. 24). In making leakable ones, such as serve for workbaskets, for storage of food, and for trays for winnowing wild rice, the birchbark is cut and the seams are sewed with basswood fiber.

Three sewing baskets were collected on the Red Lake Reservation. One measured 9 by 8½ inches at the opening and 3½ inches in depth (pl. 24, *3 a*). Two circular ones were each 5½ inches in depth. One measured 10 inches in diameter at the opening and 7 inches at the bottom; the other, 7 inches at the opening and 6 inches at the bottom.

Mākōk', trapezoidal-shaped containers (pl. 24, *3 b*), were used for storing maple sugar and wild rice, and as buckets when carrying berries long distances. Small ones were tied to the belt of the picker while picking. The handles of buckets were usually made of wood or of basswood fiber. Three that were being used for storing maple sugar were collected on the Red Lake Reservation. The depth of one was 10½ inches; the opening, 11 by 5½ inches; the base, 13 by 8½ (pl. 24, *3 b*). Another measured 5½ inches in depth, 7 by 5 inches at the opening, and 8½ by 5 inches at the base. A smaller one—one filled with maple sugar (weight 1¼ pounds)—was 3 inches deep and 4½ by 3½ inches at the base. A berry-picking bucket collected on the Lac Courte Orielle Reservation was 7 by 6½ inches and 3 inches deep.

A tray used in winnowing wild rice on the Vermilion Reservation measured 20 by 14 inches across the opening, 17 by 12 inches at the base and 6 inches in depth (pl. 24, *1*). One collected on the Red Lake Reservation was 17 by 12 across the opening and 3 inches deep (pl. 24, *3 c*). One used on the Lac Courte Orielle Reservation was 24 by 16 at the opening and 6 inches in depth.

Bark used for nonleakable containers is folded, never cut. Before present-day dishes were available, nonleakable receptacles had many uses; today they are used almost exclusively for gathering maple sap, some women making several hundred for this purpose during winter months. Sizes vary; average-size ones are approximately 18 inches in length and 9 in width. One found in a maple grove on the Red Lake Reservation is 10 by 13 inches and 5 inches deep (pl. 24, *2*, one at right).

A Red Lake informant made a nonleakable dish by cutting a piece of birchbark in rectangular shape—the size for dishes used in serving soups or liquids. She quickly passed both sides of one end several

---

[41] Cf. Densmore (1919, vol. 70, pp. 114–118) for photographs on collecting and packing birchbark.

times over a small fire on the ground (pl. 25, *1*) and promptly folded that end into two folds slightly overlapping. (The bark can be variously bent once heated.) She pierced the folds and side simultaneously with an iron awl and tied them together with basswood fiber (pl. 25, *2*). (Formerly awls were made of bone of moose or some other large animal.) She moistened the fiber with saliva by passing it back and forth between her lips several times. This made it more flexible. Next she rolled it between first finger and thumb, dried it over the fire, and passed it through the hole made by the awl. After this she heated the opposite end of the bark, folded it, and tied it in the same way (pl. 25, *3*). When completed the dish was 5 by 4½ inches and 2 inches deep (pl. 25, *4*).

A Red Lake informant not wishing to pass up some ripe chokecherries on her way home through the woods one day made a similar receptacle using a thorn of the thornapple tree as an awl.

Basswood fiber (wīgōb') is made by removing the inner bark of the basswood tree, tearing it into long strips while wet, folding these into small bundles about the length of the hand, boiling and then drying them. Dried fibers can be pulled apart into various widths—widths depending upon the use for which they are intended. Strands of the same width are tied into small bundles and stored for future use. The bark is gathered in June and July since it is most easily removed then.[42]

Basswood fiber was being used, during the period of research covered in this study, in sewing birchbark receptacles, in tying together poles of tripods or racks used in cooking, in tying floaters and sinkers to fish nets, and for tying purposes in general. One informant, in preparing warp used in making rush mats, drew two strands of the fiber between her lips to dampen them, and then with the palm of her hand rolled these over the bare shin of her right leg (pl. 19). One woman who had shins crusted from the friction of the fiber, used the thigh for rolling. Formerly basswood fiber was also used in making traps and fish nets.

Cracks in birchbark receptacles today are mended as formerly with heated resin. Resin that has oozed for a year in gashes made in spruce trees is gathered, whittled, placed in bags loosely woven of fine strands of basswood fiber, and boiled in water (pl. 13, *1*). As the heated resin comes to the top it is instantly removed—long boiling makes it brittle—poured into birchbark dishes, and stored for future use. Women usually have a supply on hand. The basswood-fiber bag serves as a sieve, retaining bark and dirt.

---

[42] Cf. also Jones (1936, vol. 22, pp. 1–14) for preparation and uses of basswood fiber by the Chippewa and other Indians of the Great Lakes region; and (1935, vol. 21, pp. 21–31) for uses of sweetgrass in handicrafts and as perfume and incense.

Mākōk′ and work baskets were sometimes decorated with designs. An informant, after drawing the outline of a spray of maple leaves on the birchbark of her mākōk′ soaked the mākōk′ in water for more than a day after which she scraped off the top layer of all the bark except the leaves. On drying, the leaves were given prominence because of their darker hue (pl. 24, *3 b*).

Porcupine quills, used in decorating birchbark and deer hides, were removed from the animal, while it was still warm, with the aid of a butcher knife. A La Pointe informant dyed quills by soaking them in a decoction made by boiling alder bark or the roots of the "owl root" (kōkōkō djībīk′). A L'Anse woman soaked hers in a decoction made by boiling mud from Copper River.

Bulrush mats were used as floor mats, the family squatting on them indoors and outdoors, especially when the ground was damp; as "tables" on which meals were served; and as coverings for wigwams (pl. 26, *1*).

Women both gathered the material and made the bulrush mats (nākōn) (cf. also Kinietz and Jones, 1942, vol. 27, pp. 525–527, pls. 1–3). Although bulrushes growing near the edge of any lake or river were usable, the ones in small lakes were choicest since they were least brittle. Those grown in rivers were not used because of their shortness, unless lake-grown ones were not available. Today, as in days past, rushes are pulled up by the roots or cut with a knife, tied in bundles, boiled until the green color has disappeared, and spread out in the sun to bleach. Bleaching continues during the sunny hours of 6 or 7 days, the rushes being turned several times each day in order to give sun exposure to all sides. They are taken in at sunset before the dew falls—dew causes them to turn yellow while in the process of bleaching. Weaving, however, is done in the morning while the dew is still on the mat; dry reeds break easily. Should any reeds become dry, the weaver squirts mouthfuls of water on them, thus keeping them pliable.

Mats used as "tables" or for squatting on were often woven in colored designs—designs "planned in the head of the weaver." On the La Pointe Reservation reeds were dyed yellow by being boiled either in a substance (probably a mineral) found in a certain creek or in decoctions of finely chopped bark and twigs of hazelnut and sumach. Red color was procured by boiling them in decoctions of roots of either the bloodroot, the "owl-plant" root (kōkōkō djībīk′), or the inner and outer bark of the wādō′pe. Hemlock bark produced a purple dye; bark of the alder tree, mahogany; black muck found in certain ponds, a black color.

On the L'Anse Reservation red dye was made by boiling either roots of a red fungus found on decayed wood or earth found in the

Copper River or bark of alder and hemlock—"the more the bark was boiled the redder the color became." Red, green, and blue streaks found in decayed roots of the maple tree made corresponding colors when boiled. One informant swished bulrush reeds in ashes of the outer bark of the poplar tree thereby making them "pitch black."

On the Lac Courte Orielle Reservation, informants had boiled root of bloodroot for a brown-orange color and bark of butternut for black. L'Anse informants had not used either of these, nor sumach. Red Lake informants had boiled black muck for black, roots of blood-root for red, and bark of alder for mahogany.[43] Some informants boiled reeds in decoctions; others soaked them over night. Boiling, said some, made them too soft. Reeds formed the woof in weaving; basswood twine, the warp (cf. also Densmore, 1929, pp. 154–161).

Mats placed around the interior of wigwams to keep drafts from blowing in were made of cattails (ápōkwā′yōk) or of cedar bark. Both bulrush and cattail mats were being made on the Mille Lacs Reservation in 1940.

DWELLINGS

The principal types of dwellings of the Chippewa were the wig-wam, the bark house, the peaked lodge, and occasionally the tipi. The framework of all types consisted of saplings, and the cover of either bark alone or of bark and rush mats (cf. also Bushnell, 1919 a, pp. 609–618).

A wigwam was constructed by driving saplings, usually peeled ironwood, securely into the ground in either a circle or in an elipse. Opposite poles were brought together in arches, overlapped, and tied with green basswood fiber (pl. 28, 2). In some instances the sides were covered with bulrush mats and the top with birchbark (pl. 26, 1; 27, 2); in others, the framework was entirely covered with bark (pl. 26, 2). Coverings at times were held in position by being over-laid with cords of basswood fiber, the ends of which were weighted with stones or pieces of wood (pls. 26, 1; 28, 4). Sometimes poles were leaned against the sides of the wigwam (pl. 27, 1). Women carried the rush mats and birchbark coverings on their backs from camp to camp as the family followed its seasonal occupation. Frame-works were left in the localities and used successive years. If bark other than that of the birch was used, the entire wigwam was left intact from season to season (pl. 26, 2).

A hide was used to cover the entrance. The upper end was fas-tened to the wigwam while the ground end was weighted horizontally with a stick or pole. (Today cloth has replaced the hide.) If the wind blew so strongly through the usual entrance, it was closed by

---

[43] For plants used as dyes, see also Densmore (1928, pp. 369–374) and Huron Smith (1932, vol. 4, pp. 424–426).

placing a pile of stones on the lower end of the hide; an opening was then made by separating the bulrush mats in the opposite side of the wigwam.

Circular wigwams housed only one family; elongated ones, one or several. An informant remembered that when a child his family occupied a wigwam with three other families, each family having a separate fireplace and tripod.

In the building of a wigwam the women selected, cut, and peeled the poles, pulled the bulrushes and made the mats, collected birchbark and sewed it together, and placed the coverings over the framework. The man drove the poles into the ground, bent them, and held them in arched position until the women had tied them.

Because of the difficulty in certain localities of finding large birch from which wide strips of bark can be removed, the bark of the elm, tamarack, Norway pine, and ash are used as substitutes. One also finds these barks used as substitute for bulrush mats. Consequently coverings for wigwams may be entirely of bark.

Wigwams or frameworks were seen on all reservations except L'Anse, either in sugar bushes, on shores of lakes producing wild rice, in blueberry patches, or near Mīdē'wiwin lodges. The framework of seven circular wigwams occupied during the Mīdē'wiwin celebration were seen near the Mīdē' lodge on the Lac Courte Orielle Reservation (1935). One was 14 feet in diameter and 6½ feet in height; its entrance was 4 feet 11 inches high and 2 feet wide. The keepers of the drum, a medicine man and his wife, occupied an elongated one nearby, covered with bulrush mats and birchbark. Plate 26, 1, shows seams between pieces of birchbark, and poles sewed to the edges to prevent tearing. When camp moved, the bark was rolled on these poles and packed on backs of women.

A wigwam (pl. 28, 4) used as an all-year-round dwelling on the Mille Lacs Reservation was 18 feet long, 17 feet wide, and 7 feet high. The framework consisted of 9 saplings extending lengthwise, 11 crosswise and 6 encircling ones. All were tied at points of junction with basswood fiber. Strips of bark of the black ash, each about 5½ feet in width, were tied to the outside lower frame; the upper ends were neatly trimmed off in zigzag edges. Sheets of birchbark about 10 feet long and 4 feet wide, made by sewing together pieces of the bark and ending them off with strips of cedar wood, were laid across the top for roofing. All coverings were held in position by being weighted down with strands of basswood fiber, to ends of which, on opposite sides of the wigwam, trunks of young trees were tied. Stones rested in several places along the trunks, adding further weight to the strands. The entrance was 30 by 69 inches.

A mother and her two daughters had erected a wigwam (pl. 28, 1) to be used as a dwelling for the summer months of 1940 near a well-traveled road (Mille Lacs Reservation). They were selling birchbark articles to tourists. The length of the wigwam was 12 feet; the width, 11 feet; the height, 5½ feet. Five saplings placed lengthwise and seven placed crosswise formed the framework. Poles were tied together with basswood fiber at points of meeting. Cattail mats, 49 inches in width, had been placed about the entire outside lower section; pressboard and tar paper covered the top. (The cattail mats had been made in the fall of 1939.) All was weighted down with poles tied to the ends of a network of basswood fiber, nine strands running lengthwise and eight crosswise. The entrance was 24 by 63 inches.

A wigwam and a tipi were erected by a 45-year-old woman, her daughter, and another woman at Mille Lacs Indian Trading Post in June 1940 (pls. 28, *3;* 29, *1, 2*). The wigwam was 12 feet long, 11 feet wide, and 6 feet high. The framework consisted of 4 saplings extending lengthwise, 4 crosswise, and 4 encircling ones. Cattail mats, 50 inches wide, covered the sides; sheets of birchbark sewed together, the roof.

The following account records additional information regarding wigwams:

Several wigwams of the more recent type were found in blueberry patches on the Red Lake Reservation in 1932. The lower section of the walls of one of these, the part traditionally covered with bulrush mats, was covered with the bark of black ash. The upper section of the walls and the roof, the sections formerly covered with birch bark, were covered with the barks of Norway pine and black ash; the top and upper sides were covered with only the bark of Norway pine. The lower bark was tied to the framework with basswood fiber, while the roof was kept in place by being weighted down with a network of twine ropes at the end of which, about six feet from the ground, poles were fastened as weights. This particular wigwam was twelve feet in diameter and eight feet in height. Another wigwam in the same blueberry patch, an elongated one, was sixteen feet long, twelve feet wide, and eight feet high. Its lower walls were of bark of black ash; the top and upper sides were of birch bark. Each wigwam had an entrance about three feet wide and six feet high. None of the wigwams had smoke holes, cooking undoubtedly having been done out-of-doors over open fires, for tripods, cinders, and flat stones—the latter used in shutting off the wind—were in evidence nearby. In the interior were platforms of lumber, elevated about a foot from the ground, which served as beds.

Mrs. Peter Everywind of Red Lake was using a wigwam for a storage house in 1932. She herself had built it. The walls were of bark of the black ash, and the roof, of that of the cedar tree. The interior upper ends had been prettily cut in zigzag pattern. "I wanted it to look nice on the inside," she said. "I built it well in every way, and I haven't had to repair it since I built it, way back in 1922."

Wigwams were seen on the White Earth Reservation in the summer of 1938 . . . Two families were occupying one as a dwelling during the spring Midē wiwin at Ponsford. Its framework, twelve by sixteen by six feet in height, was of ironwood saplings and the roof was of birch bark. The traditional bulrush mats, however, had been replaced by old blankets and pieces of calico. Eight poles laid against the outside weighted down the bark. From the center of the roof a stovepipe protruded, and an old blanket served as a door.

Skeletal frameworks of four other wigwams were found near homes. Three of these were in the wild-rice area near Rice Lake and were used by relatives of the owners during the wild-rice season. It was interesting to note that all three, although entirely exposed to the weather, were used as storage places during the summer. Two were nearly filled with birch-bark rolls and with implements used in wild rice gathering and maple sugar-making; the third contained wash tubs and firewood.

A fourth one, seen in the Ponsford area, was in the process of construction. A 30-year-old woman noted that she had completed the framework and had the birch-bark rolls for the roofing ready, but that she lacked the bulrush mats. Her mother, fifty-two years of age, had in mind to make these. The wigwam was for her aged grandparents, a grandfather probably one hundred years old and a grandmother nearly that. They had complained so many times that they were uncomfortable in their tar-paper shack. It was hot in summer and cold and full of bedbugs in winter. And she added, "The old man says before the Whites came, the Chippewa had no bedbugs nor smallpox nor tuberculosis!" It is interesting to note that Chippewa who were constructing, occupying, or owning wigwams in the summers of 1932, 1933, 1935, and 1938 were members of the Midē wiwin.

Although bark wigwams were found on all Chippewa reservations visited, few were intended for all-year-round dwellings. If found near homes, they were used for sleeping purposes during the summer months, or possibly as storage places. Those found scattered in berry patches, in sugar bushes, along lakeshores where wild rice is gathered, and in places where the Midē wiwin is held, were occupied only seasonally.[44]

The bark lodge used by the Chippewa gave the appearance of a one-room, low, gable-roof cottage. The entire framework consisted of saplings of ironwood or elm. The coverings of walls and roof were bark of the birch, cedar, Norway pine, elm, or tamarack. A 96-year-old White Earth man recalled that previous to sawmill days, nearly all the Indians in their vicinity lived in bark houses. The framework of several was seen in wild-rice camps on the same reservation in 1938. An old Lac Courte Orielle informant as a child lived in an elm bark house with a gabled roof at Jump River near Chippewa Falls, Wis.

The peaked lodge consisted of poles so planted as to form two sloping sides, giving the appearance of a high-pitched gabled roof squatting on the ground. The ends of the poles used for forming the sides were held in place by being tied to a horizontal pole at the ridge. Any of the barks used in constructing wigwams served as coverings for the sides. Each end served as an entrance; the crossing of the poles provided space for the emission of smoke. Such a lodge usually accommodated three or four families. The only peaked lodge that came to the writer's notice or was known to her informants

---

[44] Hilger, (1939, pp. 45–47). The construction of all wigwams seen by the writer conformed closely to Densmore's description (1929, pp. 22–26).

to exist on any reservation was one in which the Mīdē'wiwin ceremonial was being held on the Nett Lake Reservation in August 1939.

A tipi consisted of a conical-shaped framework of saplings covered
with overlapping layers of birchbark. The bark was held in position by being tied to the saplings with basswood fiber and weighted
down with leaning poles (pl. 29). Jenness found Parry Islanders
had "no recollection of the earlier use of dome-shaped wigwams covered with birchbark or rushes" but they remembered the peaked lodge
"with A-shaped ends and ridgepole," and the conical or tipi form
(Jenness, 1935, p. 112). A Red Lake informant remarked: "Every
Chippewa woman had to learn to build a wigwam in the old days;
it was part of the training her mother gave her. None, however,
knew how to build a tipi except those that lived near the Sioux."

Canvas-covered tipis were seen on several reservations and were
being used for storage or for sleeping purposes. Originally they had
been used in pow-wow demonstrations (Indian dances given for commercial purposes).

FUEL, FIREPLACES, AND LIGHTING

Wood was the only fuel used by the Chippewa of the early days.
It was gathered by women as needed, usually every day, and packed
on their backs in carrying straps (pl. 29, *3*, *4*).

Gilfillan (1901, vol. 9, p. 77) noted his observations:

Every day one can see, about four o'clock in the afternoon, long strings of
women, each with her ax and packing strap, going out into the woods perhaps a
mile; soon the woods are vocal with the axes; and then equally long strings
of women are seen issuing from the woods, each with her load upon her back,
and each woman packs an immense quantity. This is thrown down at the door
of the house, and brought in as needed.

A carrying strap (à'pīkȧn) used by a Red Lake informant in 1932
(pl. 29, *4*) was 16 feet long and 1½ inches wide. It had been made
by sewing two pieces of tough tanned moose hide to the ends of a
delicately tanned piece of deer hide. The moose-hide ends were used
in strapping wood; the deer hide rested across the forehead. The
forehead side had not been tanned but only closely cropped of hair
in order to leave a soft finish. The informant laid the strap on the
ground in two equal parallel lengths, about 1 foot apart, and piled
pieces of wood upon the straps some distance from the ends. She
then laid the first two fingers of her left hand (pointing toward headband) upon one strap, between wood and headband and parallel with
it, and brought the end of the strap over the wood, passed it three
times around the fingers and under the strap, withdrew her fingers,
slipped the end toward headband through the space left by the re-

moval of her fingers in such a manner as to make a half bow. She proceeded to tie the other strap in the same way. Remaining in a kneeling position, she placed the headband on her forehead, reached backward around left side with both hands, and moved the pack onto her back.

Another informant on the same reservation who had a similar strap, demonstrated its use in a similar manner and tied the bow in exactly the same way (pl. 29, *3*). "Many a stick of wood I cut and carried strapped on my back," she remarked.

Although any wood could be used for fuel, alder wood was preferred since it threw off neither sparks nor smoke.

In the old, old days, [said a Red Lake informant] an Indian chief wanted his son to marry. No one knew who the girl would be. Since many girls wanted to marry the young chief, the old chief said that she who brought the best firewood could marry him. An old woman dressed her granddaughter, whom she had adopted when a little girl, in her Indian best, combed her hair like they did in the old days, painted her face, and said to her, "Now, daughter, go and cut a bundle of dry alders, pack it to the chief's door and drop it there." Well, all the girls brought their wood; but the lucky one was the one who brought the alder.

On the La Pointe Reservation an informant made fire by striking a piece of flint held between thumb and first finger, along with some punk, with a piece of tin; the sparks falling on the punk, lit it. Some informants wrapped the flint nearly completely in punk; some used two flints and no tin.

A Lac Courte Orielle informant made fire by rotating the end of a 10-inch stick in a circular groove made in a piece of wood. The groove was ¾ of an inch in diameter and ½ inch deep; the piece of wood, 14½ inches in length. The stick rotated by being slid back and forth either between the palms of the hand like a hand drill or on a 29-inch string of a bow like a pump drill; in the latter case the left hand held the stick which had been looped into the cord of the bow, while the right moved the bow backward and forward.

Open fireplaces were used for heating and lighting wigwams and for cooking. Types were tripods and racks. Both were used in the open, but only the tripod in the wigwam (pl. 30, *1*, *2*). If two families occupied the same wigwam, two tripods were found on the center line of the wigwam, one for each family. A tripod on the Red Lake Reservation was made by resting two Juneberry saplings in the crotch of a third; all were tied together with basswood fiber. "This is made exactly like my grandmother taught me to make it," said the 70-year-old demonstrator. She then made a hanger for a kettle by chopping a small branch off an alder tree in such a way that a slice of the trunk remained on it. The trunk end, after being trimmed, served as a crotch and was placed over the junction of the tripod. The other end was notched so as to hold the handle of the kettle. A hanger could also have been made by removing all pulp but not the bark from one end of the branch and tying the branch to the junction of the tripod with the bark; the crotched end in this instance would have been used for the kettle.

Racks or elongated fireplaces served both for cooking and for drying fish or meat (p. 148). When en route or when moving, camp kettles were sometimes hung over a fire from ends of sticks that had been securely fastened into the ground at an angle in such a way as to hold the kettle over the fire. At times fish and pieces of meat were broiled at the end of sticks similarly placed.

Wigwams were also heated and lighted in the early days by means of fire located in a shallow pit in the center of the wigwam; the pit was usually encircled with stones to prevent persons from stepping into it. No light was needed in the summer months, ordinarily, for the end of dusk was bedtime; during the winter months, however, evenings were spent in visiting or storytelling for entertainment and instruction.

The fireplace in the wigwam usually gave sufficient light for ordinary work. If a woman, however, needed additional light, she stuck a piece of tightly twisted birchbark into the sliced end of a piece of wood, and set this upright in the ground. If light was needed for a short duration outside the wigwam, a lighted piece of birchbark served as torch. A cornucopia of bark filled with resin and bits of birchbark served for longer periods, such as might be required to fetch one skilled in herbs to the bedside of a sick person (Hilger, 1939, p. 150).

L'Anse and Lac Courte Orielle informants recalled seeing their homes lit by means of oil and wicks.[45] "I often saw my mother roll cord over her leg and later curl it into a dish of bear grease, or any grease. She lighted one end and let it rest on the edge of the dish," said a Lac Courte Orielle informant. His friend remarked: "My mother pulled rags through the four holes of an ordinary button, twisted the ends together and wound a string tightly around them. This made a wick which she placed into a dish of bear grease and lit." On the L'Anse Reservation oil of any fish, preferably whitefish, served as oil for lamps. Whitefish oil never froze; deer tallow did, when the weather became very cold. "Chumbs," the fatty substance found in the interior of whitefish, was boiled in water and skimmed off. Braided pieces of cotton cloth also served as wicks. One informant had placed a button on a piece of cloth, brought ends together, tied them close above the button, and then twisted the ends

---

[45] The writer believes this to have been an intrusion of European origin.

between the fingers: the weight and size of the button gave equilibrium to the wick.

La Pointe informants had not used lamps made of grease or oil and wicks: "When old Indians wanted light, they built a fire; or the fire in the wigwam served as a lamp."

GARDENING

Gardening of the traditional type, small cultivated plots of ground scattered haphazardly among tall grass or in open spaces in the woods, was seen on most reservations. In the early days garden plots were found near all winter camps. The winter camps, the permanent camps, were usually located in maple tree groves. In the spring the grass on the plots was burnt and the ground was worked with sticks. Corn, squash, pumpkins, and beans were planted and cared for until the families moved into the berry patches. After the wild rice had been harvested in the fall, families returned home and gathered their garden products.

Today traditional vegetables and many others can be seen in Chippewa gardens. A Lac du Flambeau informant had three good-sized gardens: she herself had prepared two, and a third had been prepared by her nephew's wife. The farmer of the United States Indian Service had furnished seeds of squash, beans, radishes, onions, rutabaga, lettuce, artichoke, tomatoes, carrots, and peas. The informant had also cleared grass and weeds off three small patches, about 2 by 3 feet each, leaving the grass about the patch intact, however. "This is the old way," she remarked; "the grass keeps off the sun, retains the moisture, and helps prevent early freezing." In one she had planted squash, in another lettuce, and in a third radishes.

FOOD: PREPARATION AND STORAGE [46]

Meat, fish, and fowl formed the chief sustenance of the Chippewa. These were boiled with cultivated vegetables, such as beans, corn, squash, and pumpkin, and with native ones, such as wild rice, wild potatoes, and tips of certain plants. Berries of many varieties were eaten both fresh and dried. Acorns, too, were used as food. Maple sap, refined to sugar, was used for sweetening purposes and was also eaten pure. Squash and pumpkin were baked on coals for immediate use; for winter use, the rind was removed and the pulp cut in one continuous strip and hung in the sun to dry. Dried squash and pumpkin were boiled with meat. Beans were collected from the pods in the fall and stored in birchbark containers. They were either boiled with meat alone, or with meat and corn.

---

[46] For uses of plants as food, see also Densmore (1928, pp. 306–322); Huron Smith 1932); Gilmore (1933).

Corn prepared for storage was boiled in the shucks when not quite ripe, cooled, shucks turned back and braided, and then hung up to dry (pl. 1, *1*). If treated in this manner, kernels retained their sweet taste and remained on the cobs. Several informants did not boil the corn, but removed it from stocks before it was completely dried. When in this condition shucks could also be braided. Braids of corn, about 4 feet in length, were seen hanging in kitchens or on outside walls of houses on several reservations.

Dried corn was ground in mortar with pestle, motion being a stir‑ring rather than a pounding one. A L'Anse informant rubbed corn against the walls of a stone that had been grooved by water action with a rock held so that the larger part protruded beyond the little finger. One informant had seen a mortar made by chipping and smoothing a large rock until it was bowl-shaped. Two Red Lake informants were using a section of a trunk of a tree that had been hollowed out, leaving both ends closed, however. One was 24 inches long with a trough 13 inches in length and 4 inches in depth; the other was 12 inches long, 5 inches wide, and 4 inches deep. A pestle used with the former was a continuous piece of wood shaped so as to have a handle. It weighed 1 pound 5 ounces. When mortars were being used, they were placed on buckskin so that no meal would be lost.

Formerly corn meal was used primarily for thickening soup; some informants had mixed it with water and fried it in tallow of buffalo or bear. Today it is used in soups, fried, and baked as corn bread.

Many Chippewa bake "Indian bread" by mixing wheat flour with baking powder, water, and salt, and frying it in lard. An informant squatted near her outdoor fireplace, stretched dough with both hands, poked a hole in the center with her finger, and dropped it into hot lard in a frying pan which rested on the coals (pl. 30, *1*). When the bread was well browned on one side, she flipped the pan, thereby turning the dough, and browned the other side also. She then removed it to a plate, spread fresh blueberries upon it, and served it to a grandchild.

Acorns of white oak—red oak are too bitter—were boiled in hulls, cooled, hulled, and dried in the sun. When needed they were crushed or pounded to meal, boiled with meat, and served as thick soup.

Informants and interpreters on all reservations were sun-drying blueberries, Juneberries, and chokecherries on pieces of birchbark, on roofs, or on pieces of cloth. After 2 or 3 days' drying they were stored and later cooked with wild rice and venison. Wādō'pē ("a root found between Flambeau and Hurley, Wis."), and Indian turnips, both braided by means of their leafy growth, were also dried for storage and cooked with meat when desired.

Lac Courte Orielle Indians (June 1935) were gathering milkweed shoots (4 inches or less tall) and tips of ferns, which when boiled and flavored with grease of any kind were served as vegetables. Pumpkin blossoms gathered later in the season were also boiled with meat and made "delicious soup."

A beverage served with meals was made by boiling in water either raspberry twigs and leaves, wintergreen, or "something that grows in swamps"; these had no medicinal value.

No family neglected to put in its supply of maple sugar in the early days. When the sap began to rise, groups of families moved into maple groves—unless the winter camp was located in one, which was not unusual. The time for tapping trees varied with the years and the localities; sap flow might be affected by an early spring, by nearness to Lake Superior, or by latitude. Informants were certain that at the present time tapping is never begun before March 25. The season ends by April 30.

Maple groves were not claimed by any particular family, but it was well understood that no one tapped trees that were customarily tapped each season by the same family. Should a family neglect to tap its trees for a season, another family might then do so the following season, making certain, however, that the first family did not intend to do so. Often, too, a family, knowing that it was unable to tap trees because of sickness or taboos related to death, invited another to tap its trees. Wigwams were erected in sugar bushes, each family usually having three—one for a family dwelling, one for making sugar (this one might be shared), and one for storage of utensils. Frameworks were permanent and at times coverings also (p. 138).

Maple trees were tapped; sap was collected, boiled, evaporated, and refined. (Cf. also Densmore, 1928, pp. 308–313; Winchell, 1911, p. 595; Warren, 1885, vol. 5, pp. 186, 263; Gilfillan, 1901, vol. 9, pp. 70–71; and Chamberlain, 1891, vol. 4, pp. 381–384.) "The sap must be closely watched while boiling," said a White Earth sugar maker. "Just as soon as it begins to make eyes, it is taken off the fire and worked with a small paddle that looks like a canoe paddle. When we were children we used to watch for this stage in the boiling, beg for a little sap on a piece of birchbark, drop it into the snow—if there was still snow on the ground—and let it turn to gum." An old Vermilion woman followed the custom of placing a little pinch of tobacco in the fire before eating the first maple sugar: "I do the same before eating the first wild rice or the first fish in spring. I ask Manito to grant success on all we do." After all families in a group had completed the first boiling of the sap, a feast was held in which all participated; maple sugar formed the chief food.

When I was still a child, our family moved into the woods every spring in order to make maple sugar [remarked a Lac Courte Orielle woman]. "Here we lived in wigwams. The first year we lived on this reservation, I was about 10 years old then, we tapped 800 trees. When the season was ended, we had 10 mākŏk' of maple sugar so heavy that I was not able to carry even the smallest one. They varied in size; the largest one was about 3 feet high and a foot in diameter. The sirup never fermented in these birchbark containers, and tasted good in the following spring. Some people made taffy (bȧgŏŏ'cĭgŏns) for children from maple sirup. It tasted very good. One seldom sees it today.

Wild rice, one of the staple foods of the early Chippewa, was gathered by the women in late August or early September just before it matured.[47] If gathered when ripe much is lost, for it drops readily then. As the season approached, families migrated in groups to lakes and streams producing it. It grows in mud bottoms short distances from shores of lakes or slow-moving streams.

Wild rice is an annual plant, growing from seed each year. If not destructively gathered by man or wild fowl or, as has been recently done, completely drowned out by backwaters of dams, it is perpetual once established in favorable environment.

Patches of wild rice were considered common property in the early days, but it was the custom for families to return to the same growth year after year, and others respected their rights to gather it. If families planted wild rice, which was done occasionally, others ceded their exclusive rights to it. An interpreter's mother on the La Pointe Reservation sowed wild rice every fall shortly after gathering it. It was sowed in rather shallow water. "No one has ever gone to gather rice there," she remarked. "Such patches have always been claimed by the people who sowed them, and by their descendants." A Lac Courte Orielle man remarked: "Sections of wild rice on this reservation are claimed by some because their fathers and grandfathers planted them." "At the present time (1935) on this reservation (Lac du Flambeau) people scatter rice on lake shores a few days after they have gathered it but lay no claim of ownership to these patches. They sow the rice so that Chippewa in the future—maybe relatives—will have wild rice. It must be sowed in shallow muddy water, in either spring-fed or running water like at the outlet of a lake."

The kernels of wild rice grow at the tip of a stem that at times is 15 to 20 feet long. The color is dark slate; the shape, cylindrical. Kernels differ in size and taste with localities. A Lac Courte Orielle informant gathered her rice in Aitkin County, Minn., in the fall of 1934 "for kernels there are small and better tasting than the ones around here." Kernels on the La Pointe Reservation "are finer than the ones at Red Lake."

In the middle of summer women tie the rice into bunches. When

---

[47] For detailed description of wild rice gathering, see Winchell (1911, pp. 592–594); Densmore (1928, pp. 313–317); Jenks (1900 b, pp. 1013–1137); Skinner (1921 b, pp. 101–102, 142–152); Hilger (1939, pp. 186–187); Tyrrell (1916, p. 275); and Carlson (1934, pp. 16–23, and Chambliss, 1940).

collecting it bunches are held over a canoe or boat and knocked with a paddlelike stick causing the kernels to drop.

In the early days rice was either dried on birchbark in the sun or on flat rocks heated over slow fire. After contact with Europeans it was parched in kettles, husks loosened by being pounded, and then winnowed in the wind.[48] (Cf. winnowing trays, nōckánīcīgōn, pl. 24, *1, 3 c.*) It was then stored in bags made by women of cedarbark. "Parched wild rice was cooked like Chinese rice is today with strips of meat, or boiled in soups." Children often popped it on hot stones.

The meat of deer, moose, bear, and buffalo (buffalo by those living near the prairie areas) was eaten both fresh or dried and smoked. Fresh meat was cooked with either green vegetables, dried berries, dried chokecherries, or wild rice. Meat that was not needed for immediate use was cut into strips "as thick as my thumb" and dried over a slow fire on racks or tripods used for cooking, on slanting sticks stuck into the ground, or, if a large amount was on hand, on specially erected frames (pl. *31, 1, 2*). In old days racks were sometimes 30 feet long, 3 feet wide, and 3 feet high. On the White Earth Reservation (1938) a 32-year-old informant was drying venison on a rack made by resting the corners of a lattice framework, made of split branches, in the crotches of four saplings; it stood about 2 feet from the ground. "Any green wood may be used in making the frame," she remarked; "but green wood is best because it resists the heat and will not catch fire."

Fish of various kinds were also eaten fresh; but only pike, crappies, and whitefish were smoked. Fish were split down the back, the framework of bones and entrails removed, and with belly up were placed astride on rods over a slow fire. Heads were not severed. Another way, but one in which fish needed turning, was to rest them sidewise on racks over fire—in more recent times on screens. Racks were similar to the one used by the White Earth informant, referred to above, in drying venison. On the Red Lake Reservation a piece of window screening (4 by 4 feet) rested on boxes about 1 foot above the ground. Underneath it, in a pit about one-half foot deep, a slow fire was maintained. An interpreter had smoked all the crappies she could obtain during the summer (1933) on window screening over an aspen fire. The last ones of those she stored were eaten at Christmas time.

Oak, ash, maple, or any hardwood was used for smoking purposes. These gave both meat and fish a good taste and a "nice brown color." Jack pine was not used; it left a "dirty color." Smoking fish for 8 hours over a slow fire dried and smoked them sufficiently for storage.

---

[48] Cf. Densmore (1919, vol. 70, p. 96) for photographs of poling boat through rice field and of parching wild rice.

The meat of the wolf was not eaten. That of the turtle was eaten only by men, never by women. Porcupines, skunks, rabbits, ducks, geese, and pigeons were all eaten fresh. After the quills had been removed from the back of a porcupine, "it was cleaned like a chicken: boiling water poured over it, the shorter quills plucked, and the hair singed." The meat of pups was eaten in very early days. Although many informants had heard this repeatedly and must have eaten it at the Mīdē′wiwin feast, they seemed to revolt at the idea.

Turtle eggs were considered a delicacy, and were eaten in season; no way of preserving them was known. They were boiled for 20 minutes, cooled, the shell punctured with a finger, and contents sucked. An old Lac Courte Orielle informant and several of her aged friends had walked nearly 5 miles (1935) to find a sandy lake shore, "the place where the turtles lay their eggs." Upon arrival they searched around in the sand "for little raised places, little bumps," into which they poked sticks. By the sensation, "the place will feel soft", they were able to tell whether or not eggs were present. (They found a nest with sixty.) This method of searching was necessary because of a recent rain. "It's easy to find them before a rain for one can follow the turtle's trail then; the dragging of his tail makes a line which invariably passes between his four steps. The time for hunting turtle eggs is when the first wild roses are in full bloom."

Food supplies that were not needed during a season were usually stored in caches (ásăn′sīgōwin) built near the home wigwams. Stored food might be braided corn; maple sugar and dried berries in birchbark containers; wild rice in cedar-bark bags; dried meat or fish wrapped in birchbark; and dried vegetables. "In former days our Indians dug pits after the rice season and stored in them their rice and corn and vegetables from their gardens," said a Lac Courte Orielle woman. "Then everyone went down the Yellow River to Chippewa Falls, Wis., in canoes in order to hunt. Meat was dried and smoked there, and hides were tanned; moccasins and snowshoes were made, and then all returned home."

The writer witnessed the opening of a cache by an 82-year-old Red Lake informant on August 1, 1933. An Indian wished to buy some potatoes from the informant's garden. Since these were not yet fullgrown, she was willing to sell him some stored ones. She proceeded to a grove of maple trees nearby and from a place in it removed some saplings which she had felled and placed there the previous fall. She next removed several armfuls of cornstalks and then some dead leaves. "All of this," she remarked, "was needed to 'fool' the deer! Deer won't walk on dead trees for their feet catch in them. Without these trees they could have found the cache by the feel of their feet. Any soft spot raises their suspicions." She next removed hay to about the depth of a foot, lifted out several rutabagas, and finally good-sized fine healthy-looking potatoes. The cache, 6 feet deep and nearly 3 feet square, was lined with hay to about the depth of 8 inches. "I had three of these filled with vegetables from my gardens last fall." In a new cache she was at that time storing Mason fruit jars of canned blueberries and gooseberries of the summer's growth. Each jar was so placed that it could be surrounded with hay. "I have stored my canned things that way ever since we learnt to put things up in glass jars, and I have never had any of them freeze. The food I need for winter, I keep in my house," she said. "Whatever I put in the caches stays there until the snow melts. That's the hardest time of all the year. Indians that don't provide for themselves in the fall often nearly starve in the late winter. I belong to the Pembina band, and it was seldom heard, when we still lived the Indian way, that any of us were starving." A third cache in which she had deposited canned raspberries and Juneberries of the season—8 pints of the former and 9½ quarts of the latter—was 22 inches in diameter and 12 inches deep. "When I have all my canning done, I'll tuck hay all around the jars and plenty of it on top, and then I'll cover both caches with earth, making a heap at least so high (18 inches) above the level of the ground."

Another cache on the Red Lake Reservation was 3 feet 7 inches long, 3 feet 5 inches wide, and 4 feet 2 inches deep. Potatoes had been stored in it to about 1 foot from the top in the fall of 1932. The remainder had been filled with hay which was weighted down with pieces of heavy timber. Dirt was then thrown over all to the height of 18 inches above the ground.

In a cache (4 feet square and 6 feet deep) on the Lac Courte Orielle Reservation potatoes, dried corn, maple sugar in mākōk′, and wild rice had been stored in the winter of 1934–1935. The cache was lined with hay and the food covered with mats and rugs overlaid with hay and dirt to a depth of 2 feet. Some informants had lined pits with hay, held in place by bent saplings.

"At the end of Lake Pokegema," said a Lac du Flambeau interpreter, "the people buried about two hundred pounds of wild rice last fall (1934). It was put in sacks and buried in a pit and left there until the snow was gone."

BANDS, CHIEFS, AND COUNCILS

The political unit among the Chippewa was the band. A band comprised from 5 to 50 or more families and was headed by a chief who was assisted by subchiefs. Informants were agreed that both chiefs and subchiefs received their positions normally through inheritance; this information corroborates that given by Warren and Copway, both natives (Warren, 1885, vol. 5, p. 135; Copway, 1847, p. 137; cf. also Gilfillan, 1901, vol. 9, p. 75, and Densmore, 1929, p. 131). It was not unusual, however, that men of good repute became chiefs because of merit. Informants knew of men who had been rewarded with chieftainship by the tribe for unusual courage in time of widespread illness, such as smallpox epidemics. Several additional men bore the title chief, and were considered such, because a President of the United States had awarded them with medals during visits to the White House. The power and prestige of the chief's position, however, depended upon the individual who held it.

All bands considered themselves as affiliated with either the Lake Superior Bands or the Mississippi Bands. Copway called them the Lake Bands and the Interior Bands (Copway, 1847, p. 52). A band today may be scattered over a large area. The L'Anse Band, for example, comprises all the Indians of the L'Anse Reservation, plus groups living in Michigan, near or at Marquette, Sault Ste. Marie, and Escanaba, and groups living in Wisconsin at Land O'Lakes and at Lac Vieux Desert. Lac Vieux Desert comprises 16 fullblooded families, all members of the Mĭdē'wiwin. About 75 years ago their leader, a subchief, called Chief Silver Scott, purchased a small piece of land at Lac Vieux Desert and settled there with his group.

An informant on the Lac Courte Orielle Reservation related the following:

In old days the Lac Courte Orielle band had a head chief. He had two names, Bagowas, which means "patch," like patch on a pants, and Aquewanse, which means "old man." When Bagowas died, his son, Gengwawa, became chief. After Gengwawa died, his sister's child, Peter Wolf, became chief. A son of Peter Wolf, Mike Wolf, is now the recognized chief. Since Mike is not on this reservation—he is in the Indian service in one of the Dakotas—one of the subchiefs, Anaquat, of the Chief Lake group, is acting as head chief. His duty is to represent the Lac Courte Orielle Chippewa if anything tribal turns up. If any such business turns up, a meeting is held to which all are invited, and whatever is decided upon there, Peter Anaquat will present to the agent or whoever is concerned. The tribe will uphold him in these decisions.

Subchieftainship is also inherited. There are three subchiefs on the Reservation today. Peter Anaquat is subchief of Paquawang, which includes Chief Lake on the Chippewa River. Mose Bluesky, Oshawashgogesik, is subchief of the Couderay band that lives on the Chippewa River, now called New Post. Joe White, Ashquagabow, is the subchief at Reserve. His grandfather is one of the chiefs who signed the Treaty of September 30, 1854, at La Pointe.

All the Indians on this Reservation belong to the Lac Courte Orielle Band. The Indians at Odanah, in Ashland County, are of the Chippewa tribe, but of a different band. The Chippewa at Redcliff are called the Redcliff Band or John Buffalo's Band. John Buffalo is now dead. Another band of Chippewa live at Lac du Flambeau. [Hilger, 1936, pp. 41–42.]

The Treaty of September 30, 1854, was made at La Pointe, Wis., between the seven bands of the Lake Superior Bands and the Mississippi Bands, on one side, and the United States Government on the other. The signers of the Lake Superior Bands are grouped under the following bands: La Pointe, L'Anse, Grand Portage, Fond du Lac, Lac Courte Orielle, Lac du Flambeau, and Bois Forte. Of these bands 12 first chiefs, 24 second chiefs, and 34 headmen signed the treaty. Signers of the Mississippi Bands were one head chief, one first chief, eight second chiefs, and five headmen (Kappler, 1904, pp. 648–652).

The origin of the Lac Courte Orielle Band was described (1935) by the 91-year-old wife of a descendant of the founder as follows:

An old man who lived on the Point tells this story: One time an old woman was going to the Point and a little boy followed her. He fell into the water (Little Lake Couderay) and was spirited away through a hole in the bank; the spirit who did this came from the West. They consulted the medicine man regarding the lost boy. They even held a Medicine Dance during which they threw into the water traps, maple sugar, utensils, pots, quilts, in fact the best of everything. The medicine man told them that the boy would be delivered the next day, and the next day the boy popped out of the water! It is believed that all our people and our chiefs came from this boy. After the boy grew older, he became a medicine man. He prophesied what would happen to these people—that there would be priests and a church here. This happened six generations before any white man came. This boy's name was Omȧgȧn'dip, which means, "scabby head," and from him all the Couderay Band of Indians came. When the great-grandson of Omȧgȧn'dip, named Bȧ'gŭŏs, died, his son George became chief; upon the latter's death, his small son became chief. Due to his minority, two men were appointed to act as guardians of the band. The boy died; after this, one of the guardians was looked up to as chief.

No extraordinary respects were paid to a chief. Nor was his son given any preparation for the office: he was treated like other children and was expected to grow up to be a man of good character and good sense. If he lacked these qualities, he might not be greatly esteemed by the people but he would not thereby lose his position. A chief's main duties were to preside at council meetings (councils consisting of all men and women past puberty); of making decisions regarding the general welfare of the tribe, such as petitioning the United States Government for favors or redress; of settling small disputes among his people; of representing the band at annuity payments, at signing of treaties, and at large gatherings of many tribes. The chief's responsibility is exemplified in a "Petition of the head chiefs of the Chippewa Tribe of Indians on Lake Superior," dated February 7, 1849. It reads as follows:

That our people, to-wit, sixteen bands, desire a donation of twenty-four sections of land, covering the graves of our fathers, our sugar orchards, and our rice lakes and rivers, at seven different places now occupied by us as villages, viz.: At View Desert, or Old Garden, three sections; at Trout Lake, four sections; at Lake Coteré, four sections; at La Pointe, four sections; at Ontonagon, three sections; at La Ance, three sections; and at Pah-po-goh-mony, three sections.

That we desire these lands for the purpose specified. [Jenks, 1900 b, pt. 2, p. 1097.]

No informants had ever heard of women chiefs among their people. That women, however, acted as chiefs and were permitted to sign treaties, is a matter of record:

The head chief of the Pillagers, Flatmouth, has for several years resided in Canada. His sister, Ruth Flatmouth, is in her brother's absence the acknowledged Queen, or leader of the Pillagers; two other women of hereditary right acted as leaders of their respective bands, and at the request of the chiefs were permitted to sign the agreements. [U. S. House Exec. Doc., 1889–90, p. 26.]

Women not only expressed their opinions at council meetings, but were often called upon for information.

MARRIAGE CUSTOMS

GENTES

Warren, a native Chippewa, wrote that the Algies of which his people formed one of the principal branches were as a body divided into several large families, each of which was known and perpetuated by a symbol of some bird, animal, fish, or reptile, and called by them totem or dō'dăm. He notes that the descent was invariably along the male line; and that intermarriage never took place between persons of the same symbol or family, "even, should they belong to different and distinct tribes, as they consider one another related by the closest ties of blood and call one another by the nearest terms of consanguinity" (Warren, 1885, vol. 5, p. 34). Informants on all reservations were agreed that the dō'dăm was patrilinear. Such remarks as the following were typical: "The dō'dăm is invariably inherited from the father." "Children belong to the dō'dăm of their father; never to that of their mother." "I have five boys and five girls and all belong to the wolf dō'dăm, their father's dō'dăm." "You are always a member of your father's dō'dăm; never of your mother's."

Traditions of the Mīdē'wiwin teach that originally there were five dō'dăms among the Chippewa. Today the Chippewa recognize many more. Warren lists 21 by name (Warren, 1885, vol. 5, pp. 44–45). Mooney and Thomas record that among some of the Chippewa the gentes were associated in five phratries (in Hodge, 1907, pt. 1, p. 279). Jones notes that there "was a large number of clans, and some of them seemed to have been grouped under a feeble form of phratry (Jones, 1906, p. 136). Informants, both men and women, who contributed to this work belonged to the following gentes: wild cat, bear, eagle, martin, bullhead, kingfisher, crane, loon, wăbīcă'cīnă (unidentified four-footed animal), wolf, fish, sturgeon, lynx, pickerel, caribou, lion, and bird. Warren lists, in addition, catfish, reindeer, merman, pike, rattlesnake, moose, black duck or cormorant, goose, sucker, whitefish, beaver, gull, hawk.[49]

Since white fathers held no membership in any gentes, their children were said to belong to the eagle dō′dȧm, the eagle having been assigned to them, it was thought, because it symbolized the United States, and white men were associated with the United States. It may have been a mere coincidence that all informants and interpreters who were members of the eagle gentes had white feathers, or it may indicate the validity of the eagle gentes.

Each gentes, as noted before, is designated and perpetuated by the symbol of some animal. Animals so symbolized are treated with friendliness but are not considered sacred, nor are any taboos associated with them. "They are killed, skinned, and eaten like other animals."

A L'Anse informant found inspiration in his dō′dȧmic symbol. "The children take their dō′dȧm from the father," he said. "I took mine from my father; he took it from his father, and so on, three or four generations back. My dō′dȧm is the deer. The deer is smart and quick. When a deer wants to drink, he goes up the river a little way from where he crossed, because he won't drink the water that has washed his traces. The deer is my companion; I follow his life. I never need a compass to go through the woods, for I am able to find my way just like the deer."

A Red Lake interpreter said:

I can't be a member of a dō′dȧm, I am told, because I have too much white blood; my father's father was a white man. Last year there was a wake 5 miles from here and my neighbor and I attended it. While there she said to me, "Let's go and see my clan." (She belongs to the bear clan; these people had caught three bear cubs somewhere last winter, and had kept one.) She said to the woman who had the wake, and the cub, "I want to see my clan; where is it?" The woman also belongs to the bear clan. The cub was resting on an army cot, and looked well cared for; it was being fed canned milk from a bottle with nipple. My neighbor talked to the cub in a very friendly way and said that had she known he was there she would have brought him some maple sugar. Many of those who belonged to the bear clan had brought maple sugar; they consider their clan animal something very special. I sat on the bed too and began to pet the cub, but he scratched me and bit my arm. The woman said to me, "You're not of his clan; that's why he is ugly to you." They had no mercurochrome, so I rubbed my arm with kerosene from the lamp.

All informants were emphatic in stating that the gentes were exogamous: intermarriage was never permitted between members of the same gentes, whether of their own tribe or band or those of another

[49] Warren (1885, vol. 5, pp. 44–45); cf. also Winchell (1911, pp. 602–606. For names of sibs of the Ojibway of the Lake of the Woods, see Cooper (1936, p. 4). These sibs, too were patrilineal and exogamous.

Chippewa tribe or band. All members of the same gentes, no matter where found, were considered related by the closest ties and called themselves brothers and sisters.

My father was a white man and therefore did not belong to any clan. Clan members are as brothers and sisters. Long ago all clans must have been blood relatives and, therefore, all clan members must have blood relationship today. Any member of the Wolf Clan, for instance, in any one of the bands today, must be related to all members of the Wolf Clan in all the Chippewa tribe. Today when two meet, and they discover that they are members of the same clan, they grab each other by the arm and say, "Oh! you are my relative." Animals represented in these totems or clans, such as the Bear Clan, Wolf Clan, etc., are not considered sacred. They are killed and eaten as are other animals.[50]

"You can marry a member of your mother's dō'dăm, but never of your father's," said a Red Lake informant. "You are brother or sister to all of your father's dō'dăm. This is distinct from blood relationship." The oldest Nett Lake informant was a member of the caribou dō'dăm: "So was my father," she added. "My husband was a bullhead." When asked what might have happened had she married a caribou, she hesitated a few moments appearing to be thinking the matter through and finally answered, "I wouldn't have been so foolish as to marry a caribou, a man of my own dō'dăm!" The oldest Mille Lacs informant remarked: "A member of the Wolf Clan on the Cass Lake Reservation would be like brother and sister to members of the Wolf Clan on this reservation."

Some children were told early in life of their dō'dămic membership; some learnt it only upon inquiry. "When I began to understand, I was told I had a dō'dăm." "I must have been about 3 years old when I was told I belonged to my father's clan—at least I was very, very little." "My daughter, who is 16 now, asked me the other day of what dō'dăm she was a member; the man who has asked to marry her wanted to know." Most informants could not recall when they first learnt of their membership, "but it was long before marriage entered my head, and I knew always that I couldn't marry a loon." "I was small when I was told about my dō'dăm. We were out fishing and somebody held up a bullhead and said to me, 'This is your dō'dăm.' We have great respect for our dō'dăm, but we eat them; I have often eaten bullhead."

Jenness recorded regarding the Ojibway of Parry Island: "Marriage between parallel cousins was disallowed because they belonged to the same clan, and the clan was an exogamous unit; but cross-cousin marriage, i. e., the union of the children of a brother and sister, was both permissible and common" (Jenness, 1935, p. 98). Landes speaks of cross-cousin marriages among the Ojibwa of western Ontario. She notes that the custom of arrangement of marriage by parents "is per-

[50] Hilger (1936, p. 41). Cf. Bushnell (1905, pp. 69–73), for ceremonial and social gathering of the Kingfisher clan.

haps most common among those Ojibwa who prefer the cross-cousin form of marriage, when a brother and sister agree to propose the marriage of their respective children" (Landes, 1938 b, pp. 51–52). Hallowell writes: ". . . we have two positive statements that among the more remote Ojibwa, at least, cross-cousin marriage was actually practiced in certain bands as late as the first half of the nineteenth century." [51]

Cross-cousin marriage was not found among the Chippewa included in this study. Informants were emphatic in their denial of such a custom. An old Lac Courte Orielle man, the officiating minister of the Mīdē'wiwin ceremonials, remarked: "In the olden days, that was strictly against the customs of the Chippewa of the Great Lakes region; never was it heard that the children of a sister married the children of her brother." Another man informant on the same reservation added: "The children of one of my sisters could not have married the children of another sister; the same applies to my children and those of my brother. They were considered brothers and sisters. However, the children of a man and his sister were considered a little different: they were considered related in the same way as such children are today—they were first cousins. But neither were such children allowed to marry each other. A Red Lake informant, a very old woman, said with much emphasis that "the relationship between a brother's children and the children of his sister was a sacred relationship, and never would they have been allowed to marry."

COURTING

Men were of marriageable age as soon as they were able to supply food for a family. "A boy had to be a good hunter and a good worker to get married; he was that usually at about 20." "If a man had shown that he was a good hunter and a good trapper, well then he was considered ready to marry a girl; he might then be given one." "A girl admired a boy more for his successes in hunting than for anything else."

A girl was of marriageable age as soon after puberty as she was able to do all the work expected of a housewife, such as building wigwams, gathering wood, tanning hides, drying meat and fish, and cooking food. Some informants were married as early as 14 years, knowing at that age how to do all the work of an adult woman. Pierz wrote in 1855: "Girls marry early, most of them being married at 14 or 15 years of age" (Pierz, 1855, p. 24—writer's translation). An

---

[51] Cf. Hallowell (1928, p. 522) for quotation from Duncan Cameron found in L. R. Masson, Les Bourgeois de la Compagnie du Nord-Quest (circa) vol. 2, p. 247, and one from H. Y. Hind, Explorations in the interior of Labrador Peninsula, London, 1863. Hallowell notes that Hind had previously explored in the Red River and published Narrative of the Canadian Red River Exporing Expedition, etc., 1860.

87-year-old Red Lake man said: "I was 25 when I was married the first time; my wife was 30. She died after 12 years, and the next one I married was 14." The girl that was admired most by the men was one that was "quiet, didn't run around, and was a good worker; 'good worker' was the virtue most sought by men."

Courting if defined as an endeavor to gain the affections of a person by wooing can hardly be said to have existed among the Chippewa. Informants agreed that formerly girls past puberty had to remain continuously in their mother's presence or in that of some older woman. Pierz made a similar observation: "I saw, too, among the pagans the most praiseworthy care and watchfulness extended to the morals of the girls. Girls are constantly with their mothers who warn them early of the possibility of being led astray" (Pierz, 1855, p. 22). An old Red Lake woman collaborated when saying: "In old days a boy and a girl never walked together. If a man liked a girl he went to see her in the presence of her parents and then only in daytime, never at night." "You never saw a man and a girl alone by themselves. It was awful to see a boy and a girl walk together." "There wasn't any courting in the old days; at sundown everybody was in the tent." On the Lac Courte Orielle Reservation (1935) a young mother was "keeping an eye" on her oldest daughter, a 16-year-old girl. Their home was a 2-room house. The daughter had been told that she and her boy friend might sit in the bedroom while the mother stayed in the kitchen. They were not to get out of sight, however, but were to stay in line with the open doorway. The mother continued: "Her boy friend is 25. He just never sees the girl unless I'm around: I watch her all the time. When they are together, they sit around and read the papers like you saw them do today. He asked my husband last spring to marry her, but was told she was too young. When she is a little older my husband and I will talk it over with his parents. He is her lover all right because she gets clothes and things from him. He has to go to CCC soon."

Densmore's informants, too, noted that girls were closely observed. She wrote:

The young maidens of the Chippewa were closely guarded and were modest in their behavior toward the young men of the tribe. If a young man wished to call upon a young woman he talked first with the older people who lived next to the door of the lodge. He might then proceed to the middle of the lodge, where the young woman lived, and talk with the girl in a low tone, but she was not allowed to leave the lodge with him. If a young man came to call rather late in the evening when the fire had burned low, the mother or grandmother would rise and stir up the fire so that it burned brightly, then fill her pipe and sit up and smoke. The young man could continue his call, but was conscious of being watched. The young man played the "courting flute" in the evenings, but it was never permitted that a young girl leave the lodge in response to the flute.

If a young man's intentions were serious, he killed a deer or some other animal and brought it to the girl's parents. This was to indicate his ability and intention to provide well for his family. If the parents approved of the young man, they asked him to stay and share the feast. This was understood as an acceptance of his wish to marry their daughter, and he was allowed to come and go with more freedom than formerly. [Densmore, 1929, p. 72.]

Two informants (Red Lake and Lac Courte Orielle Reservations) had heard that long ago, "long before our time," the pretty tunes of the flute were used by young men to make girls aware of their presence. Flutes were made of cedar twigs or sumach stalks. Thomas L. Mc-Kenney, when en route with Governor Lewis Cass in 1826, heard such a flute and wrote:

Nothing can be more mournful in its tones. It was night, and a calm rested on everything; and it was moonlight, all of which added to its effect. We saw the Indian who was playing it, sitting on a rock. . . . We afterwards learned that this Indian was in love, and that he would sit there all night indulging in this sentimental method of softening the heart of his mistress, whose lodge he took care should be opposite his place of melody, and within reach of his monotonous but pensive strains. [Winchell, 1911, p. 602.]

If a young man was serious in his intentions, he killed a deer or some other animal and brought it to the lodge of the girl's parents. This signified his intention of providing well for his family. Armstrong wrote in 1892:

Leaving it outside, he enters the wigwam, saying nothing, but lights his pipe and makes himself at home. Should there be more than one girl in the lodge at the time, he has a sign by which his choice is made known. If the girl does not like his appearance she remains where she is, but if he is agreeable to her fancy she takes a knife and proceeds to skin the animal and take charge of the meat, after which the suitor takes his leave. The parents of the girl, being advised of what is going by the presence of the meat not of their killing, commence systematic proceedings to ascertain the young man's habits, his ability as a hunter, warrior, etc., and if satisfied with them they proceed to the young man's parents, who are now for the first time aware of the youth's aspirations and they in turn make inquiry as to the character, etc., of their prospective daughter-in-law. If all is satisfactory the young man is given permission by the girl's parents to visit her, but all he or she has to say must be said in the common wigwam and before all who happen to be present. [Armstrong, 1892, pp. 103–104.]

MARRIAGE

Many old informants had been told by grandmothers that a girl in their day did not know the man she married until the day of marriage. Often she had not even seen him; parents made all arrangements. The girl's wishes regarding a man were usually taken into consideration, however, although some informants related forced marriages. "That seems to have been the Indian way of long ago; that's the way I was married. He asked my parents for me before I had ever seen him; I didn't want to marry him; he was sickly then already. My mother made me marry him. We lived with her 3 years, when he died. He was a good man; he never became angry. But he was sickly. I had one child by my first husband." "I got my old man because my parents made me take him. He brought many things to my parents, including food. There was no marriage ceremony nor any other celebration; they just made me live with him."

A medicine man on the Lac Courte Orielle Reservation told of his second marriage: "My first wife died. She was a good woman; I admired her. I went to her uncle (her parents were dead) and asked for her sister. I gave many things to her uncle: quilts that I had received at dances, as well as food. The girl's brother asked her nicely to marry me, and so she did. There was no marriage ceremony."

A Red Lake informant was married at 20. He said:

I found out that her parents approved of me and so I went to her place and stayed there. And that was the marriage—nothing like now. Here is the way it started: I went out hunting and brought home much meat, for I had killed a buffalo. The mother of the girl came to our lodge to visit about that time and my mother gave her all the meat she could carry on her back. That's why she approved of me when I came. But I was not well acquainted with the girl, although I knew who she was, for we were neighbors. I used to meet her going places but would always pass her by. She was much younger than I. We were not related: her dō'dăm was the wăbīcă'cīnă (a small animal); mine, the loon. You couldn't marry into your dō'dăm. Years ago no one carried on courtship for years like they do now.

The Chippewa had no marriage ceremony. Marriage consisted of eating together and of sharing the fur robe used as bedding. When parents had settled upon the marriage or when the man had received the consent of the girl's parents, he went to the latter's wigwam with all his belongings "and that was all." The couple usually shared the wigwam of the girl's parents for a year. If all was satisfactory, they built a wigwam for themselves after that. Moving into their own wigwam was called bākānīī'kwe, meaning "being separated from the home wigwam."

The following two accounts were related by Red Lake informants:

Marriage depended on old folks. I wasn't my own boss; I didn't choose to marry my old man. When my mother told me "You have to marry; I have chosen your man for you, and he is a good man, for I saw how he treated his first wife," I broke down and cried for days. I cried for days! I cried every time they mentioned him! In those days we didn't answer back or refuse; so I cried. He was a widower with a child, and I didn't want him. My uncles and aunts tried to persuade me to marry him. My uncle from Pembina Reservation [Canada] came to visit just then, and they must have asked him, without my knowledge, to talk to me about this man. He took me aside, and talked to me. He said, "You're growing up to be a big girl now and you ought to get married. He is a good man; you couldn't do any better." (Good husband meant that he had taken good care of his wife and that he was a good hunter.) Then I said to him, "All right." This was 2 years after I had become an old woman, and I think I began to be that way at 14. After I gave my consent my man brought a blanket filled with clothes—all he could carry. Among them

I remember were two shawls and some tanned deer hides that his mother had tanned. (We wore dresses made of buckskin then; no one wore calico dresses.) But I didn't like him; I never spoke to him. My mother cooked for him; and I didn't even eat when he did. I must have been foolish! I never suffered so much. I would sit up most of the night and did not want to sleep with him; but they made me. [The interpreter inserted that she had felt the same way about her own marriage]. When fall came, he went hunting for furs. My mother said to me, "You go along?" I said, "Let him go!" He prepared to go and took his boy. My mother said, "You have to go with him! Pack your things!" I cried, but followed him. We camped, and the first night he brought in a black bear. In all he killed three bears on this trip. From that time on I liked him; I helped him skin his game. He never said an impatient word to me, and I was therefore good to his son. The boy didn't live very long. There was never any wedding ceremony in those old days, and seldom did a man leave his wife, or a wife leave her husband. I always thought only death should separate married people.

My man came to my parents' house and asked my folks to marry me. But my folks didn't like me to marry him because he was a Red Laker, they wanted to return to Pembina [Canada], and take me back with them. After he left, my nose began to bleed. It bled for 2 days and 2 nights. This man was a "grand medicine" man. My parents called in another "grand medicine" man, an old one, to find out what this one had done to me. This man said that the first "grand medicine" man had been displeased and had caused my nose to bleed; that he had in mind to kill me that way; that the first one would have to come back and fumigate me. My mother called the first one and had him fumigate me with Indian medicine. He heated two big stones, placed some herbs on these, and covered my head with a blanket in such a way as to enclose the stones. After that my mother gave me to him. And now you know how I got my old man.

LOVE CHARMS

Love charms (kȧcībī'djīgȧns or māsīnākō'djīgȧns) were bought from medicine men or medicine women who were gifted with the power to make them. The charm, or talisman, was carried on the person of the one wishing to influence another, and contained besides love "medicine," hair, fingernail parings, or bits of clothing of the person to be charmed.

When I was young, some old men had charms for sale [said a Lac Courte Oreille informant]. A love charm consisted of a small piece of wood about an inch long shaped like a person, and either a hair of the person to be charmed or a piece of his clothing. All was tied into a small piece of buckskin. Both men and women who wished to charm another person carried these near their own person. For example, if some woman here at New Post had such a charm— one containing hair or a small piece of clothing of a man at Reserve— the first thoughts of the man over there on awakening would be of her. He would also dream of her and want to be with her so badly that he might come over here in his stocking feet forgetting to put on his shoes!

"My husband, when still young and a pagan (Mīdē'), worked at a lumber camp where my parents had a lodge," said a Lac du Flambeau interpreter. "I had noticed that in the pocket of his jacket he carried a little cloth bag. So one day when he wasn't around, I pulled it out and upon examining it found a piece of my shawl about half the size of my thumbnail in it. I knew then that he was charming me, and that's how I began to like him. There must have been something in me too that charmed him!"

Polyandry was not found among the Chippewa; polygyny, however, was an established custom but practiced only by men who were able to support several families. Such men might be chiefs, headmen, medicine men, and those who by reason of their hunting and trapping abilities could easily support more than one family. Informants on every reservation gave names of old men who had had two simultaneous wives; and several that had had three or four. A Lac du Flambeau informant had married his second wife 10 years after the marriage to his first wife, both wives living in the same wigwam and each rearing a family. "When one would go away berry-picking, the other would nurse the babies of both. One did the cooking; the other the sewing, generally. The oldest wife finally left him."

One Red Lake man had four simultaneous wives, living two in a wigwam. Densmore visited a wigwam housing two wives and wrote:

A man might have two or three wives and all lived in the same lodge, each having her appointed part of the lodge. The writer witnessed a ceremony in the house of a Chippewa at Grand Portage who had two wives. Two of his sons lived with him and the family seemed to be living harmoniously. A Canadian Chippewa said that many Indians had two wives, adding that "the man sat between them." He said that in old times some men had five wives, and that one was the "head wife" and the only one who had children. [Densmore, 1929, p. 73.]

Gilfillan (1901, vol. 9, p. 84) notes that sometimes the wives were sisters, and that usually the man had two separate homes or wigwams for his two families: sometimes they lived in one dwelling.

Most informants had been married several times. Some had deserted their partners or had been deserted by them; others had lost a partner by death. Widows were expected to obtain permission to remarry. The following relates to the custom of being released from widowhood:

If a husband dies, his wife must stay single for a year and continue living in her home as if her husband were still living there. At the end of the year, the woman is dressed up and painted. The medicine man comes and so do the dead husband's parents and relatives. One of two conditions will be placed before the woman: First, her husband's parents, or, if these are dead, his nearest relatives may accept the presents the woman offers them. If they accept them, she is released and is free to marry anyone of her own choice. Or, secondly, the parents or relatives may present her with a husband right there, and she must accept him. Her husband's relatives have that right. Should the widow marry before this ceremony, or be seen with a man, her relatives will violently upbraid her. A certain woman here had one braid cut on one side to remind her that she had done something wrong. One woman had a gash cut in her throat. Another had a gash cut in her face. Men fall under the same restrictions laid down for women. [Hilger, 1936, pp. 47–48.]

SEPARATIONS

Separations between husbands and wives were part of the Chippewa culture pattern. Either partner could leave and return to the parental home, or could marry another person. Warren (1885, vol. 5, pp. 253–254) relates that a certain chief who had married for the first time at 30, marrying a widow by whom he had one son, left her after 2 years and married a girl 14 by whom he had a family of 6 children.

Gilfillan writes:

It is quite common for a husband, after having lived with a woman for a long time and raised quite a family, to abandon her and his children without any cause, and to take another woman and begin to rear a new family. A man, for instance, will abandon his wife and children at Leech Lake, and go to Red Lake, 75 miles distant, and take a new wife there. Or he may do so in the same village. In such circumstances he never does anything to support the wife and children he has abandoned. I have never known a man in such a case to do the slightest thing for the children. [Gilfillan, 1901, vol. 9, p. 85.]

INFIDELITY

Infidelity on the part of the wife was punishable, even with death; generally either the wife or the paramour was killed. The mother of a Vermilion Lake informant had told her daughter a story in order to teach her to be faithful to her husband: "Young Chippewa braves went to war to fight the Sioux. When they came back, one found his wife married to another brave. So he said to him, 'We'll each have half of her.' They took her to the woods and cut her right down the middle and each one took one-half." The husband of an unfaithful wife usually disfigured the woman's face so no man would desire her. Informants knew of men who had cut gashes with flint stones in the cheeks of their unfaithful wives and pressed out the flesh in order to cause permanent scars. "That's what they did to women; but it was quite all right for men to have two wives!" remarked a Nett Lake interpreter.

SUMMARY

Child life among primitive Chippewa began with birth and ended with puberty. Although approximately 280 secondary sources contain information related to Chippewa culture, only very scanty and scattered material is found in them regarding child life. Exceptions are Densmore's Chippewa Customs (1929), Jenness' The Ojibway Indians of Parry Island (1935), and Landes' The Ojibwa Woman (1938 b). These contain some information. The following summary is based on data which the writer collected at intervals from 1932–40 during interviews with 96 Chippewa informants on 9 Chippewa reservations: 5 in Minnesota (Red Lake, White Earth, Nett Lake, Vermilion Lake, and Mille Lacs); 3 in Wisconsin (Lac Courte Orielle, La Pointe, and Lac du Flambeau); and 1 in Michigan (L'Anse).

Prenatal period.—Childless couples were not well thought of. The cause of inherent sterility was not known; herbal decoctions taken orally might produce it artificially. Fertility also could be produced by drinking a potion. On the Mille Lacs Reservation both husband and wife drank it; on other reservations only women. Artificial limitation of families was not known; but abstinence was practiced.

Some informants believed the child a human being from the moment of conception; others, not until the fetus gave signs of life; still others had never heard anyone tell. No methods were known by which sex could be produced either at conception or during pregnancy. Sex, it was thought, could be predicted from the contour of the pregnant mother's body, the location and the movements of the fetus, and by a type of affinity. Parents had no preference regarding sex of children; mothers hoped that some would be girls since daughters more often than sons cared for aged parents. Children born with certain physical traits, such as a patch of gray hair or a birthmark, were considered reincarnated.

Except on the Mille Lacs Reservation the husband of a pregnant woman was not hampered by food taboos or prescriptions, and only on the Lac Courte Orielle were restraints placed on his conduct. The pregnant woman, on the contrary, was circumscribed by numerous restraints in both food and conduct.

Although methods for induced abortions were known, they were seldom resorted to; they were viewed with great disfavor. Old informants today speak of them in whispers. An induced aborted fetus was not given burial rites; a spontaneously aborted one was given burial the same as an adult person. When a spontaneous abortion was feared, the mother submitted to fumigation as a preventive.

Birth.—A birth in the late fall or winter took place in the home wigwam. If, however, there were preadolescent children in the home, the mother retired to a small wigwam built for this purpose some distance from home. If birth occurred in the spring or summer or when en route, the mother retired to a place in the open where privacy was assured. Midwives or the woman's mother or sisters attended the birth. Certain midwives were also capable of delivering still-births.

The husband was present at birth only when no women were available or when some strong person's assistance was needed; other male persons were never present. The husband could in no magical way assist at birth. Shamans, either men or women, were summoned if labor was unusually difficult.

Women worked until the onset of labor. When labor began herbal medication was administered orally. The child was delivered while the mother knelt on a thin layer of grass or hay spread either on the ground or on a bulrush mat. She either pulled on a rope or braced herself on a horizontally elevated sapling. Most mothers returned to work within a day after birth.

The navel cord was sewed into a beaded buckskin bag. Beadwork was of no particular design nor were bags of a prescribed shape. Girls' bags differed in no way from boys'. The bag was hung on the bow of the cradleboard along with toys. Later it was either given to the child or disposed of by the father if a boy's, or the mother if a girl's, in order to bring magical favors of occupational dexterity upon the child.

No meaning was attached to the caul on Vermilion Lake, Nett Lake, and White Earth Reservations; on L'Anse, Red Lake, and Lac Courte Orielle, a child so born was considered favored with good luck. Neither significance nor treatment was accorded the fontanels. The placenta was hung in the crotch of a tree; never buried or burnt.

A baby's first bath, administered on the day of birth, was given in an herbal decoction contained in a nonleakable birchbark receptacle. Since this type of bath was thought to promote a strong constitution, the mother gave it repeatedly during babyhood.

Neither mother nor baby was subjected to purification ceremonials. The day following birth, or very soon after, parents invited guests to a meal to celebrate the baby's arrival.

Postnatal interests.—In the very early day nose rings and earrings were worn by both sexes; more recently only earrings. Many informants had holes pierced in lobes and along edges of ears. Ears were pierced unceremonially on day of birth or at any time.

Babies were tied to cradleboards to develop erect posture, to permit mothers to transport them on backs when traveling, and to keep them safely in place while mothers worked. When older they were tightly and snugly wrapped in buckskin and laid in hammocks or swings. When old enough to stand the strain, a baby was carried on its mother's back seated in its mother's blanket or shawl. Rabbitskins, swamp moss, or down of cattail served as diapers. To prevent chafing the baby was powdered with ashes of cedar bark, charcoal of cedar crushed to powder, or finely ground decayed root or wood of cedar or Norway pine. Lullabies were conventional songs of nonsense syllables.

A child's first clothes were the rabbit and weasel skins in which it was wrapped when in its cradleboard. When old enough to creep it wore a slip of softly tanned deer hide, or preferably fawn hide. In warm weather it wore no clothing at all. It was given its first moccasins when about able to walk. A hole, about the size of a blueberry, was cut into the soles of these. Neglecting the hole might cause the child to grow up to be lazy, "so lazy that it would not even wear out the soles of its moccasins". At night babies were wrapped in rabbit-skin blankets.

Clenching fists during first days of life was not significant; but allowing an infant to touch fingers of one hand with those of the other was like counting the days it had still to live. This was to be guarded against. No significance was attached to either the advent or the loss of a first tooth, nor to a child's first word. Since, however, a child that talked early was considered intelligent, it might be fed raw brains of any small bird, the belief being that this developed early speech. Not a child's first steps but its first walk, at least half the length of the wigwam, was celebrated. If this happened at home, the parents gave a feast; if it walked to neighbors, the neighbors gave it. On Nett Lake and Vermilion Lake Reservations a child's first portage on foot was celebrated with a feast.

Nursing and weaning.—Babies were nursed immediately after birth. If the mother died or her condition did not permit nursing, the child sucked porridge from a small hole punched in the bladder of an animal. The porridge was made by boiling wild rice or corn meal in fish or meat broth. Babies were nursed whenever they cried, and not at set intervals. Commonly children were nursed for 2 years; some nursed 4 or 5 or more years, two at times nursing together. Never were any nursed while the mother was pregnant. Babies nursed while in their mothers' arms or in cradleboards; older children stood while nursing. A child was usually weaned by being separated from its mother; at times, by being frightened by nipples blackened with charcoal.

Atypical conditions.—Twins as well as their families were respected in the community. Twins were thought to be related to the spirit world; but no supernatural powers were ascribed to them. One case of quadruplets was known; supernatural powers had been ascribed to these.

Sick or weak babies were bathed in a herbal decoction or given a purgative potion. Nursing mothers also chewed a purgative root, passing it, through milk secretion, to the child. The purgative values of the same root, when heated and placed on the child's abdomen, were thought to penetrate the intestines. Furthermore, a sickly child or one that cried a great deal might be given a dream-name by an old and healthy person—all children, irrespective of health, were given a dream name shortly after birth. If the child continued to ail, it might be given a third and a fourth name, but no namer might do so twice. If all remedies failed the child was admitted to the Mīdē′wiwin, the native religion. Two ailing children, 4 and 5 years of age, were admitted on the White Earth Reservation in June 1938; a 1-year-old child, on Nett Lake Reservation in August 1939.

The Chippewa practiced neither head nor body deformation. If a child was born deformed it was said that the mother had been frightened while carrying the child. Incest was decidedly an unusual event. Illegitimacy was rare. A child born out of wedlock was called "a stolen child" or "a child conceived in sneaky ways." Although parents of both the paramour and his partner felt disgraced, the unmarried mother was allowed to care for the child in her parental home. Infanticide was not conventional.

At no time did the Chippewa enslave people or treat them as servants. Adoption of children prevailed even though both parents of the child were living. Adults, too, were adopted. In the case of small children the parents' consent was necessary. A dying mother might arrange for the adoption of her children. There were no adoption ceremonials.

Naming a child.—Chippewa names originated in dreams. They were given to children ceremonially by a person of either sex. Each child was named shortly after birth. Ailing children might be given several additional names successively. An unfailing rule was that the namer had to be a person grown old in continuous good health. Names of informants were Coming-over-the-hill, Morning-at-dawn, Ice-feathered-woman, One-that-can-walk, Round-old-woman, and One-that-can-climb. Many children were given a pet name. No names were given at puberty.

Prepuberty fasts.—Both boys and girls spent some days in silent commune with the spirit world while abstaining from food and drink. A child at about the age of reason abstained wandering about the woods from sunrise to sunset for one day. A child from about 7 to 9 years spent from 1 to 4 successive days thus; those from 10 to 12 years, from 4 to 10 days. A 10-day fast was participated in more often by boys than by girls. The reward was usually supernatural or shamanistic powers. Parents often chose the occasion for fasting for younger children, the determinant being a dream of the previous night. A 10-day fast was an entirely voluntary affair.

All fasters had cheeks blackened with charcoal, but without design. Older boys usually fasted on platforms or in nests in trees at some distance from home. Girls and younger boys walked about the woods.

Upon the faster's return the mother—or if she were dead, the grandmother or aunts—prepared a feast and invited guests. Nearly all
informants were emphatic in saying that eligibility for fasting ended
with a girl's first menses and a boy's change of voice.

Fasting in early childhood provided contact with the spiritual
world; when a little older, a medium in a guardian spirit who usually
took the form of a person, an animal, an inanimate object, or an
activity of nature. If a faster was not thus favored, power could be
procured only by joining the Mīdē′wiwin. The guardian's prerogatives were to give advice, knowledge, and power. Powers were of
various kinds: the producing of rains or winds; success in war;
knowledge of medicinal properties of plants; prediction of future
events or discovering causes for past ones; and the uses of magic.
After a successful fast the faster kept his power, as directed by his
vision or dream, in a "medicine bundle." This bundle was an integral
part of the faster's spiritual life and could be used for his personal
benefit.

Puberty customs.—Although well defined customs ushered a girl
into her maturity, few girls received previous instructions regarding
the occurrence or the significance of it. During her first menses, but
not during any succeeding ones, a girl's cheeks and forehead were
blackened with charcoal, but without design. Her hair was tied back
or completely covered. She was thus isolated in a small wigwam built
either by herself or her mother, or by both of them, at a little distance
from home. A small stick was given her with which to relieve any
itching feeling. She cooked her own food, but under no circumstances
was she allowed to eat food in season. Doing so would destroy the
growth or production of it. She was kept busy with beadwork and
sewing. Her mother and older women instructed her regarding the
potentialities of motherhood as well as proper conduct and responsibilities in her newly acquired membership among "old women."
During all succeeding menses she was not to touch plants since it
withered them; nor babies, nor clothes belonging to her father or
brothers, since it crippled them. She was not to cross the path of
anyone, since it paralyzed him. Puberty of informants, interpreters,
and their daughters had occurred between the ages of 12 and 15.

After isolation the girl bathed herself—not even hands or face had
been washed during isolation—washed her clothes, and walked to the
home wigwam over a path of cedar boughs or bark to a feast-day meal
prepared by her mother. The old women who had acted as instructors
during her isolation were guests. After the feast she was free to
mingle with the people, but was not yet permitted to gather or prepare
food in season. This taboo was removed if she was fed a small quantity of the food by some one else. After puberty a girl was not per-

mitted out of sight of her mother or an older woman designated by the mother.

There was no puberty fast or rite for boys. Boys might be inspired to a prolonged fast at puberty, but it was merely incidental; it was not conventional to do so.

With the change of voice a boy's boyhood ended. With a girl's puberty isolation, her girlhood ended. Childhood had ended for both. Both must now learn the techniques of adult occupations. The boy must learn to make bows and arrows, learn to hunt large game, to build canoes. He must participate in government. The girl must learn to weave mats, tan hides, make birchbark receptacles, design beadwork, build wigwams, make snowshoes, harvest wild rice, make maple sugar, and dry meat, fish, berries, and fruit.

Training children.—Chippewa children learned conformity to conventional tribal standards, the mental content of the tribal culture pattern and the customs and beliefs regarding religion, health, politics, economics, and social life. They were lectured to, counseled, presented with ideals, and allowed to listen in when elders conversed. They imitated their elders in play, participated with them according to their capacities in serious work, and were nonparticipant observers at ceremonials.

Parents, but more especially grandparents and older persons, were the chief instructors. Instructions were usually given when an occasion presented itself; sometimes it was a planned affair.

Although praise, reward, punishment, scolding, and frightening played a part in the training of the child, no great emphasis was laid upon them. Children were not ridiculed for failures. A child that walked away from a group that was being instructed gave evidence thereby that it would not lead a good life. If parents discerned a child as one of promise, it was sent to bed without food some evening. Upon rising in the morning it was handed both charcoal and food. If it chose charcoal, parents felt encouraged; if bread, they knew they had been mistaken.

Training in religion and supernatural power.—The child was taught the belief in a Supreme Being called Kī'cē Măn'itō, the Great Spirit. The Great Spirit was meditated upon and addressed formally in prayer during the Mīdē'wiwin ceremonial. Help was sought more generally from minor deities of lesser powers that dwelt in nature and from individual guardian spirits. Tobacco was the usual ceremonial offering for minor deities; it was seldom offered to the Great Spirit.

The Mīdē'wiwin of the Chippewa was their "mode of worshiping the Great Spirit, and securing life in this and a future world, and of conciliating the lesser spirits, who in their belief, people earth. sky, and waters."

Any person, including children and infants, could be admitted at any celebration. Children are admited only to the first of the four or more degrees. This degree did not carry with it magical power known as "grand medicine." Celebrations were always held in fall and spring and could in addition be held at any time of the year as a thanksgiving offering or as a petition for the restoration of health.

Belief in life after death.—Chippewa traditions taught that the spirits of their children and adults after death went westward. Both burial and mourning customs evidenced a belief in life after death. Spontaneously aborted fetuses, stillbirths, and children were given burials in the same manner as adults. Parents offered food at the grave of a child and kept fire burning there for several nights following burial, in the same manner as was done for adults. The customs of mourning for a departed child, too, did not differ from those for a mature person.

Training in health measures.—Shamanistic powers were always exercised when sickness was ascribed to evil powers; in all other cases, only when natural remedies, such as potions of herbs, roots, and barks, bloodletting, sweating, and tattooing, failed.

Children were never taught the secrets of the curative powers of the shaman. They might be eyewitnesses to cures ascribed to shamanistic procedures, however. They might, too, be witnesses in the collection and preparations of herbalists, bloodletters, and tattooers. But knowledge of the ingredients used by them was not shared with children. Children might obtain knowledge of medicinal values of herbs, roots, and barks in prepuberty dreams, but such knowledge was not exercised until adulthood was reached. Children participated in sweat baths with adults.

Baths in herbal and root decoctions were given to babies to strengthen them physically. As they grew older, they were given charcoal to eat for the same purpose. The Chippewa had no means of establishing immunity to disease.

Moral training.—Emphasis was placed upon children being kind and respectful to older people. They were instructed and trained to share the superfluous. A child was not only taught honesty formally but was made to return articles not belonging to it. A lying child was told it was making a wrong beginning in life; a boasting or a tale-bearing one was not listened to. Quarrels between children of the same family were ignored; but children quarreling with neighboring children were forbidden to play with them again. Most hurting denunciations were "you dog" or "you ghost."

Mental training.—The native language was learnt by imitation or by hearing elders speak it. The sign language was not taught to children. Only a few adults in each band learnt it so that the band might communicate with Plains area tribes. Neither were children taught the ideograms or pictographs which their elders used in sending messages, recording events, and making maps designed for travel.

Diversions.—Chippewa children were given much freedom. They therefore spent much time in play. Their developmental age was not unlike that of white children: when small each played with toys as an individual; when a little older, boys and girls played together in games and in imitation of elders; when older still, sexes excluded each other in play; when approaching puberty both boys and girls had chums.

Children did not participate in social dances of elders but were nonparticipant observers and readily imitated them. A favorite diversion of elders was visiting, children sitting by and listening in. Topics of conversation might be gossip, legends, historic events, travels, or visits of other tribes.

Vocational training.—Birchbark canoes of various sizes were used for travel during the summer and whenever the rivers and lakes were free of ice; for fishing, hunting, berrying, and wild-rice gathering; and for moving household goods and families. Canoe making was a man's job; women, however, often assisted. Boys past puberty were expected to help and to learn thereby.

Winter travel was done by both men and women on snowshoes. Toboggans were used by trappers and hunters to haul game and furs.

Hunting provided both food and clothing. It was the man's chief occupation throughout the year, but especially in winter when the furs were heavier and the animals were not bearing young. A boy's first successful hunt in killing an animal used as food, probably some fowl or small fur-bearing animal, was celebrated by the parents with a feast to which all the village was invited. The game was served as part of the main dish.

Foetal inclusions were used as hunting charms. Hunters who had tutelary powers related to hunting exercised them in their own favor. Meeting an owl when hunting was a bad omen.

Deer were shot, impounded, or snared. At night they were enticed by torchlight; in the daytime, by the "deer call." Artificial saltlicks brought them into open spaces. Bears were caught in deadfalls. Wolves, foxes, and rabbits were snared. Wolves were also trapped. Beavers were speared.

Fish, both fresh and smoked, were important foods. In the fall, groups of families moved to lake shores to fish for winter storage. Nets, fishhooks, spearheads, and traps were used in fishing. Women usually used nets which they made of inner bark of basswood or of nettles.

Adult clothing was made from finely tanned hides of deer, moose, elk, or bear, and of dressed skins of rabbit, beaver, and other small fur-bearing animals. Children's clothing was made of delicately tanned hides of fawn and of skins of beaver, squirrel, and rabbit. Dressing skins and tanning hides was a woman's work, with girls past puberty assisting. Blankets worn by adults and used as bed coverings were of rabbitskins.

Women made receptacles, both leakable and nonleakable, of birchbark. These were used as work baskets, storage containers, winnowing trays, and buckets for carrying water, collecting sap, and gathering berries. Women made mats of bulrushes to be used as wigwam coverings, floor mats upon which to squat, and "tables" off which to eat.

The type of dwelling most generally used by the Chippewa was the wigwam. It was a circular or elongated framework of saplings covered with bark or with bark and bulrush mats. Other types of dwellings, but less frequently used, were the bark house, the peaked lodge, and, occasionally, the tipi.

Wood was the only fuel used. Women gathered it daily and packed it on their backs in carrying straps. Fire was made by striking two stones or by rotating a wooden fire drill. Punk served as tinder. Cooking was done over an open fireplace, either in or outside the wigwam. In winter the fireplace gave also heat and light to the wigwam. If additional light was needed, torches were used.

Gardening consisted of cultivating corn, squash, pumpkins, and beans in small plots scattered haphazardly in tall grass and in open spaces in the woods.

Chief foods were meat, fish, wild rice, berries, maple sugar, cultivated vegetables, and corn. Food not needed for immediate use was often stored in caches.

Every Chippewa was a member of a band, a political unit of 5 to 50 families. A band was headed by a chief who was assisted by subchiefs. Generally chiefs and subchiefs inherited their positions. The title could, however, be bestowed on any man of good repute, because of merit. All bands were affiliated with either the Lake Superior Bands or the Mississippi Bands. No unusual deference was shown a chief. Sons of chiefs were not given any preparation for the office. They were expected to grow up to be men of good character and good sense; lacking these they would not be respected by the people. They would not thereby, however, lose their rights to their inheritance of the chieftainship.

A chief's main duties were to preside at council meetings, to make decisions regarding the general welfare of the tribe, to settle disputes among his people, and to represent his band at annuity payments, signing of treaties, and at large gatherings of many tribes. Women probably acted as chiefs on occasions. They did express their opinions at council meetings and were often called upon for information. Council meetings consisted of all men and women past puberty.

Marriage.—The gentes of the Chippewa were exogamic. This exogamy extended to all members of one's gens in any Chippewa tribe anywhere. Cross-cousin marriages were not permitted, according to informants of the present study; Jenness and Landes found them among the Canadian Ojibwa.

A man was of marriageable age as soon as he was able to supply by hunting enough food to support a family; a girl, as soon after puberty as she was able to do all the work expected of a housewife.

Courting was not institutional; girls were closely guarded after puberty. A lover, however, might make his presence known by playing a flute near the home of the girl. If he had serious intentions, he might bring a deer or some other large animal that he had killed while hunting to the home of the girl's parents, signifying thereby that he had in mind to provide well for his family. Love charms were carried by men and women who wished to draw upon themselves the affections of another.

A girl was usually not acquainted with the man whom she married, but her wishes regarding him were generally taken into consideration. Sometimes a girl was forced into marriage. There was no marriage ceremony. Eating together and sharing the fur robe used as bedding signified that the couple was married. During the first year of married life the couple usually shared the wigwam of the girl's parents. If at the end of the year all was satisfactory, the couple built its own wigwam.

Polyandry did not exist among the Chippewa; polygyny was institutional, the number of wives depending on the ability of the man to support the families. None were known to informants to have more than four wives; many had two. Densmore was told of one man who had five. Successive marriages were general, owing to death or desertion. Widows were expected to obtain permission to remarry. Separations were institutional, either party leaving the other and either returning to the parental home or marrying another person.

Punishing the unfaithful wife was conventional. Generally either the wife or her paramour was killed. If the wife was not killed, her husband disfigured her face so badly that he felt certain no other man would again desire her.

SOME PLANTS USED BY THE CHIPPEWA

Alder (*Alnus incana* [L.] Moench)

Artichoke (*Helianthus tuberosus* L.)

Ash (*Fraxinus quadrangulata* Michx.)

Aspen (*Populus grandidentata* Michx.)

Balsam (*Abies balsamea* [L.] Mill.)

Basswood (*Tilia americana* L.)

Beans (*Phaseolus vulgaris* L.)

Birch (*Betula alba* L. and *Betula papyrifera* Marsh.)

Blackberry (*Rubus cubatus* Focke)

Black raspberry (*Rubus occidentalis* L.)

Bloodroot (*Sanguinaria canadensis* L.)

Blueberry (*Vaccinium vacillans* Kalm)

Boneset (*Eupatorium perfoliatum* L.)

Bulrush (*Scirpus validus* Vahl.)

Butternut (*Juglans cinerea* L.)

Carrot (*Daucus carota* L.)

Catnip (*Nepeta cataria* L.)

Cattail (*Typha latifolia* L.)

Cedar (*Juniperus virginiana* L.)

Chokecherry (*Prunus virginiana* L.)

Corn (*Zea mays* L.)

Dogwood, red (*Cornus stolonifera* Michx.)

Elder (*Sambucus canadensis* L.)

Elm (*Ulmus americana* L.)

False solomon's-seal (*Smilacina stellata* L.)

Fern (*Phegopteris hexagonoptera* Michx.)

Gooseberry (*Ribes oxyacanthoides* L.)

Hazelnut (*Corylus americana* Walt.)

Hemlock (*Tsuga canadensis* [L.] Carr.)

Indian turnip (*Arisaema triphyllum* [L.] Schott)

Ironwood (*Carpinus caroliniana* Walt.)

Jack pine (*Pinus banksiana* Lamb.)

Juneberry (*Amelanchier canadensis* [L.] Medic.)

Lettuce (*Lactuca sativa* L.)

Maidenhair (*Adiantum pedatum* L.)

Maple (*Acer saccharum* Marsh.)

Milkweed (*Asclepias syriaca* L.)

Nettle (*Urtica gracilis* Ait.)

Norway or red pine (*Pinus resinosa* Ait.)

Oak (*Quercus bicolor* Willd. and *Q. stellata* Wang.)

Onion (*Allium cepa* L.)

Peas (*Pisum sativum* L.)

Poison ivy (*Rhus toxicodendron* L.)

Potato (*Solanum tuberosum* L.)

Pumpkins (*Cucurbita pepo* L.)

Radishes (*Raphanus sativus* L.)

Raspberry (*Rubus idaeus* L.)

Rutabaga (*Brassica campestris* L.)

Sarsaparilla (*Aralia nudicaulis* L.)

Slippery elm (*Ulmus fulva* Michx.)

Snake root (*Aristolochia serpentaria* L.)

Spruce (*Picea rubra* [DuRoi] Dietr.)

Squash (*Cucurbita maxima* Duchesne)

Sumac (*Rhus typhina* L.)

Tamarack (*Larix laricina* [DuRoi] Koch)

Tomato (*Lycopersicum esculentum* Mill.)

White pine (*Pinus strobus* L.)

Wild currant (*Ribes floridum* L'Her.)

Wild potato (*Glycine apios* L.)

Wild rice (*Zizania aquatica* L.)

Wild rose (*Rosa pratincola* Greene)

Wild strawberry (*Fragaria virginia* Duchesne)

Wintergreen (*Gaultheria procumbens* L.)

BIBLIOGRAPHY

ARMSTRONG, BENJAMINE G.
    1892. Early life among the Indians. Ashland, Wis.
ARNOLD, JOHN B.
    1923. A story of Grand Portage and vicinity. Minneapolis.
BABBITT, Miss FRANC E.
    1888. Illustrative notes concerning the Minnesota Ojibwas. Amer. Assoc.
        Adv. Sci. Proc., vol. 36, pp. 303–307.

BARAGA, FREDERIC.
    1917. A lecture delivered in 1863.   Acta et Dicta, vol. 5, July.
    1878. A dictionary of the Ojibwa languages.   Montreal.
BARRETT, SAMUEL ALFRED.
    1911. The dream dance of the Chippewa and Menominee Indians of Northern
        Wisconsin.   Bull. Public Mus. City of Milwaukee, vol. 1, pp. 251–406.
BELTRAMI, J. C.
    1828. Pilgrimage in Europe and America leading to the discovery of the
        sources of the Mississippi and Bloody River; with a description of
        the whole course of the former and of the Ohio.   Vol. 2.   London.
BERNARD, M.
    1929. Religion and magic among the Cass Lake Ojibwa.   Primitive Man, vol.
        2, pp. 52–55.
BLACKBIRD, ANDREW J.
    1887. History of the Ottawa and Chippewa Indians of Michigan.   A grammar
        of their language, and personal and family history of the author,
        Andrew J. Blackbird, late United States interpreter.   Ypsilanti,
        Mich.
BLACKWOOD, BEATRICE.
    1929. Tales of the Chippewa Indians.   Folk-lore, vol. 40, pp. 315–344.
        London.
BLAIR, EMMA HELEN, EDITOR.
    1911–12. The Indian tribes of the upper Mississippi Valley and region of the
        Great Lakes, as described by Nicolas Perrot, French commandant
        in the Northwest; Bacqueville de la Potherie, French Royal Com-
        mander to Canada; Morrell Marston, American Army officer;
        and Thomas Forsyth, United States Indian Agent at Fort Arm-
        strong.   2 vols.   Cleveland.
BLAKESLEE, ALLEN D.
    1890. The religious customs of the Ojibway Indians.   (From the dictated
        account of Rev. S. G. Wright.)   Hayward, Wis.
BOAS, FRANZ.
    1911. Handbook of American Indian languages.   Bur. Amer. Ethnol. Bull.
        40, pt. 1.
BOND, J. WESLEY.
    1856. Minnesota and its resources.   Philadelphia.
BOTTINEAU, JEAN BAPTISTE.   See IN MEMORIAM.
BRECK, JAMES LLOYD.
    1910. Chippeway pictures from the territory of Minnesota, 1857.   Hartford.
BROWN, T. T.
    1930. Plant games and toys of Chippewa children.   Wisconsin Archeologist,
        n. s., vol. 9, pp. 185–186.
BURDEN, HAROLD NELSON.
    1895. Manitoulin; or church work among the Ojibway Indians and lumber-
        men, resident upon the Island or its vicinity.   London.
BURTON, FREDERICK R.
    1909. American primitive music with especial attention to the songs of the
        Ojibways.   New York.
BUSHNELL, DAVID I., JR.
    1905. An Ojibway ceremony.   Amer. Anthrop., n. s., vol. 7, pp. 69–73.
    1919 a. Ojibway habitations and other structures.   Ann. Rep. Smithsonian
        Inst. for 1917.

BUSHNELL, DAVID I., Jr.—Continued
  1919 b. Native villages and village sites east of the Mississippi. Bur. Amer.
      Ethnol. Bull. 69.
  1922. Villages of the Algonquian, Siouan, and Caddoan tribes. Bur. Amer.
      Ethnol. Bull. 77.
  1927. Burials of the Algonquian, Siouan, and Caddoan tribes. Bur. Amer.
      Ethnol. Bull. 83.
CALKINS, HIRAM.
  1855. Indian nomenclature of northern Wisconsin, with a sketch of the
      manners and customs of the Chippewas. Wisconsin State Hist. Soc.
      Ann. Rep. and Coll., 1854. Vol. 1, pp. 119–126.
CAMPBELL, GEORGE M.
  1940. Original Indian dictionary of the Ojibway or Chippewa language.
CAPPEL, JEANNE L'STRANGE.
  1930. Chippewa tales, retold by Wa-be-no O-pee-chee. Los Angeles.
CARLSON, E. J.
  1934. Indian rice camps, White Earth Reservation. Indians at Work, vol. 2,
      No. 7, pp. 16–23.
CARVER, JONATHAN.
  1779 a. Travels through the interior parts of North America, in the years
      1766, 1767, and 1768. London.
  1779 b. Travels through the interior parts of North America, 1779. Dublin.
CASTILE, HENRY A.
  1915. Minnesota, its story and biography. Vol. 1. Chicago.
CATLIN, GEORGE.
  1852 a. Adventures of Ojibbeway and Ioway Indians in England, France,
      and Belgium. London.
  1852 b. Adventures of the Ojibway and Ioway Indians in England, France,
      and Belgium; being notes of eight years' travels and residence in
      Europe with his North American Indian collection. 2 vols.
  1926. North American Indians, being letters and notes on their manners,
      customs, and conditions, written during eight years' travel amongst
      the wildest tribes of Indians in North America, 1832–1839. 2 vols.
CHAMBERLAIN, ALEXANDER FRANCIS.
  1888. Notes on the history, customs, and beliefs of the Mississaugas. Journ.
      Amer. Folklore. July.
  1889. Tales of the Mississaugas. Journ. Amer. Folklore, vol. 2, pp. 141–147.
  1891. Maple sugar and the Indians. Amer. Anthrop., vol. 4, pp. 381–384.
CHAMBLISS, CHARLES E.
  1940. The botany and history of *Zizania aquatica* L. ("wild rice"). Journ.
      Washington Acad. Sci., vol. 30, pp. 185–205, illus. (Reprinted In
      Smithsonian Ann. Rep. for 1940, pp. 369–382.)
CHARLEVOIX, PIERRE FRANCOIS XAVIER DE.
  1763. Letters to the Duchess of Lesdiguieres; giving an account of a voyage
      to Canada, and travels through that vast country, and Louisiana,
      to the Gulf of Mexico. London.
  1766. A voyage to North America: Undertaken by command of the present
      King of France. Containing the geographical description and na-
      tural history of Canada and Louisiana. With customs, manners,
      trade and religion of the inhabitants. Dublin.
  1923. Journal of a voyage to North America. Chicago. (Original edition:
      London, 1761.)

CHIPPEWA INDIANS IN MINNESOTA, message from the President of the United States, transmitting a communication from the Secretary of the Interior relative to the Chippewa Indians in the State of Minnesota, March 6, 1890. U. S. House Ex. Doc. No. 247, 51st Congress, 1st Sess.

COLEMAN, Sister BERNARD.
 1937. The religion of the Ojibwa of Northern Minnesota. Primitive Man, vol. 10, pp. 33–57.
 1929. Religion and magic among the Cass Lake Ojibwa. Primitive Man, vol. 2, pp. 52–53.
 1947. Decorative designs of the Ojibwa of northern Minnesota. Cath. Univ. Amer.

CONSTITUTION AND BY-LAWS OF THE MINNESOTA CHIPPEWA. 1936. Washington.

COOPER, JOHN MONTGOMERY.
 1936. Notes on the ethnology of the Otchipwe of Lake of the Woods and Rainy Lake. Catholic Univ. Amer., Anthrop. Ser. No. 3.

COPE, LEONA.
 1919. Calendars of the Indians north of Mexico. Univ. Calif. Publ. Amer. Archaeol. and Ethnol., vol. 16, No. 4, pp. 119–176.

COPWAY, GEORGE.
 1874. The life, history, and travels of Kah-ge-ga-gah-bowh (George Copway) a young Indian chief of the Ojibwa nation, a convert to the Christian faith. Albany.
 1851. The traditional history and characteristic sketches of the Ojibway nation. Boston.
 1860. Indian life and Indian history. Boston.

CORPORATE CHARTER OF THE MINNESOTA CHIPPEWA TRIBE OF THE CONSOLIDATED CHIPPEWA AGENCY. Washington. 1938.

CULIN, STEWART.
 1907. Games of the North American Indians. 24th Ann. Rep. Bur. Amer. Ethnol., 1902–3.

CULKIN, WILLIAM.
 1915. Tribal dance of the Ojibway Indians. Minnesota Hist. Bull., vol. 1, pp. 83–93.

CURTIS, EDWARD S.
 1907–30. The North American Indian, being a series of volumes picturing and describing the Indians of the United States and Alaska. (Ed. by Frederick Webb Hodge.) Cambridge.

DALLY, NATHAN.
 1931. Tracks and trails; or incidents in the life of a Minnesota territorial pioneer. Walker, Minn.

DAVIDSON, J. A.
 1945. Ojibwa songs. Jour. Amer. Folklore, vol. 58, pp. 303–305.

DAVIDSON, J. N.
 1895. In unnamed Wisconsin studies in the history of the region between Lake Michigan and the Mississippi. To which is appended a memoir of Mrs. Harriet Wheeler. Milwaukee.

DENSMORE, FRANCES.
 1907. An Ojibwa prayer ceremony. Amer. Anthrop., vol. 9, pp. 443–444.
 1910. Chippewa music. Bur. Amer. Ethnol. Bull. 45.
 1913. Chippewa music. Bur. Amer. Ethnol. Bul. 53.
 1918. Study of Chippewa material culture. Smithsonian Misc. Coll., vol. 68, pp. 95–100.

DENSMORE, FRANCES—Continued
  1919. Material culture among the Chippewa. Smithsonian Misc. Coll., vol. 70, pp. 114–118.
  1920. Material culture of the Chippewa of Canada. Explorations and Field Work of the Smithsonian Inst. in 1919.
  1928. Uses of plants by the Chippewa Indians. 44th Ann. Rep. Bur. Amer. Ethnol., 1926–27, pp. 275–397.
  1929. Chippewa customs. Bur. Amer. Ethnol. Bul. 86.
  1941. Native art of the Chippewa. Amer. Anthrop., vol. 43, pp. 678–681.
DUCATEL, I. I.
  1877. A fortnight among the Chippewas of Lake Superior. Ed. by W. W. Beach. Indian Miscellany, pp. 361–378. Albany. (Reprinted from N. S. Catholic Magazine, January and February 1846.)
EASTMAN, A. C.
  1911. Life and handicrafts of the Northern Ojibways. Southern Workman, vol. 40, pp. 273–278.
ENGELHARDT, ZEPHYRIN.
  1901. Anishinabe Negamod. A collection of hymns in Ottawa and Chippewa languages. Harbor Springs, Mich.
ELLIOTT, RICHARD R.
  1896. The Chippewas of Lake Superior. Amer. Catholic Quart. Rev., vol. 21, pp. 354–373.
  1897. The Chippewas and Ottawas. Amer. Catholic Quart. Rev., vol. 22, pp. 18–46.
EWING, CHARLES.
  1873. Petition of the Catholic Church for the agency of the Chippewas of Lake Superior. Washington.
FLANNERY, REGINA.
  1940. The cultural position of the Spanish River Indians. Primitive Man, vol. 13, pp. 1–25.
FOLWELL, WILLIAM WATTS.
  1921–26. A history of Minnesota. 4 vols.
FRIEDL, E.
  1944. Note on birchbark transparencies. Amer. Anthrop., vol. 46, pp. 149–150 (bibliog.).
GENERAL INDEX, ANNUAL REPORTS OF THE BUREAU OF AMERICAN ETHNOLOGY, Volumes 1–48 (1879 to 1933), compiled by Biren Bonnerjea. 48th Ann. Rep. Bur. Amer. Ethnol., 1930–31, pp. 25–1221. 1933.
GILFILLAN, JOSEPH A.
  1901. The Ojibways in Minnesota. Coll. Minn. Hist. Soc., vol. 9.
  1902. Ojibwa characteristics. Southern Workman, vol. 31, pp. 260–262.
  1904. The Ojibway, a novel of Indian life of the period of the early advance of civilization in the great Northwest. New York and Washington.
GILLIN, J.
  1942. Acquired drives in culture contact; Flambeau band of Chippewa Indians. Amer. Anthrop., vol. 44, pp. 545–554 (bibliog.).
GILLIN, J., and RAIMY, V.
  1940. Acculturation and personality; field work with the Lac du Flambeau band of Chippewa in northern Wisconsin. Amer. Sociological Rev., vol. 5, pp. 371–380 (bibliog.).
GILMORE, MELVIN RANDOLPH.
  1933. Some Chippewa uses of plants. Mich. Acad. Sci., Art, and Lit. Pap., vol. 17, pp. 119–143.

GLAZIER, WILLARD.
    1891. Down the great river; embracing an account of the discovery of the true
        source of the Mississippi, together with views, descriptive and pic-
        torial, of the cities, towns, and villages and scenery on the banks
        of the river, as seen during a canoe voyage of over three thousand
        miles from its head waters to the Gulf of Mexico. Philadelphia.
GODSELL, P. H.
    1932. The Ojibwa Indian. Canadian Geol. Journ., vol. 4, pp. 51–66.
GRANT, JOHN CHARLES BODEAU.
    1929. Anthropometry of the Cree and Saulteaux Indians in northeastern
        Manitoba. Canadian Geol. Surv. Bull. 59, Anthrop. Ser. No. 13.
HALF-BREED SCRIP OF CHIPPEWAS OF LAKE SUPERIOR.
    1874. Washington.
HALLOWELL, A. IRVING.
    1928. Was cross-cousin marriage practiced by the North-Central Algonkian?
        Proc. 23rd Int. Congr. Amer., pp. 519–544. Philadelphia.
    1934 a. Some empirical aspects of Northern Saulteaux religion. Amer.
        Anthrop., vol. 36.
    1934 b. Culture and mental disorder. Journ. Abnormal and Social Psychol-
        ogy, vol. 29, pp. 1–9.
    1936 a. Psychic stresses and culture patterns. Amer. Journ. Psychiatry,
        vol. 92, pp. 1291–1310.
    1936 b. The passing of the Midewiwin in the Lake Winnipeg region. Amer.
        Anthrop., n. s., vol. 38, pp. 32–51.
    1937 a. Temporal orientation in western civilization and in a preliterate
        society. Amer. Anthrop., vol. 39. pp. 647–670.
    1937 b. Cross-cousin marriage in the Lake Winnipeg area. 25th Anniversary
        Studies: Philadelphia Anthrop. Soc., pp. 95–110. (Edited by D. S.
        Davidson.)
    1938 a. Fear and anxiety as cultural and individual variables in a primitive
        society. Journ. Soc. Psychology, vol. 9, pp. 25–47.
    1938 b. Shabwan: A dissocial Indian girl. Amer. Journ. Orthopsychiatry,
        vol. 8, pp. 329–340.
    1938 c. The incidence, character and decline of polygyny among the Lake
        Winnipeg Cree and Saulteaux. Amer. Anthrop., vol. 40, pp. 235–
        256.
    1938 d. Notes on the material culture of the Island Lake Saulteaux. Journ.
        Soc. Amér., n. s., Paris, vol. 30, pp. 129–140.
    1939. Sin, sex, and sickness in Saulteaux belief. Brit. Journ. Med. Psychology,
        vol. 18, pp. 191–197.
    1940 a. Aggression in Saulteaux society. Psychiatry, vol. 3, pp. 395–407.
    1940 b. The spirits of the dead in Saulteaux life and thought. Journ. Roy.
        Anthrop. Inst., vol. 70, pp. 29–51.
    1941. The social function of anxiety in a primitive society. Amer. Sociological
        Rev., vol. 4, pp. 869–881.
    1942 a. Some psychological aspects of measurement among the Saulteaux.
        Amer. Anthrop., vol. 44, pp. 62–77.
    1942 b. The role of conjuring in Saulteaux society. Philadelphia.
    1946. Concordance of Ojibwa narratives in the published works of Henry
        R. Schoolcraft. Vol. 59, pp. 136–153 (bibliog.).
HAMMOND, J. H.
    1904. The Ojibway of Lakes Huron and Sinicoe. Ann. Archeol. Rep. Min-
        ister Ed. Ontario, pp. 71–73.

HART, IRVING HARLOW.
1928. The story of Beengwa, daughter of a Chippewa warrior. Minnesota History, vol. 9, pp. 319–330.
HASKETH, JOHN.
1923. History of the Turtle Mountain Chippewa. North Dakota State Hist. Soc. Coll., vol. 5, pp. 85–124.
HEARD, ISAAC V. D.
1865. History of the Sioux war and massacres of 1862 and 1863. New York.
HENRY, ALEXANDER.
1921. Travels and adventures in Canada. Edited by M. M. Quaife. Chicago.
HILGER, SISTER M. INEZ.
1935 a. Indian women preparing bulrush mats. Indians at Work, vol. 2, No. 2, p. 41. July 1.
1935 b. Indian women making birch-bark receptacles. Indians at Work, vol. 3, No. 3, pp. 19–21. September 15.
1935 c. A "Peace and Friendship" medal. Minnesota History, vol. 16, pp. 321–323. September.
1936 a. Chippewa customs. Primitive Man, vol. 9, pp. 17–24. April.
1936 b. Chippewa hunting and fishing customs. Minnesota Conservationist, pp. 2–3, 17–19. April.
1936 c. In the early days of Wisconsin, an amalgamation of Chippewa and European cultures. Wisconsin Archeologist, vol. 16, pp. 32–49, n. s., June.
1936 d. Chippewa pre-natal food and conduct taboos. Primitive Man, vol. 9, pp. 46–48. July.
1936 e. Letters and documents of Bishop Baraga extant in the Chippewa country. Records Amer. Catholic Hist. Soc., vol. 47, pp. 292–302.
1937 a. Chippewa interpretation of natural phenomena. Scientific Monthly, vol. 45, pp. 178–179.
1937 b. Some phases of Chippewa material culture. Anthropos, vol. 32, pp. 780–782.
1939. Social survey of one hundred and fifty Chippewa Indian families on the White Earth Reservation of Minnesota. Washington.
HODGE, FREDERICK WEBB, EDITOR.
1907, 1910. Handbook of American Indians North of Mexico. Bur. Amer. Ethnol. Bull. 30, pts. 1 and 2.
HOFFMAN, W. J.
1891. The Mide'wiwin or "Grand Medicine Society" of the Ojibwa. 7th Ann. Rep. Bur. Amer. Ethnol., 1885–1886.
1888. Pictography and shamanistic rites of the Ojibwas. Amer. Anthrop., vol. 1, pp. 209–229.
1889. Notes on Ojibwa folk-lore. Amer. Anthrop., vol. 2, pp. 215–223.
1890. Remarks on Ojibwa ball play. Amer. Anthrop., vol. 3, pp. 133–135.
HOUGHTON, DOUGLAS.
1928. Michigan Historical Society Geological Reports, 1837–1845.
HRDLIČKA, ALEŠ.
1916. Anthropology of the Chippewa. In Holmes Anniversary Volume, pp. 198–227. (Edited by F. W. Hodge; printed by the G. W. Bryan Press. Washington.)
HUGOLIN, PÈRE.
1907. L'idee spiritualiste et l'idee morale chez les Chippewa. Int. Congr. Amer., 15th sess., Quebec, 1906. Compte rendu, vol. 1, pp. 329–335.

HULBERT, THOMAS.
    1846. Hymns in the Chippewa and Ottawa language to which is appended a
        short summary of Christian doctrine.
IN MEMORIAM, JEAN BAPTISTE BOTTINEAU.
    1912. Obit. Dec. 1st, 1911. Washington.
JENKS, ALBERT ERNEST.
    1900 a. The childhood of Ji-shib. Chicago.
    1900 b. The wild-rice gatherers of the upper lakes. 19th Ann. Rep. Bur.
        Amer. Ethnol., 1897–1898, pt. 2, pp. 1013–1137.
    1902. The bear-maiden. An Ojibway folk-tale from Lac Courte Orielle
        Reservation, Wisconsin. Amer. Folklore Assoc. Journ. vol. 15,
        pp. 33–35.
JENNESS, DIAMOND.
    1932. The Indians of Canada. Nat. Mus. Canada Bull. 65.
    1935. The Ojibway Indians of Parry Island, their social and religious life.
        Nat. Mus. Canada Bull. 78, Anthrop. Ser. No. 17.
JESUIT RELATIONS AND ALLIED DOCUMENTS.
    1897. Vols. 1 and 12. Cleveland.
JOHNSON, FREDERICK.
    1929. Notes on the Ojibwa and Potawatomi of the Parry Island Reserva-
        tion, Ontario. Mus. Amer. Ind., Heye Foundation, Notes and Mono-
        graphs, vol. 6, pp. 193–215. New York.
JONES, PETER.
    1860. Life and journal of Kah-ke-wa-quo-na-by (Rev. Peter Jones), Wesleyan
        Missionary. Toronto.
    [186?] History of the Ojibway Indians. London. 2d issue (First published
        in 1861. Cf. Sabin).
JONES, VOLNEY H.
    1934. A Chippewa method of manufacturing wooden brooms. Mich. Acad.
        Sci. Papers, vol. 20, pp. 23–30.
    1935. Some Chippewa and Ottawa uses of sweet grass. Mich Acad. Sci.
        Papers, vol. 21, pp. 21–31.
    1936. Notes on the preparation and uses of basswood fiber by the Indians of
        the Great Lakes region. Mich. Acad. Sci. Papers, vol. 22, pp. 1–14.
JONES, WILLIAM.
    1906. Central Algonkin. Annual Archeological Report, 1905, in Appendix
        to the Rep. Minister Ed. Ontario, pp. 136–146. Toronto.
    1919. Ojibway texts. (Edited by Truman Michelson.) Amer. Ethnol. Soc.
        Publ., 1915, vol. 7.
JOSSELIN DE JONG, J. P. B.
    1913. Original Odzibwe texts with English translations, notes and vocab-
        ulary. In Baessler-archivische Beiheft 5. Leipzig.
KAPPLER, CHARLES, EDITOR.
    1903–29. Indian affairs: laws and treaties. 4 vols.
KARPEINSKI, LOUIS C.
    1931. Map and bibliography of Michigan and Great Lakes region, 1804–1880.
KEATING, WILLIAM HYPOLITUS.
    1825. Narrative of an expedition to the source of St. Peter's River, Lake
        Winnepeck, Lake of the Woods, etc., performed in the year 1823.
        London.
KELLOGG, LOUISE PHELPS, EDITOR.
    1917. Early narrative of the Northwest, 1634–1699. New York.

KINIETZ, W. VERNON.
    1940. The Indian tribes of the western Great Lakes, 1615–1760. Occasional
        Contrib. from Museum Anthrop. Univ. Mich., No. 10, pp. xiv–427.
KINIETZ, W. VERNON, and JONES, VOLNEY H.
    1942. Notes on the manufacture of rush mats among the Chippewa.
        Papers, Mich. Acad. Sci., Arts, and Letters, 1941, vol. 27.
KINNEY, JAY P.
    1937. A continent lost—a civilization won: Indian land tenure in America.
        Baltimore.
KOHL, JOHANN G.
    1859. Kitschi-Gami; order Erzählungen vom Obern-See. Ein Bietrag zur
        Charakteristik der Amerikanischen Indianer. (Wraxall trans.)
        Bremen.
LAFLEUR, L. J.
    1940. On the Mide' of the Ojibway. Amer. Anthrop., n. s., vol. 42, pp. 706–
        708.
LAIDLAW, G. E.
    1915–22. Ojibway myths and tales. Ann. Archeol. Rep., App. Rep. Minister
        Ed. Ontario. 1915, pp. 71–90; 1920, pp. 66–85; 1921–22, pp. 84–99.
        Toronto.
    1922. Ojibway myths and tales. Wisconsin Archeologist, n. s., vol. 1, pp.
        28–38.
LANDES, RUTH.
    1937 a. Ojibwa sociology. New York.
    1937 b. The personality of the Ojibwa. Character and Personality, vol. 6,
        pp. 51–60.
    1937 c. The Ojibwa of Canada. In Cooperation and competition among
        primitive peoples, ed. by Margaret Mead. pp. 87–126.
    1938 a. The abnormal among the Ojibwa Indians. Journ. Abnormal and
        Social Psychology, vol. 33, pp. 14–33.
    1938 b. The Ojibwa woman. New York.
LATHROP, STANLEY EDWARDS.
    1905. A historical sketch of the Old Mission, and its missionaries to the
        Ojibway Indians on Madeline Island, Lake Superior, Wisconsin.
        Ashland, Wis.
LINDERMAN, FRANK BIRD.
    1915. Indian why stories; sparks from War Eagles' lodge fire. New York.
    1920. Indian old-man stories; more sparks from War Eagles' lodge fire.
        New York.
LIPS, J. E.
    1937. Notes on some Ojibway traps. Ethnos, vol. 2, pp. 354–360.
LISTS SHOWING THE DEGREE OF INDIAN BLOOD OF CERTAIN PERSONS HOLDING LAND
    UPON THE WHITE EARTH RESERVATION IN MINNESOTA AND A LIST SHOWING
    THE DATE OF CERTAIN PERSONS WHO HELD LAND UPON SUCH RESERVATION.
    Washington. 1911.
LONG, JOHN.
    1904. Journal, 1768–1782. Cleveland.
    1791. Voyages and travels of an Indian interpreter and trader describing
        the manner and customs of the North American Indians. London.
LOWIE, ROBERT H.
    1917. Ojibwa. In Hastings' Encyclopedia on Religion and Ethics, vol. 9,
        pp. 454–458. Edinburgh.

LYFORD, CARRIE A.
   1943. The crafts of the Ojibwa. Office of Indian Affairs. Indian Hand-
      crafts, 5.
MASON, OTIS TUFTON.
   1896. Primitive travel and transportation. In Rep. U. S. Nat. Mus. for
      1894.
MAUN-GWA-DANS.
   1848. An account of the Chippewa Indians who have been travelling among
      the Whites, in the United States, England, Ireland, Scotland, France
      and Belgium. Boston.
McCLINCHEY, FLORENCE.
   1929. Joe Pete, a story of Indian life in northern Michigan. New York.
McGEE, W J
   1898. Ojibwa feather symbolism. Amer. Anthrop., vol. 11, pp. 177-180.
McKENNEY, THOMAS LORAINE.
   1827. Sketches of a tour to the lakes, of the character and customs of the
      Chippeway Indians, and of incidents connected with the treaty of
      Fond du Lac. Baltimore.
   1846. Memories, official and personal: With sketches of travels among
      northern and southern Indians; embracing a war excursion and
      descriptions of scenes along the western borders. New York.
McKINSEY, SHIRLEY
   MS. Report of 1937-1938 based on a survey of the six Chippewa reservations
      under the Consolidated Chippewa Agency. Duluth. 1938.
MEANS, PHILIP AINSWORTH.
   1917. Preliminary survey of the remains of the Chippewa settlements on
      the La Pointe Island, Wisconsin. Smithsonian Misc. Coll., vol.
      66, No. 14.
MEDICINAL PLANT RESOURCES OF MINNESOTA.
   1942. St. Paul.
MEMORIAL OF THE CHIPPEWAY, POTTAWATOMY, AND OTTAWA INDIANS OF WALPOLE
ISLAND.
   1869. Ontario.
MICHELSON, TRUMAN.
   1912. Preliminary report on the linguistic classification of the Algonquian
      tribes. 28th Ann. Rep. Bur. Amer. Ethnol. 1906-07, pp. 221-290.
   1926. Studies of the Fox and Ojibwa Indians. Smithsonian Misc. Coll., vol.
      78, No. 1, pp. 111-113.
   1934. Maiden sacrifice among the Ojibwa. Amer. Anthrop., vol. 36, pp.
      628-629.
MILES, NELSON APPLETON.
   1896. Personal recollections and observations. Chicago.
MINNESOTA IN THREE CENTURIES, 1655-1908.
   1908. 2 vols. Minneapolis.
MONCKTON, ELIZABETH.
   1904. The white canoe and other legends of the Ojibways. New York.
MOONEY, JAMES, and THOMAS, CYRUS.
   1907. Article on Chippewa. In Handbook of American Indians North of
      Mexico. Bur. Amer. Ethnol. Bull. 30, pt. 1, pp. 277-281.
MORSE, RICHARD E.
   1857. The Chippewas of Lake Superior. In Wisconsin State Hist. Soc. Ann.
      Rep. and Coll., 1856, vol. 3, pp. 338-369.

NEILL, EDWARD DUFFIELD.
  1885. History of the Ojibways and their connection with fur traders, based upon official and other documents. *In* Minnesota Hist. Soc. Coll., 1885, vol. 5, pp. 395–510.
  1887. The last French post in the valley of the upper Mississippi near Frontenac, Minnesota. St. Paul.
O'BRIEN, FRANK G.
  1904. Minnesota pioneer sketches, from personal recollections and observations of a pioneer resident. Minneapolis.
OJIBWAY AND ENGLISH EASY READER.
  1906. Toronto.
OLIPHANT, LAURENCE.
  1885. Minnesota and the far West. Edinburgh and London.
ORR, R. B.
  1915. The Mississauges. Ann. Archeol. Rep. Minister Ed. Ontario, pp. 7–18.
  1918. The Chippewa Indians. Ann. Archeol. Rep. Minister Ed. Ontario, pp. 0–23.
  1920. Snowshoes. Ann. Archeol. Rep. Minister Ed. Ontario. Toronto.
OSBORN, E. B.
  1900. Greater Canada. New York.
PARKMAN, FRANCIS.
  1908. The Jesuits in North America in the seventeenth century. Boston.
PERROT, NICOLAS. *See* HODGE, F. W., 1907.
PHILLIPS, RICHARD.
  1807. A collection of modern and contemporary voyages and travels. Vol. 6, No. 4. London.
PHONETIC TRANSCRIPTION OF INDIAN LANGUAGES.
  1916. Report of Committee of American Anthropological Association. Smithsonian Misc. Coll., vol. 66, No. 6.
PIERZ, FRANZ.
  1855. Die Indianer in Nord-Amerika, ihre Lebensweise, Sitten, Gebräuche, etc. St. Louis.
PILLING, JAMES CONSTANTINE.
  1891. Bibliography of the Algonquian languages. Bur. Amer. Ethnol. Bull. 13.
PITEZEL, JOHN H.
  1860. Lights and shades of missionary life. Cincinnati.
PRUD'HOMME, L. A.
  1916. Pierre Gaultier de Varennes, Sieur de la Verendrye, Captain of Marines, Chevalier of the Military Order of St. Louis, Discoverer of the North-West 1685–1749. Bull. Hist. Soc. St. Boniface, Manitoba, vol. 5, pt. 2.
RADIN, PAUL.
  1914 a. An introductive enquiry in the study of Ojibwa religion. Pap. and Rec. Ontario Hist. Soc., vol. 12, pp. 210–218.
  1914 b. Some aspects of puberty fasting among the Ojibwa. Canadian Dept. Mines, Geol. Surv. Mus. Bull. No. 2, Anthrop. Ser. No. 2.
  1914 c. Some myths and tales of the Ojibwa of southeastern Ontario. Anthrop. Ser. Dept. Mines of Canada, Mem. 48, No. 2.
  1924. Ojibwa ethnological chit-chat. Amer. Anthrop. n. s., vol. 26, pp. 491–530.

RADIN, PAUL, and REAGAN, ALBERT B.
    1928. Ojibwa myths and tales. Journ. Amer. Folklore, vol. 41, pp. 61–146.
    1936. Ojibwa and Ottawa puberty dreams. *In* Essays in Anthropology Presented to A. L. Kroeber, pp. 233–264.
REAGAN, ALBERT B.
    1919. Some games of the Bois Fort Ojibwa. Amer. Anthrop. n. s., vol. 21, pp. 264–278.
    1921 a. Wild or Indian rice. Proc. Indiana Acad. Sci., 1919, pp. 241–242.
    1921 b. Some Chippewa medicinal receipts. Amer. Anthrop., n. s., vol. 23, pp. 246–249.
    1922. Medicine songs of George Farmer. Amer. Anthrop., vol. 24, pp. 332–369.
    1923. Rainy Lakes Indians. Wisconsin Archeologist, vol. 2, pp. 140–147.
    1924. The Bois Fort Chippewa. Wisconsin Archeologist, n. s., vol. 3, pp. 101–132.
    1927. Picture writings of the Chippewa Indians. Wisconsin Archeologist, vol. 6, pp. 80–83.
    1928. Plants used by the Bois Fort Chippewa Indians of Minnesota. Wisconsin Archeologist, vol. 7, pp. 230–248.
    1934. The O-ge-che-dah or Head-men dance of the Bois Fort Indians. Americana, vol. 28, pp. 302–306. (Amer. Hist. Soc.)
REID, A. P.
    1873. Religious beliefs of the Ojibois or Sauteux Indians. Journ. Roy. Anthrop. Inst., vol. 3, pp. 106–113.
REPPLIER, AGNES.
    1929. Père Marquette. New York.
RICHARDSON, JOHN.
    1924. Tecumseh and Richardson; the story of a trip to Walpole Island and Fort Sarnia. Toronto.
RIGGS, STEPHEN R.
    1887. Protestant missions in the Northwest. Coll. Minnesota Hist. Soc., vol. 6, pt. 1, pp. 117–188.
RITZENTHALER, R.
    1943. Impact of war on an Indian community. Amer. Anthrop., vol. 45, pp. 325–326.
    1945 a. Acquisition of surnames by the Chippewa Indians. Amer. Anthrop., vol. 47, pp. 175–177.
    1945 b. Totemic insult among the Wisconsin Chippewa. Amer. Anthrop., vol. 47, pp. 322–324.
    1945. c. Ceremonial destruction of sickness by the Wisconsin Chippewa. Amer. Anthrop., vol. 47, pp. 320–322.
ROGERS, ROBERT.
    1765. A concise account of North America . . . Also of the interior of westerly parts of the country, upon the rivers of St. Lawrence, the Mississippi, Charistino, and Great Lakes. London.
    1918. Journal (Ed. Wm. L. Clements) Worcester. (*Reprinted from* Proc. Amer. Antiq. Soc. for Oct. 1918.)
SAGATOO, MARY A.
    1897. Wah Sash Kah Moqua; or thirty-three years among the Indians. Boston.

SCHOOLCRAFT, HENRY ROWE.
    1834. Narrative of an expedition through the upper Mississippi to Itasca
          Lake, the actual source of the river; embracing an exploratory trip
          through the St. Croix and Burntwood (or Broule) Rivers: in 1832.
          New York.
    1855. Summary narrative of an exploratory expedition to the source of the
          Mississippi River, in 1820. Philadelphia.
SCHMIDT, WILHELM.
    1934. Der Ursprung der Gottesidee. II Teil, V Band, pp. 555–564. Muenster.
SHORT HISTORY AND DESCRIPTION OF THE OJIBBEWAY INDIANS NOW ON A VISIT TO
    ENGLAND . . .
    1844. London.
SKINNER, ALANSON.
    1908–10. Ojibway and Cree of Central Canada. Amer. Mus. Journ., vol. 10,
          pp. 9–18.
    1911. Notes on the Eastern Cree and the Northern Saulteaux. Amer. Mus.
          Nat. Hist. Anthrop. Pap., vol. 0, pt. 1.
    1914 a. Political organization, cults and ceremonies of the Plains Ojibway
          and Plains Cree Indians. -Amer. Mus. Nat. Hist. Anthrop. Pap.,
          vol. 11, pt. 4.
    1014 b. The cultural position of the Plains Ojibway. Amer. Anthrop., vol.
          16, pp. 314–318.
    1919. Plains Ojibway tales. Journ. Amer. Folklore, vol. 32, pp. 208–305.
    1920. Medicine ceremony of the Menomini, Iowa, Whapeton Dakota, with
          notes on the ceremony among the Ponco, Bungi Ojibwa and Pota-
          watomi. Mus. Amer. Ind. Heye Found. Notes and Monographs,
          vol. 4. New York.
    1921 a. The sun dance of the Plains Ojibway. Amer. Mus. Nat Hist.
          Anthrop. Pap., vol. 16, pp. 311–315.
    1921. b. Material culture of the Menomini. Mus. Amer. Ind. Heye Found.,
          Notes and Monographs, Misc. Publ. No. 20. New York.
SMITH, HARLAN INGERSOLL.
    1906. Some Ojibwa myths and traditions. Journ. Amer. Folklore, vol. 19,
          pp. 215–230.
SMITH, HURON HERBERT.
    1932. Ethnobotany of the Ojibwa Indians. Bull. Public Mus. City of Mil-
          waukee, vol. 4, No. 3.
SMITH, WILLIAM RUDOLPH.
    1927. Incidents of a journey from Pennsylvania to Wisconsin Territory, in
          1837. Chicago.
SNELLING, WILLIAM JOSEPH.
    1830. Tales of the Northwest; or sketches of Indian life and character, by
          a resident beyond the frontier. Boston.
    1868. Early days at Prairie du Chien and the Winnebago outbreak of 1827.
          Wisconsin State Hist. Soc. Rep. and Coll., 1867–1869.
SOCIAL AND ECONOMIC SURVEY OF 1934 OF THE CONSOLIDATED CHIPPEWA AGENCY.
    Ms. United States Bureau of Indian Affairs.
SOME OJIBWAY BUFFALO ROBES. Univ. Pa. Mus. Journ., vol. 7, pp. 93–96. 1916.
SPECK, FRANK C.
    1915. Family hunting territories and social life of various Algonkian bands
          of the Ottawa valley. Includes myths and folklore of the Timiskam-
          ing Algonquin and Timagami Ojibwa. Canadian Geol. Surv. Mem.
          70–71, Anthrop. Ser., Nos. 8 and 9.

STICKNEY, J. D.
    1914. The Warren family history and genealogy as compiled by Mr. J. D. Stickney, Paris, France. St. Paul.
SWEET, GEORGE W.
    1894. Incidents of the threatened outbreak of Hole-in-the-Day and other Ojibways at time of Sioux massacre of 1862. Minn. Hist. Soc. Coll., vol. 6, pp. 401–408.
TANNER, JOHN.
    1830. Narrative of the captivity and adventures of John Tanner (U. S. interpreter at the Sault de Ste. Marie) during thirty years residence among the Indians in the interior of North America. Edited by Edwin James. New York.
THOMAS, CYRUS. See Mooney, James.
TOMKINS, WILLIAM.
    1926. Universal Indian sign language of the Plains Indians of North America, together with a dictionary of synonyms covering the basic words represented also by a codification of pictographic word symbols of the Ojibway and Sioux nations. San Diego.
TYRRELL, J. B.
    1916. David Thompson's narrative of his explorations in western America. Toronto.
UNITED STATES CONGRESS. SENATE COMMITTEE ON INDIAN AFFAIRS.
    1934. Survey of conditions of the Indians of the United States; hearings . . . 73d Congress, 1933.
UNITED STATES CONGRESSIONAL HOUSE COMMITTEE ON EXPENDITURES IN THE INTERIOR DEPARTMENT.
    1913. Report in the matter of the investigation of the White Earth Reservation . . . Minnesota . . . from July 25, 1911, to March 28, 1912.
UNITED STATES HOUSE EXECUTIVE DOCUMENTS No. 247. 51ST CONGRESS, 1ST SESSION. VOL. 32.
    1889–90.
UNITED STATES OFFICE OF INDIAN AFFAIRS.
    1940. Annual report. Statistical suppl. Washington.
UNITED STATES STATUTES AT LARGE. VOL. 43, CHAPTER 233; VOL 48, CHAPTER 147.
VAN CLEVE, CHARLOTTE OUISCONSIN.
    1888. Three score years and ten, life-long memories of Fort Snelling, Minnesota, and other parts of the West. Minneapolis.
VAN DUSEN, C.
    1867. The Indian chief: An account of the labors, loses, sufferings, and oppression of Ke-zig-ko-e-ne-ne (David Sawyer) a chief of the Ojibbeway Indians in Canada west. London.
VERWYST, CHRYSOSTOMUS.
    1886. Missionary labors of Father Marquette, Menard, and Allouez in the Lake Superior region. Chicago.
    1900. Life and labors of Rt. Rev. Frederic Baraga, First Bishop of Marquette, Michigan. Milwaukee.
    1901. Chippewa exercises, being a practical introduction into the study of the Chippewa language. Harbor Springs.
WARREN, WILLIAM.
    1885. History of the Ojibways. Coll. Minnesota Hist. Soc., vol. 5.
WATRIN, BENNO, EDITOR.
    1930. The Ponsfordian, 1880–1930. A collection of historical data dealing especially with pioneer days of Ponsford, Becker County, Minn. Park Rapids.

WHIPPLE, HENRY BENJAMIN.
    1901. Civilization and Christianization of the Ojibways of Minnesota. Coll.
        Minnesota Hist. Soc., vol. 9.
WINCHELL, N. H., EDITOR.
    1911. The aborigines of Minnesota, a report based on the collection of Jacob
        V. Brower, and on the field surveys and notes of Alfred J. Hill and
        Theodore H. Lewis. St. Paul.
WILSON, EDWARD FRANCIS.
    1886. Missionary work among the Ojibway Indians. London and New York.
WISSLER, CLARK.
    1922. The American Indian, an introduction to the anthropology of the New
        World. New York.
YOUNG, EGERTON RYERSON.
    1890. By canoe and dog-train among the Cree and Saulteaux Indians.
        Toronto.
    1897. On the Indian trail; stories of missionary work among the Cree and
        Saulteaux Indians. New York.
ZSCHOKKE, HERMAN.
    1881 a. Ein Besuch bei den Chippewas-Indianern in der Reservation White
        Earth in Nordamerika. Berichte der Leopoldinenstiftung in
        Kaiserthume Oesterreich. LI. Heft.
    1881 b. Nach Nordamerika und Canada, Schilderungen von Land und Leuten.
        Würzburg.

INFORMANTS, RED LAKE RESERVATION, 1933.

1, John Baptist Thunder and daughter, Jane Bonga. *2*, Charley Johnson.
3, Angeline Highlanding. *4*, Ella Badboy.

MOTHERS CARRYING BABIES IN CRADLE BOARD.

1, Mrs. Howard Pete, Vermilion Lake Reservation, 1939. *2*, Woman in Ponemah village, Red Lake Reservation, 1933. *3*, Baby ready for cradle board, Mille Lacs Reservation, 1940.

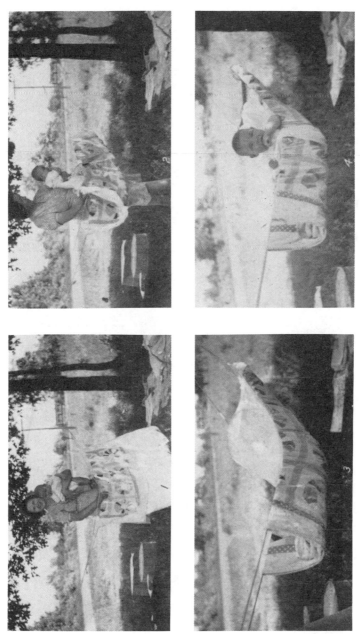

MILDRED HILL PUTTING SON JIMMY TO SLEEP IN A HAMMOCK, MILLE LACS RESERVATION, 1940.

1 and 2, Preparing hammock. 3, Baby asleep in hammock. Notice netting over hoop as a protection against flies and insects. 4, Baby after its nap. Notice stick holding ropes apart at head end.

MILLE LACS RESERVATION BABY TRANSPORTED ON MOTHER'S BACK, 1940.

1, Swinging to mother's back.   *2*, Carrying baby on back.   *3*, Dropping baby off back.

CHIPPEWA CHILDREN.

1 and 2, White Earth Reservation, 1938.   3, Red Lake Reservation, 1933.

MĪDĒ'WIWIN CELEBRATION, WHITE EARTH RESERVATION, 1938.

1, Man and woman dancing; man in white shirt beating drum. Notice two poles near man beating drum; upon each pole rests a bird carved of wood. *2,* Old people resting between dances. Young mother holding her child, one of two for whom Mīdē'wiwin was being celebrated. Pails and calico cloth on rod are offerings.

CHIPPEWA BURIALS.

1, Burials near home, Red Lake Reservation, 1933.   *2*, Mīdē'wiwin cemetery, White Earth Reservation, 1938.   *3*, Mīdē'wiwin cemetery, Lac Courte Orielle Reservation, 1935.

CHIPPEWA BURIALS.

1, Grave with cloth covering, Red Lake Reservation, 1933. *2*, Burials near home, Lac du Flambeau Reservation, 1935.

BURIALS, MILLE LACS RESERVATION, 1940.

1, Cemetery. *2,* Birchbark covering. *3,* Notice small platform. *4,* Birchbark covering weighted down with stones. Notice do′dam marker in foreground to right.

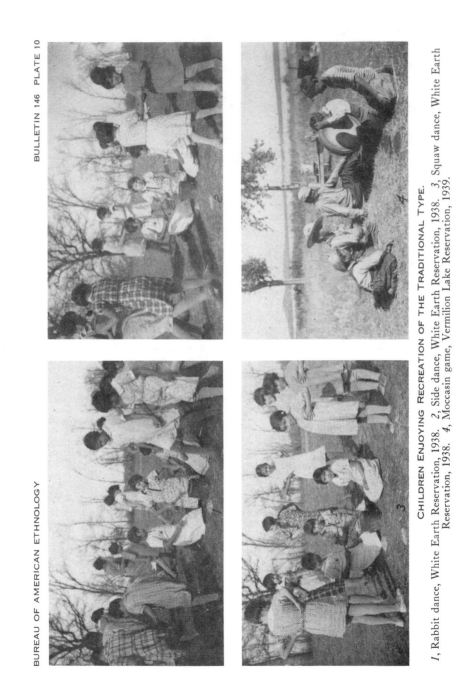

CHILDREN ENJOYING RECREATION OF THE TRADITIONAL TYPE.

1, Rabbit dance, White Earth Reservation, 1938. *2,* Side dance, White Earth Reservation, 1938. *3,* Squaw dance, White Earth Reservation, 1938. *4,* Moccasin game, Vermilion Lake Reservation, 1939.

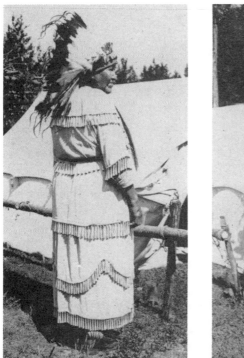 

POW-WOW PARTICIPANTS, RED LAKE RESERVATION, 1933.
1, Wife of Amos Big Bird.   *2*, Amos Big Bird.

DANCE HALL, RED LAKE RESERVATION. 1933.
1, Interior.   *2*, Exterior.

MAKING BIRCHBARK CANOE, MILLE LACS RESERVATION, 1940.

1, Boiling spruce resin for mending cracks in birchbark. *2*, Frying boiled spruce resin mixed with charcoal in grease. *3*, Split roots of spruce used in sewing. *4*, Preparing ground by leveling it.

MAKING BIRCHBARK CANOE, MILLE LACS RESERVATION, 1940—CONTINUED.

1, Placing birchbark. *2,* Shaping canoe by means of poles and framework for bow or stern. *3,* Placing bark into position by means of second set of poles.

MAKING BIRCHBARK CANOE, MILLE LACS RESERVATION, 1940—CONTINUED.
1, Framework for either bow or stern.   *2*, Binding edges with split roots of spruce.

MAKING BIRCHBARK CANOE, MILLE LACS RESERVATION, 1940—CONTINUED.

1, Canoe ready for gunwales, ribs, flooring, and binding of edges. *2*, Filling cracks in bark with pitch. *3*, Placing ribs and flooring.

MAKING BIRCHBARK CANOE, MILLE LACS RESERVATION, 1940—CONTINUED.

1, Canoe ready for use. *2*, Transporting canoe. *3*, Canoe on exhibition at Mille Lacs
Indian Trading Post, Onamia, Minn.

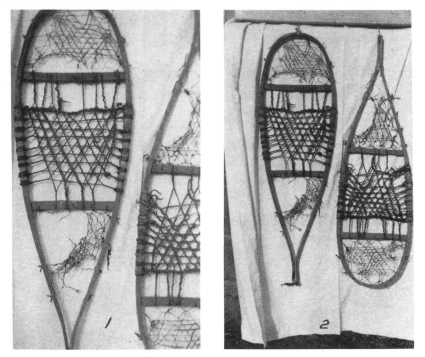

MAN'S SNOWSHOES COLLECTED ON LAC COURTE ORIELLE RESERVATION, 1935.

JOSEPHINE GURNEAU MAKING CORD OF BASSWOOD FIBER, RED LAKE RESERVATION, 1933.

1, Rolling strands of basswood fiber. *2*, Softening strands by moistening.

FISHING

1, Fish nets being hung to dry, Red Lake Reservation, 1933. *2*, Shuttle and sample of
fish net made on Red Lake Reservation, 1933.

FISHING.

1, A haul of fish, Red Lake Reservation, 1932.   *2*, Fish nets drying, L'Anse Reservation,
1935.

EMMA MARTIN TANNING DEER HIDE, LAC COURTE ORIELLE RESERVATION, 1935.
1, Wringing hide after soaking.   *2*, Last wringing of hide.   *3*, Second scraping of hide.
4, Stretching hide.

EMMA MARTIN TANNING DEER HIDE, LAC COURTE ORIELLE RESERVATION, 1935—CONTINUED.

1, Hide stretched for final scraping.   *2*, Final scraping of hide.   *3*, Smoking hide.

BIRCHBARK RECEPTACLES.

1, Anna Knott making wild-rice winnowing trays and teaching daughter to make them, Vermilion Lake Reservation, 1939.   *2*, Nonleakable birchbark receptacles, Red Lake Reservation, August 1933.   *3, a*, Work basket; *b*, mākōk'; *c*, winnowing basket: Red Lake Reservation, 1933.

MARY GURNEAU MAKING NONLEAKABLE BIRCHBARK RECEPTACLE, RED LAKE
RESERVATION, AUGUST 1932.

1, Holding bark over fire.   *2*, Fastening folded end.   *3*, Folding opposite end.
4, Completed receptacle.

WIGWAMS.

1, Mishiman and wife and their wigwam covered with birchbark and bulrush mats, Lac Courte Orielle Reservation, 1935.   2, Wigwam entirely covered with bark, Red Lake Reservation, 1932.

WIGWAMS.

1, White Earth Reservation, 1938.   *2*, Lac du Flambeau Reservation, 1935.   *3*, Lac du
Flambeau Reservation, 1922.

WIGWAMS, MILLE LACS RESERVATION, 1940.

1, Coverings of cattail mats, tar paper, and flattened cardboard boxes. *2*, Wigwam frame. *3*, Coverings of cattail mats and birchbark. *4*, Coverings of black ash and birchbark.

TIPI. WOMEN PACKING WOOD, RED LAKE RESERVATION.

1, Tipi covered with birchbark—entrance view, Mille Lacs Reservation, 1940. *2*, Same as *1;* rear view. *3*, Nancy Cain, 1939. *4*, Mrs. Peter Everywind, 1932.

BUREAU OF AMERICAN ETHNOLOGY

FIREPLACES.   COLLECTING HERBS.

1, Mabel Daisy, Red Lake Reservation, 1932.   *2*, Red Lake Reservation, 1933.   *3*, Gathering medicinal herbs, roots, and bark, Lac Courte Orielle Reservation, 1935.

FIREPLACES.

1 and *2*, Lac du Flambeau Reservation, 1935 and 1934.   *3*, Mille Lacs Reservation, 1940.

United States Bureau of Indian Affairs,
x, xii, 33, 34, 70, 93, 144, 152
United States House Executive Documents, 153
United States Indian Agency, 35
United States Indian Service, 144, 151
Urtica gracilis Ait., 173
Utensils, buried with dead, 80, 85
    cooking, 128

Vaccinium vacillans Kalm., 173
Vanoss, Andrew, informant, xiii
Vases, 83
Vashow, Mrs. Ed., informant, xiv
Vegetables, 146
    dried, 149
    garden, 87, 171
Venison, 8, 29, 38, 87, 145, 148
Vermilion Lake Reservation, Minnesota,
x, xii, xiii, 16, 17, 22, 23, 24, 25, 26, 27,
30, 32, 38, 53, 59, 60, 69, 75, 82, 97, 106,
111, 112, 113, 116, 117, 120, 121, 133,
134, 146, 162, 163, 164, 165
Visiting, form of diversion, 114, 115,
170
Vocational training and domestic economy, 115–153, 170–172

Wallis, Dr. Wilson D., xii
War dance, 70
Warren, William, 63, 101, 115, 146, 150,
151, 153, 154, 162
Waterbuckets, birchbark, 171
Water gods, 43, 62, 107
Watersmeet, 74
Watrin, Benno, Benedictine priest, xi,
101
Waukon, 62
Weaning, 29, 165
Weasel degree, 68
Weasel grave marker, 83
Weasels, 124
    skin, use of, 21, 26, 65, 68, 69, 165
Weather predictions, 106
Weaving, blanket, 26, 27
    mat, 136
Weeping, restraint of, 79
Wein, Sarah, informant, xiii
Weinzierl, Mrs. Emily, xii
Whip, 113
Whipping, rare, 99
White Earth reservation, Minnesota, ix,
x, xi, xiii, 3, 17, 21, 24, 32, 36, 64, 65,
66, 67, 68, 69, 75, 77, 85, 96, 101, 110,
114, 115, 122, 139, 140, 146, 148, 163,
164, 166
Whitefish, 8, 50, 75, 101, 128, 129
    oil, used in lamps, 143
    smoked, 148
Whitefish people, 70
White, Joe, subchief, 151
Widowers, restrictions of, 162

Widowhood, release from, 161, 162
Widows, regulations for, 161, 162, 172
Wife, 83
Wigwam, 50, 56, 58, 76, 77, 78, 128, 137,
138, 139, 142, 143, 146, 147, 149, 158,
159, 168, 171, 172
    birchbark, 128, 138, 140, 171
    ceremonial, 66, 67, 69
    circular, 138, 171
    construction of, 137, 138, 139
    divination, 75, 76, 77
    dome-shaped, 75, 88, 96
    elongated, 139, 171
    family, 19, 26, 50, 52, 54, 56, 128,
        138, 161, 163, 172
    menstrual, 50, 52, 53, 54, 129, 167
    Mīdē'wiwin, 66, 67, 84, 138
    Shaman's, 76, 77
    sweating, 96
    temporary, for use at birth, 12, 163
Wilcox, Roy P., xii
"Will-o'-the-wisp," magic use of, 71
Williams, Mr. and Mrs. Pat, informants,
xiv
"Willow, red" (*Cornus stolonifera*), 63
    See also Dogwood, red.
Willow switch, 112
Wilson, Mr., informant, xiii
Wilson, Mrs., informant, xiii
Winchell, N. H., 158
Windě'gō, mythical being, 114
Winds, spirits of, 60, 61
Winnebago, 33, 77, 113, 114
Wintergreen (*Gaultheria procumbens*
L.), 173
    tea from, 146
Wives, multiple, 161
Wolf, 101, 149
Wolf, Angeline, informant, xiii
Wolf clan, 155
Wolf, guardian spirit, 45, 46
Wolf, Mike, Chippewa chief, 151
Wolf, Peter, Chippewa chief, 151
Wolves, 124, 170
Women chiefs, 153, 172
Women, ornaments worn by, 20, 21
    pregnant, 28, 165
    punishment of, 162
    tasks of, 52, 55, 115, 116, 129, 130,
        137, 138, 141, 147, 156, 170, 171
    work during pregnancy, 9, 164
Wood carriers, leather, 130, 140, 141, 171
Woodchuck, taboos regarding, 7
Wood, fuel, 141, 142, 171
Work, 109, 116, 120, 168, 170
    taught by parents, 56, 57
Writing, picture, 108

Yellow River, Wisconsin, 149

Zea mays L., 144, 145, 149, 150, 171, 173
Zizania aquatica L., 173